Rudbeckia

ECHINOPS

Ligularia

Japonica

SALVIA

20

ALSTROEMERIA

22

30

OBERON

Phlox

31

Achillea

Veronica

Stachys

NEPETA SIX

STACHYS LANATA

PAPAVER

MAY QUEEN

NEPETA

SIX HILLS GIANT

~~SCABIOSA~~

IRIS GERM.

GOLDEN

LILIUM

ELEGANS SANGUINEUM

Phlox

orange

“For me, Mien Ruys was a genius in designing planting plans—on a par with her illustrious predecessors Gertrude Jekyll and Vita Sackville-West. She is an inspiring example! Her principles are as valuable and functional today as they were in her own day: long-flowering plants which provide ornamental value after, and even before, they flower; groups of different sizes, consecutive flowering seasons, and a variety of flower shapes. These are golden rules which improve every planting plan’s success rate and will be beneficial to every planting designer—whether they are beginners or more experienced.”

Jacqueline van der Kloet

“Some gardens you merely visit, *Tuinen Mien Ruys* is more like a pilgrimage to the revolutionary birthplace of modern landscape design. It’s remarkable to think that much of what we commonly accept about western gardens today dates back to the design experiments conducted here by Mien Ruys over her long lifetime. This is where I discovered the full creative possibilities of her maxim *Wild planting in a strong design*, an idea that deeply inspired the original Dutch Wave and continues to be piercingly relevant today.”

Tony Spencer, The New Perennialist

“I came across Mien Ruys early in my career, through her book on perennials and by visiting her garden. The tall, sturdy plants I discovered in Dedemsvaart were an inspiration to me. They led me to start collecting plants, which formed the basis for the assortment of plants in our nursery. As a designer, I chose a different path—one that did not exactly meet with Mien’s approval. Never one to mince words, she let it be known through other people that she missed structure in my work.”

Piet Oudolf

Conny den Hollander

THE GARDENS OF MIEN RUYS

Strong Design, Lush Planting, and the Origins of the Modernist Garden

Timber Press
Portland, OR

CONTENTS

PREFACE

When I changed careers in 2010 and started as a trainee at Mien Ruys Gardens, I had little experience of working in a garden, but you learn a lot by being willing and showing an interest. I found my way in the Gardens by doing, observing, and asking questions. After working for several years under the guidance of my predecessor, Tineke Grin, I took over from her as head gardener. I'm still grateful to her that, despite my limited knowledge and experience, she recognized that there was a gardener in me. Looking back, changing careers was the best decision ever; it feels like the greatest gift I could have been given.

During the year and a half that I've spent working on this book, I've traveled back through 100 years reliving the history of Mien Ruys and her Gardens. The result is a story of her life, her work, and the period in which she lived. But, above all, it is the story of the Gardens, which Mien Ruys began in her parents' kitchen garden in 1924. It was her "first act of landscaping."

I never knew Mien Ruys personally. She had died by the time I became really entranced by her gardens. Everything in this book is based on her books and publications, the video and audio recordings there are of her, the books and articles written about her life and work, and the stories of people who knew her. This book contains my interpretation of all these sources; the text has been written from my perspective and based on my experiences. My intention was to record the story of a talented women and her gardens. Someone who was ahead of her time and who—as a woman—managed to become a respected and successful garden designer and landscape architect. I do not pretend that this book is complete or will always resonate with other people's experiences. I hope that it paints a captivating portrait of a resolute woman who spent 70 years creating gardens in Dedemsvaart that, even today, attract thousands of visitors every year.

The Gardens hold an extraordinary beauty for me. Mien Ruys's style—the contrast between a clear-cut design and the looseness and lushness of the plants—creates a sense of peace and connection with nature. The history of this spot, which has developed over 100 years, is tangible and makes the Gardens a balanced, green oasis. This book is also intended to motivate you to bring nature into your own garden and enjoy it—something that Mien Ruys advocated for many years. Working and living in a green environment, with your hands in the soil is—for me at least—therapeutic. Experiencing the wonder of the awakening, burgeoning, and eventually dying plants every year makes you humble and thankful for the power of nature. I hope that I have conveyed this love through this book.

Conny den Hollander
Garden and landscape designer and head gardener at Mien Ruys Gardens

WHERE IT STARTED

ORIGINS IN DEDEMSVAART

The story of Mien Ruys Gardens actually began in the nineteenth century. For centuries, a large part of the northeast Netherlands had been uncultivated land, comprising peat moors and wilderness. In the first half of the nineteenth century, a canal was dug in Overijssel, between Gramsbergen and Hasselt, and named the Dedemsvaart after its initiator, Baron van Dedem. The manually dug canal provided drainage for the peat moor, drying it out so that the peat could be extracted and utilized. The peat, which was used widely as fuel at the time, was transported by canal to Hasselt and from there distributed throughout the Netherlands. A fen community developed as a settlement alongside the canal, becoming known as the village of Dedemsvaart. As the peat was dug up, reclaimed peatland appeared; the upper layer of peat became mixed with the sand that lay beneath the peat moor. This fertile soil was ideal for agriculture and horticulture. Peat extraction brought in a lot of money for the peat cutters or peatland owners: the *nouveau riche* of the nineteenth century. Huge, stately villas were built along the canal from the peat proceeds.

Bonne Ruys and the Moerheim Nursery

In 1869, Mien Ruys's grandfather, Jan Daniël Ruys, had to move out of the house he and his family had been renting in Kampen when it was required for a new tenant. He had no choice but to look for somewhere else to live. His brother-in-law, Arend Berends, the son of one of the peatland owners in Dedemsvaart, had recently bought ten hectares of land and the villa known as *Huize Moerheim* (Moerheim House) along the Dedemsvaart canal. He offered the house to his brother-in-law, an offer Jan Daniël was happy to accept.

Jan Daniël's son, Bonne Ruys, born in 1865, was only four when his parents went to live in Dedemsvaart. Once Bonne started school, it became clear that book-learning wasn't his strong suit, but he knew at a young age that he wanted to be a grower. Bonne's enthusiasm had arisen from his time spent at the nearby nursery garden, Tottenham, where he and his friend François van der Elst could often be found. The owner, Mr. Jongkindt Conick, had named his nursery after the suburban district of Tottenham in London, where he had learned his trade from the nurseryman Thomas Ware. On the advice of Jongkindt Conick, Bonne went to a boarding school in Brussels to study foreign languages. They would prove useful to him as a future nurseryman. After he finished boarding school in 1882, Bonne went to work as one of the apprentices at the Tottenham nursery despite repeated attempts by his father to persuade him to continue his studies.

There was no formal way of obtaining a professional qualification to become a grower at that time, and so a practical

▲ Canal diggers at work in the Dedemsvaart. The canal was dug out by hand.

▼ The New Moerheim villa beside the Dedemsvaart canal

apprenticeship was the only way to learn. The job did not carry much prestige, as Bonne recalled in his memoirs: “Anyone who was too dumb to study had to become a grower or a mayor.”

Bonne spent 1885 and 1886 working in various nurseries abroad, first in England and later in Germany. When there was no more work to be found in Germany, a lack of money forced him to return home. Back in the Netherlands, he worked for a seed and fruit merchant in Zwijndrecht. One of the owners of this company, Mr. Van Namen, visited Dedemsvaart in 1887 and advised Jan Daniël to allow Bonne to start his own nursery there. The fertile soil and Bonne’s interests were sure to make it a success. Jan Daniël took the advice to heart and offered his son a plot of land. Bonne still had his doubts because of the poor road connections from Dedemsvaart, but the suitable soil and his father’s commercial support settled

B. RUYS.

Zaadhandel — Kweekerij „Moerheim” Dedemsvaart.

Prijscourant en Bestellijst van Zaden.

BESTELLING van ……………………

te ……………………

door tusschenkomst van den Agent ……………………

N.B. *Men gelieve in de daarvoor bestemde kolom, in te vullen,* **liefst in centen,** *hoeveel van elke soort wordt verlangd.*

Van alle soorten, waarvan de prijs per pakje niet afzonderlijk is genoteerd, worden ook **pakjes van 5 cents** *geleverd.*

Daar het mij is gebleken, dat somtijds zaden van twijfelachtige hoedanigheid worden verkocht als van mij afkomstig, zoo lette men er op dat **alle zakjes zijn voorzien van mijn firma-stempel.**

GROENTEZADEN.	Prijs p. Lood centen.	In te vullen in centen.
Andijvie, echte vroege krop	15	
„ breedblad volhart late	15	
Augurken, kleine groene scherpe	15	
[illegible] gewone lange gele	15	
„ lange gele tros p. pakje 10 ct.	25	
„ „ groene	15	
Bloemkool, fijne vroege p. pakje 10 ct.	20	
„ Utrechtsche kortbeen „ „ „ „	20	
„ Italiaansche reuzen late „ „ „ „	30	
Witte kool, fijne vroege	10	
„ „ groote late	10	
Roode kool, kleine Utrechtsche zwartroode	10	
„ „ groote late	10	
Kapperkool, met blauwe randen	15	
Savoye kool, groote gele	10	
„ „ Bloemendaalsche gele	10	
„ „ groote groene late	10	
„ „ kleine groene	10	
Spruitkool, Brusselsche hooge	10	
„ „ lage	10	
Boerenkool, lage groene	10	
„ hooge „	10	
„ bonte of dessert- p. pakje 10 cent	30	
Kool- of Knolrapen, gele	10	
„ „ „ witte	10	
Koolrabi, groene boven den grond	15	
„ blauwe „ „ „	15	
Knollen of Rapen, platte witte mei	10	
„ „ „ ronde gele herfst	10	
„ „ „ lange Nijmeegsche witte	10	
Rammenas, ronde zwarte	10	
„ lange „	10	
Transporteere		

	Prijs p. Lood centen.	In te vullen in centen.
Per Transport		
Prei, dikke Brabantsche	16	
„ reuzen van Carentan	20	
Kropsalade, vroege zomer	15	
„ bonte Chili *extra*	15	
„ zwarte Duitsche	15	
Snijselderij, fijne snij	10	
Knolselderij, extra dikke kortlof	10	
Peterselie, gewone snij	15	
„ fijne krul	15	
Uien, platte stroogele N.-Holl.	16	
„ „ bloedroode	16	
„ kleine witte (voor den inmaak)	15	
Zuring, breedblad	10	
Boonenkruid	5	
Kervel	5	
Pimpernel p. pakje 5 cent		
Dille „ „ 10 „		
Salie „ „ 10 „		
Dragon „ „ 40 „		
	Prijs p. 2 Lood centen.	
Radijs, witte broei	10	
„ roode en witte gemengd	10	
„ roode witpuntige extra	10	
Raapstelen	10	
Postelein, groene	10	
„ gele	15	
Bieten of Krooten, fijne zwartroode	10	
„ „ „ bleekblad donkerroode	10	
Snijbeet of Winterspinazie, goudgele	10	
Spinazie, breedblad scherpzaad 1½ ons 10 cent		
½ ons	5	
„ „ rondzaad „ „ 10 cent	5	
Snijsalade, blanke dunsel	10	
„ fransche latuw	15	
„ kruldunsel	15	
Veldsalade, Noord-Hollandsche	10	
Schorseneren, lange zwarte	10	
„ Russische reuzen	20	
Wortelen, vroege zomer (of deuvik)	10	
„ zomer (Hoornsche)	10	
Transporteere		

Pricelist and order form for Moerheim nursery

the matter. Unable to think of a better name, Bonne Ruys named the nursery after his family home: Moerheim, which literally means “peatland house.” And so, in 1888, Moerheim Nursery was born. Bonne began by growing a variety of plants. He bought vegetable seeds from various seed merchants, but also perennials, shrubs, roses, and conifers from Tottenham nursery. He was particularly successful at cultivating seeds in the early years. He drew up a “pricelist”—a catalog of the seeds he had for sale—which he initially printed himself. Bonne noticed that the seed of a German legume variety produced a single plant with unusual, large white flowers. The flowers developed into larger pods than those of the other plants. He was greatly saddened to see that these unusually large pods had also attracted the attention of birds, who had made a feast of them. He was only able to save a few pods, which he cherished, sowed, multiplied, and eventually marketed. He named the legume “*Moerheims reuzenpeul*” or Moerheim’s giant pea, enabling him to publicize the name of his nursery at the same time.

Bonne continued to expand his nursery in the years that followed, and he began focusing more on growing perennials. He tried to make the descriptions in his catalog of perennials—unique for its time—as detailed and appealing as possible. Planting perennials in gardens was quite unusual in the Netherlands in the early twentieth century, and interest in doing so was slow to emerge. Perennials were much more prevalent in gardens in England. Bonne therefore traveled regularly to England to establish contacts, acquire customers, and procure plants he could cultivate himself. Bonne’s interests lay mainly in hybridizing, selecting, multiplying, and marketing perennials.

He found an unusual plant with a large, double flower head in a bed of *Campanula persicifolia*. By multiplying and cultivating it, he grew his first perennial cultivar. He put this plant onto the market around 1900 under the name of *Campanula persicifolia* ‘Moerheimii’. This name and that of the Moerheim giant pea played a major role in publicizing the Moerheim nursery throughout the world.

In the meantime, Bonne had met Engelina Fledderus, a clergyman’s daughter from Hellendoorn. When he made a profit for the first time in 1892, he decided that it gave

Bonne Ruys

him a good basis for marriage. He and Engelina became engaged and then married in 1896. They moved into one half of his parental home, while Bonne's mother and sister lived in the other half. By 1900, Bonne and Engelina had two children, and Huize Moerheim had become a bit too small. Bonne decided to build a new house close by with the appropriate name of *Nieuw-Moerheim* (New Moerheim). They went on to have another six children.

As a grower, Bonne Ruys proved to be enterprising, innovative, and a visionary as well. He often traveled abroad, had many contacts in the growers' world, and regularly welcomed grower acquaintances in his own home. Some of the famous names in his circle of acquaintances included the German growers Karl Foerster and Georg Arends and the English growers William Robinson and Gertrude Jekyll, famous for her cottage gardens. Bonne spoke many languages, including Danish and Swedish. He was one of the first to use an American card system for his administration and to open a checking account for the business. As the years went on, Moerheim grew to become a well-known nursery internationally, particularly for perennials and roses. As early as 1896, he was given the title of "Purveyor to the Royal Household" after he supplied the plants for Het Loo Palace, and from 1904, the nursery was permitted to be called *Koninklijk Kwekerij Moerheim* or "Moerheim Royal Nursery." A significant part of his market was in other countries, such as England, Germany, and the Scandinavian countries, but after World War I, the popularity of perennial borders grew in the Netherlands too. Moerheim Nursery undoubtedly played a major role in promoting perennials, and this was partly due to its extensive, stylishly designed catalogs. After Bonne's first successful selective breeding of the white *Campanula*, many more well-known bred strains of perennials followed, such as *Phlox* and *Delphinium.* A number of these cultivars are still available, including his first cultivar *Campanula persicifolia* 'Moerheimii'. When Bonne died in 1950, the nursery had grown to cover some 40 hectares and was one of the major employers in Dedemsvaart.

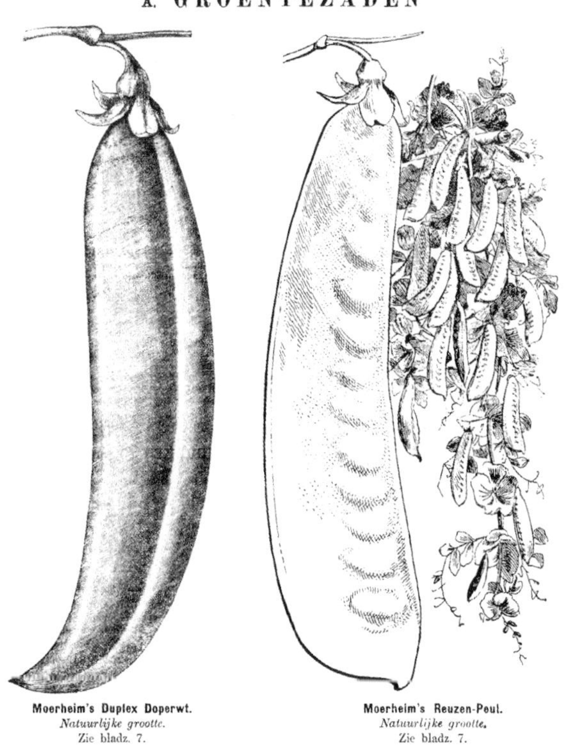

Moerheim's giant pea

1900–1930

THE NETHERLANDS IN THE EARLY TWENTIETH CENTURY

Dutch society in the early years of the twentieth century was still very traditional. The church played a major role in society, which was divided into different social classes. The division of roles between men and women was simple: men worked, and women looked after the children and ran the home. The upper middle class began campaigning for better working conditions and housing for the working classes. Particularly women from the higher social classes were expected to support those who were less well-off. Despite this traditionally structured society, the struggle for the emancipation of workers and of women gradually began to take shape.

The Netherlands remained neutral during World War I (1914–1918), but nonetheless, the effects of the war were felt in the economy. Food and fuel became scarce and trade with other countries slumped. The Spanish Flu in 1917 was a second onslaught for the population in Europe, and the Netherlands was no exception. As these gloomy years came to an end, people felt the need for change: they wanted to dance, make music, party the night away, and shake off the old standards and values. The roaring twenties made their entrance, particularly among young, better-off people in the large cities. The economy improved and prosperity grew. A milestone was reached in the emancipation of women in the Netherlands: following years of effort by a group of progressive women, women became eligible for election in 1917 and entitled to vote in 1919.

The Ruys family in 1911

Mien Ruys's Early Years

Wilhelmina Jacoba Ruys (known as Mien) was born on April 12, 1904, as Bonne and Engelina's fifth child. She and her three brothers and four sisters grew up in the parental home of Nieuw-Moerheim and the adjoining nursery. Mien loved being outdoors and was quoted in 1987 as saying "I was able to say *Potentilla* before I could say table and chair": an illustration of how she spent her youth amongst all these hectares of plants.

The Ruys family was one of the more well-off and the Dutch Reformed Church featured broadly in their lives. Despite the traditional environment in which they lived, Bonne and Engelina had modern ideas and broad interests. Not only their sons, but also their daughters were encouraged to learn and study, something that was not yet common in those days. From a young age, Mien was interested in the natural world and loved drawing. After primary school in Dedemsvaart, she continued her studies in various places, including a boarding school for general development in Bussum. Here, she was instructed in languages and literature and had lessons in household tasks. Despite her parents' modern opinions, some knowledge of how to run a household was always considered desirable for daughters. This was one of the reasons for sending her to this school. Mien Ruys later spoke of this in an interview: "Mother said: 'You have so little aptitude for housekeeping. I believe you are the only one who needs to learn something about it.' But I might as well not have gone at all because as soon as the subject of household tasks came up, I mentally drew a curtain and withdrew. I learned nothing about it."

Mien in Search of Her Identity

In her twenties, Mien often felt lonely and unsure of herself. She had no close friends in Dedemsvaart. There were few suitable candidates for marriage, and winters were particularly long, boring, and depressing. There was little to do apart from skating and reading books. She was happy in her work, but the compulsory household duties held no charms for her. As a woman, she felt restricted and would have preferred to be a man, because men were free, could have adventures and go out into the world. The natural world was her comfort, certainly once she had distanced herself from religion. She frequently left the house to take walks in the countryside. She had a difficult relationship with men. At one point, she fell in love with the artist Reinhard Heinemann, whom she had met at an exhibition in Nijmegen. When she learned that he was married, it took Mien several months to get over it. Her older sister Lotte had studied in Utrecht and lived in Amsterdam. Mien often went to visit her and got to know the progressive, artistic circles in which the independent Lotte moved. The two sisters took taxi rides through Amsterdam, with Lotte pointing out the city's different architectural styles. Mien enjoyed these trips, and they taught her how to observe.

Mien Ruys at about the age of four

The Moerheim catalog in 1921

"Today My Career Has Begun"

When Mien left school at the age of 19 in 1923, she knew for certain that her future lay in the nursery garden. Her love of nature meant that she wanted to work outside, but after she had spent a few weeks exerting herself in the nursery, she reconsidered. She decided she wanted to become a landscape gardener but had her doubts because she thought it was more a job for men. In 1916, when international trade collapsed during World War I, Bonne had set up a landscape gardening studio where designs and planting plans for individual customers were drawn up. Mien set to work in the design studio, in addition to her compulsory household tasks. She wrote in her diary: "Today my career has begun." At first, her work involved equipping the Moerheim stands for trade fairs and exhibitions, adding details to designs, and helping to plant borders. Mien's older sister Ina had taken classes in landscape gardening in England and worked as a draughtswoman in the studio. When Ina went to England for a while, Mien took over her work. In addition to her vast knowledge of plants acquired as she was growing up, she turned out to have a talent for design too. From then on, she devoted herself to designing gardens, particularly for villas. She also had a talent for writing. When she was asked to write something for the magazine *Buiten* (*Outdoors*) in 1925, she consulted her mother about whether she should do it. Her mother answered: "You write the most entertaining letters of all my eight children, so just say yes."

Growers and landscape gardeners from other countries frequently came to visit the nursery. Dedemsvaart did not have a suitable hotel, so the guests often stayed with the Ruys family. They introduced Mien to their world and encouraged her to study further. The Netherlands did not have an appropriate study program at the time, and learning from the available books was not enough for her. Through her father's contacts, she was granted a traineeship in the landscape gardening studio of Wallace and Sons' nursery in Tunbridge Wells in England in 1928. There she met Gertrude Jekyll (1843–1932), who became an inspiration not just because of her borders, but also because she was one of the first to collaborate with an architect, Edwin Lutyens. Mien visited her for a second time in 1931. Gertrude Jekyll was already well into her eighties and almost blind. Mien wandered around her garden for hours picking sprigs from plants that were new to her. While the two drank tea together, Gertrude Jekyll felt the sprigs and was able to identify the plants. They exchanged plants. Gertrude gave Mien *Sedum telephium* 'Munstead Dark Red' while Mien gave her the new *Helenium* 'Moerheim Beauty'.

> "The period in Berlin had a major influence on her development."

MUNSTEAD WOOD,
GODALMING.

July 22 1931

Dear Miss Ruys

It will give me the greatest pleasure to receive you next Wednesday the 29th. I hope it may suit you to let your visit be in the afternoon & will you please go everywhere as you will – The upper part of the ground is woodland which may be pleasant to wander in if the day is hot. The flowery part is below the house & lawn – I only wish your visit might have been in the later summer, for the greater part of what you will see is preparation for effect in August & September.

I hope you will come in

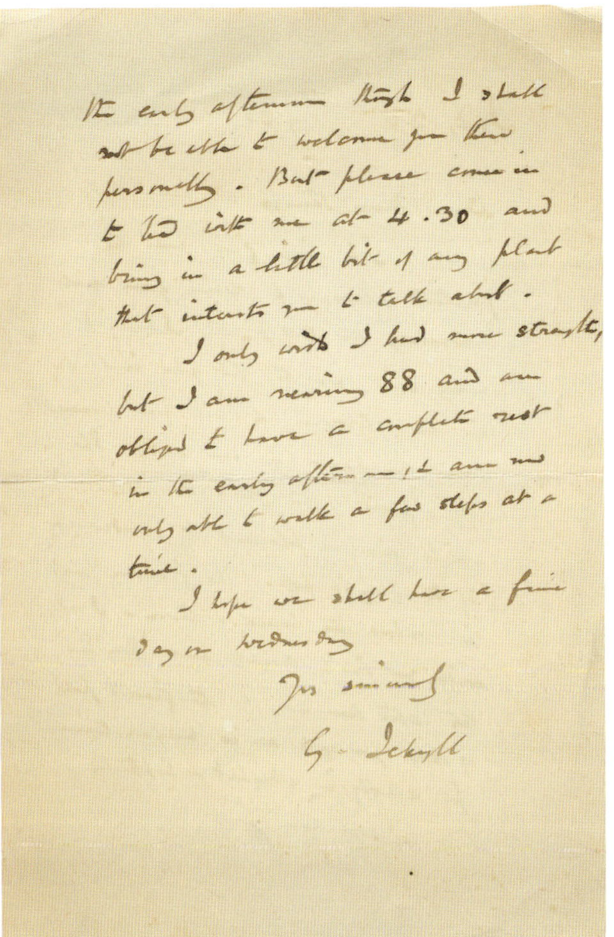

the early afternoon though I shall not be able to welcome you there personally. But please come in to tea with me at 4.30 and bring in a little bit of any plant that interests you to talk about.

I only wish I had more strength, but I am nearing 88 and am obliged to have a complete rest in the early afternoon, & am now only able to walk a few steps at a time.

I hope we shall have a fine day on Wednesday.

Yours sincerely

G. Jekyll

Letter from Gertrude Jekyll to Mien in 1931

A modern, architectural style of landscape gardening combined with copious planting was being developed in Germany at that time. This combination captured Mien Ruys's imagination. She got to know ambassadors of this style, including the German couple Hermann Mattern and Herta Hammerbacher, an architect and a landscape gardener who were collaborating with the grower Karl Foerster. When a group from the *Deutsche Dendrologische Gesellschaft* stayed in her parents' house, one of the members, the landscape gardener Camillo Schneider, advised Mien to go to Germany to study. She left for Berlin in 1929 to attend lectures on *Gartenkunst* (garden design) for a few months at the new *Institut für Gartengestaltung*, which also admitted women. She delighted in lively, cosmopolitan Berlin, its culture, art, architecture, and not least, in her freedom. In the company of a friend she had met on her train journey, she visited museums and theaters, and they took walks in the countryside around Berlin. The period in Berlin had a major influence on her development. After seeing Bertolt Brecht's *Threepenny Opera*, an indictment of capitalism, she resolved to become a socialist. "I sat through it all with my hair on end from dismay. I had been so protected and spoilt when growing up, I had no idea of the terrible things that were actually going on."

▲ The Wilderness Garden around 1932

◀ The path to the former nursery

▼ *Epimedium ×rubrum*

Wilderness Garden (1924)

"It soon became clear to me that cultivating plants was not where my interests lay, but rather what to do with all these plants." When Mien Ruys left school in 1923, the nursery was full of stool beds for propagating perennials, which were then sold as soon as they were ready. Mien wanted to acquire some experience situating the plants in the garden. There was little information recorded about this at that time. She was given permission to lay out an experimental garden in her parents' orchard. The shape of the garden was at least as important to her as the plants in it. She chose a minimalist, simple shape in which the plants were to create the effect of a wilderness.
A perpendicular line crossed the sight line from the house toward the nursery. She dug a square pond where the two lines crossed. Cement-and-gravel tiles from the nursery measuring 40 × 60 centimeters were used for the paths and the edge of the pond. There was no water supply, so the water for the pond had to come from the Dedemsvaart canal: a long way to walk. The front garden on the other side of the house, the road, and then the tram rails had to be crossed before one reached the canal. So that she didn't have to carry the water herself, she harnessed the family's cow with a yoke and milking pails to transport the water from the canal to the pond. She realized that the fruit trees made the garden a shady spot and so duly took account of that when choosing plants. She chose plants from the nursery that could withstand shade, such as columbine, primula, and bleeding heart (*Dicentra spectabilis*). One year on, it was clear that this decision had been wrong. Nearly all the plants had died. Dedemsvaart's acidic, peaty soil was unsuitable for these mainly lime-loving species. This was a valuable lesson. When choosing plants, the deciding factor would have to be the type of soil rather than choosing plants she liked and then altering the soil to suit them. Furthermore, the plants were not compatible with the idea she had in mind. Strong plants such as periwinkle, ferns, *Symphytum* (comfrey), and honesty were more appropriate, as well as a few exotic plants such as *Hosta*, *Rodgersia*, and *Brunnera*. The decision to plant these proved to work, and the ground was soon covered. It was low maintenance too, since there was no need to weed, water, or add manure due to their thick growth, the shady spot, and the falling leaves that made the soil rich in humus. This balance was upset by a storm 40 years later. Several large oak trees and old apple trees were toppled, allowing more light to get in. The damage caused by the fallen trees had to be cleared away, which disturbed the soil. The consequence of the change in light and disturbance of the soil was an explosion of weeds, "as if all hell had broken loose," as Mien said later. It took many years of systematic weeding before the balance was restored.

The Wilderness Garden was Mien's first experimental garden in Dedemsvaart. More were to follow. It is noteworthy that at a very young age she chose a minimalist, geometric shape to contrast with lush, informal vegetation. It illustrates her sense of style, and this design method would be emblematic for the rest of her life. Her good friend Rosette Zandvoort later called this experiment "her first steps on the path to garden design."

Old Experimental Garden (1927)

"The next step was to take over the entire kitchen garden," Mien Ruys wrote in *Mijn Tuinen* (*My Gardens*) in 1987. Following her first experiment in her parents' orchard, it was now the turn of the kitchen garden to be experimented on with plants. This spot had hardly any shade from trees, and therefore got far more sun. She created a large south-facing border, 30 × 4 meters backed with a palisade. Here too she used the concrete tiles from the nursery, this time in a double row along the border. A door was cut in the fence on one side of the border, while the little bridge to the nursery formed the end of the other side of the border. The path along the border adjoined a large lawn, in the right proportion to the mighty border. The lawn was bound on the northern side by a curved shrubbery. To soften the minimalist, hard lines of the border somewhat, she planted little island groups of perennials and ornamental grasses in the lawn on the other side of the tiled path. A pedestal supporting a sundial marked the start of the border. The pedestal came from an old country estate and was brought to Dedemsvaart by the steam tram that used to run between Zwolle and Coevorden. The exact date is unknown, but it was probably sometime in the 1930s. After the tram conductor had rolled the pedestal from the tram into the garden of the family home, it lay there for months waiting for Mien to have a flash of inspiration about what to do with it. This inspiration came, and the pedestal was planted in the ground upside down at the start of the tiled path in the Old Experimental Garden. She asked the local smith to make a sundial to put on top of it. The sundial told the time for many years until the plants around it grew so high that they blocked out much of the sun's rays. Although the sundial no longer functions, it has stood in exactly the same place for over 100 years.

The large border in the Old Experimental Garden was designed by Mien in the period during which she was mainly creating designs for the gardens of large villas. It is an example of a traditional English border with groups of perennials set out from low to high. This type of planting was still in its infancy but became increasingly fashionable. Moerheim Nursery certainly played a major part in this, as one of the few growers of perennials in the Netherlands.

▲ The sundial in the Old Experimental Garden in 1930

▶ The large border in 2022 (above) and in 1935 (below). The *Yucca filamentosa* in the foreground was replaced by *Molinia caerulea* subsp. *arundinacea* 'Transparent'.

pages 32–33: The large border in July 2015 featuring *Salvia*, *Solidago*, *Achillea*, and *Helenium*

ABOUT PLANTING COMPOSITION

Mien Ruys planted the Old Experimental Garden in 1927 with a large, south-facing border of perennials, four meters deep and over 30 meters long. There was little knowledge of using perennials in those days, and the large border was an opportunity for Mien to acquire experience in working with them. She learned a lot about the use of color, flower shapes, flowering schedules, combinations, and maintaining perennials, including how much sun the plants could withstand. The knowledge this experiment provided was very useful for the planting plans she went on to make and the books she wrote. Her first book, *Borders. Hoe men ze maakt en onderhoudt* (*Borders: How to Create and Maintain Them*, 1939) contains photos of the border as examples to accompany the tips she provided about "arranging the plants." In the updated version of this book, published in 1959, *Het gebruik en de verzorging van vaste planten in onze tuin* (*The Use and Care of Perennials in Our Garden*), she even called these tips "The seven commandments for composition." Many of the plants she describes in these books can be found in the planting plan for the large border. Part of this planting plan is reproduced as an example of a south-facing border in a large garden in her book *Het Vaste Planten Boek* (*About Perennials*), published in 1950.

There is no record of exactly what the large border looked like in the first period. The oldest planting plan dates from 1948, and her first notes on this border are from 1950. The old plans and notes indicate that plants were regularly moved, added to, and replaced, but to this day, the majority of the species still appear in every planting plan.

The Seven Commandments When Drawing Up a Planting Plan

The seven commandments Mien Ruys stuck to in her planting plans are described below. Their implementation can be seen in the planting of the large border.

1. Plant large groups of a single species.
2. Select plants that flower for a long time or remain attractive after flowering.
3. Vary the sizes of the groups.
4. Choose colors wisely.
5. Choose plants that will flower consecutively.
6. Choose plants of different heights.
7. Alternate vertical and horizontal shapes.

Size of Group

Mien Ruys was inspired by what she saw in nature but did not think that a border should attempt to copy nature. The plants she used in the borders were grown for their color and shape and did not have the natural look of native plants. Very large groups of the same species, as are found in nature, were therefore unsuitable for gardens, but small groups of plants made a "spotty impression"

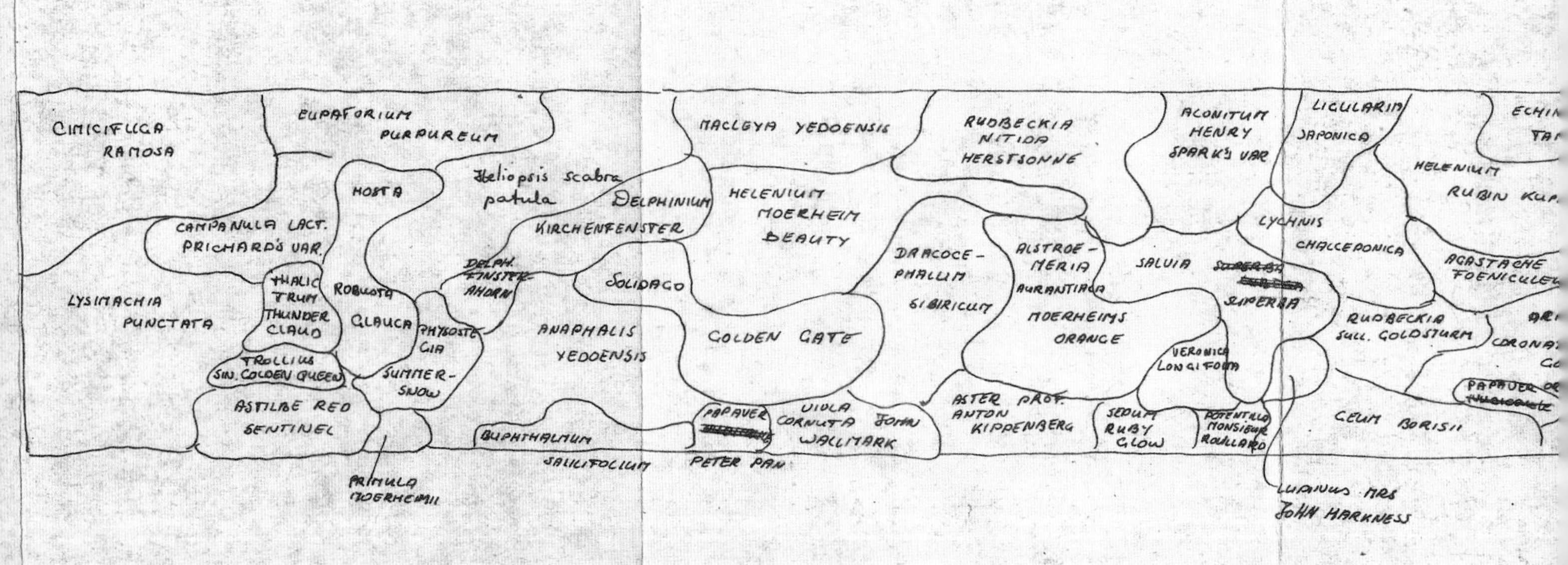

and had too little impact in terms of color, she found. So plant large groups of one species, but then again, not too large, to create the right effect. And another thing: don't make all the groups the same size. She assembled large groups of species that flowered for a long time; smaller groups of plants that have a shorter flowering season were planted in between them. The biggest groups in her large border measured as much as four square meters, while the smaller groups were less than one square meter. An example from the 1948 planting plan contained a large group (measuring over four square meters) of *Salvia nemorosa*, a plant that remains attractive after flowering and can even flower a second time if the blooms are dead-headed after they finish flowering the first time. *Trollius chinensis* 'Golden Queen', a plant with striking orange flowers from May to June but which then leaves a bloom gap, was given a bed of less than one square meter.

Flower Color

Mien thought it was important to create a powerful effect with color by planting large groups of a single species. Choosing contrasting or harmonious colors was, in her opinion, a matter of taste. However, she did not believe that all colors could be used indiscriminately as in nature. In a garden, certain combinations could definitely clash. At first, she planted pale colors (such as pink, lilac, and pale yellow) at the beginning and end of the large border and bright colors (such as orange, red, yellow, blue, and purple) in the middle. But when she looked along the border, both the lilac and pink of the pale colors and the

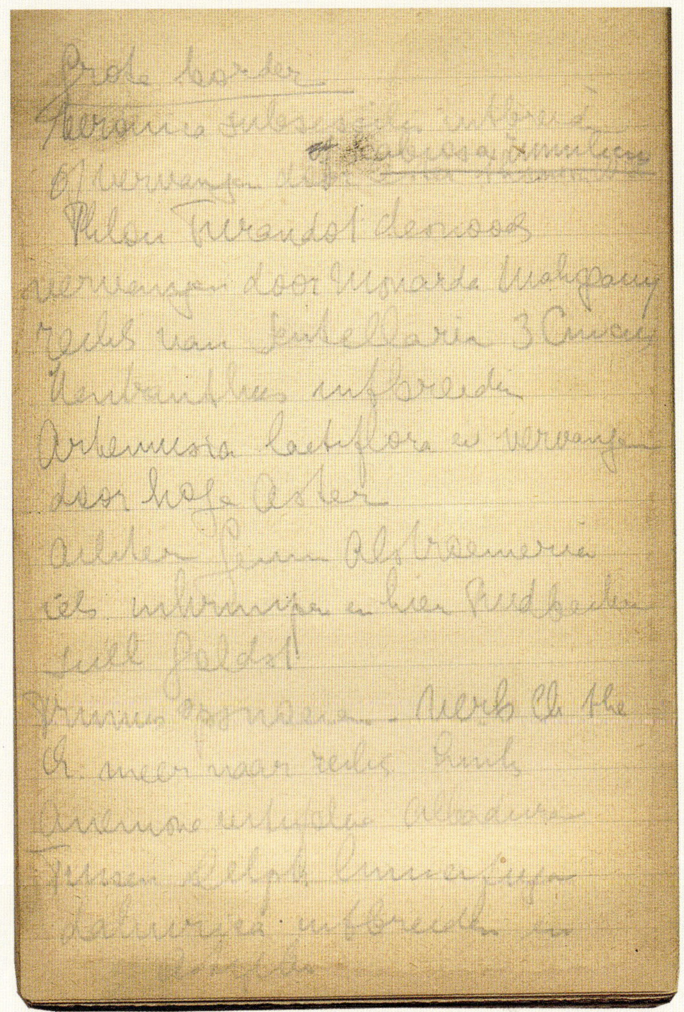

▲ Mien Ruys's note about maintaining the large border in 1950

▼ Planting plan for the large border in 1965

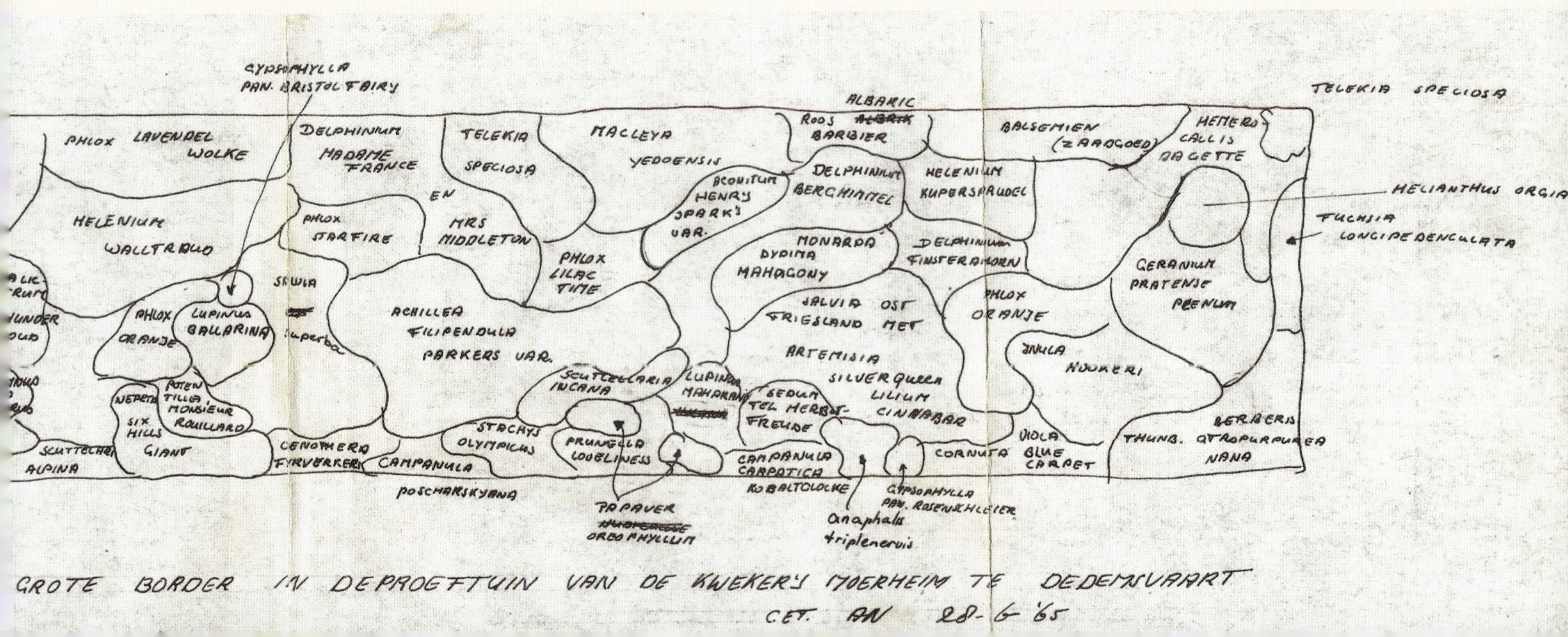

orange and red of the bright colors were visible, and this was jarring to her. She learned from this that it is better to stick to one color palette for plants you can see all at once: choose colors that go together. She divided color combinations into two groups: bright, contrasting colors such as yellow, orange, red, purple, and blue, next to harmonizing colors such as carmine red, pink, lilac, and purple. The smaller the border, the more important she thought it was to stick to this. She kept to this arrangement for her "Ready-to-make Borders" too.

She chose bright colors for the large border: yellow, orange, red, purple, and blue. To soften the strong color contrasts of the flowers, she added gray-leaved plants such as *Artemisia* and *Anaphalis* as a transitional shade. She was cautious about using white. In the early years, she planted a group of large-bloomed, white oxeye daisies with gypsophila about halfway along the border. When she showed the border to an English friend, the first thing he said was: "How can you put that white in there? Don't you know that white isn't a color in the middle of all these colors and will leave a gap?" She immediately saw what he meant and was surprised that she had not seen it herself earlier. The oxeye daisies are therefore nowhere to be seen in the oldest planting plan from 1948. She did continue to use the fine gypsophila; she felt it was "like a little cloud floating among the plants."

Flowering Season

Mien believed that you ought to put a limit on the flowering season as well as on colors. "If you try to include spring, summer, fall, and winter in a design, you will lose the connection and large gaps will form," she said about this in *Mijn Tuinen* (*My Gardens*) in 1987. One of the commandments was: choose plants that will flower consecutively, from the beginning of June to the end of September, making sure that you plant a late-flowering species in front of an early-flowering species to cover any bare spots. And select plants that flower for a long time or remain attractive after flowering—because of their foliage, for example. This will prevent gaps in the border. She preferred to plant spring-flowering plants in a corner close to the house, combined with small shrubs. Gaps in the border cannot be entirely avoided, even when these principles are followed. Annuals such as *Zinnia*, *Tagetes*, and *Nicotiana* can then be used to fill in the empty spaces. For the large border, Mien chose June, July, and August as the flowering season. A short flowering season isn't a problem in a large garden such as the Old Experimental Garden, because the shrubs across from the border flower in spring. This decision means there is a profusion of flowers in the summer months, clearly displaying her use of contrast in color and flower shape.

Layout

A traditional border has a front and a back. The front is often a path or lawn, while the back is bounded by a high hedge or fence, as in the large border. The layout of the planting runs from front to back in a line from low to high. The shortest plants are at the front. Some of them, such as *Geum coccineum* 'Borisii', grow no taller than 30 centimeters. The tallest plants are at the back, and some of them even reach a height of over two meters, such as *Eupatorium purpureum.* The layout in between does not follow a strict line, because plants are never exactly the same height. Add some variety to the contours by planting tall, rarefied plants in between the low plants to provide a whimsical effect. Mien did this by using *Verbena bonariensis* or *Verbena hastata*, for example. She did not plant ornamental grasses in the large border, but rather in the wavy-edged islands on the other side of the path. Here she chose rarefied grasses and elegant, ascending forms, such as *Helictotrichon sempervirens*, *Yucca filamentosa,* and *Iris germanica*, as a graceful transition to the extensive lawn.

▼ The spent flowers of *Helenium* covered in hoarfrost

► View of the Old Experimental Garden in fall

Flower Shape

When choosing plants, she not only considered the flower color to be important, but also the flower shape. Vertical and horizontal forms had to be alternated, because too many bushy plants like *Helenium* would be too bulky, and too many spiky, ascending flowers give a choppy effect. From a distance, the contour of the plants should look like the silhouette of a city, "in which ascending towers interrupt the massive building blocks." In the large border, she combined the violet-blue, spiky *Salvia nemorosa* 'Ostfriesland', the yellow rosettes of *Achillea filipendulina* 'Coronation Gold', and the coppery-red *Helenium* 'Moerheim Beauty'—a typical Mien Ruys combination with a wide contrast in flower color and shape.

The Large Border over the Years

Based on Mien's notebooks, there seemed to always be something that needed to be changed in the large border: plants that had to be cut back, such as *Eupatorium*; regularly dug up, treated with manure, and replanted, such as *Aconitum*; and added to, such as *Delphinium*. Plants that did not live up to her expectations were replaced by others. New plant genera were tried out; other species were replaced by improved cultivars. In fact, the large border continued to be an experiment for almost 80 years, until the Old Experimental Garden received the status of a site of historic interest. This did not mean that no more changes could be made to the plants, because maintenance and alterations due to new circumstances are always needed. The parameters, however, remain the same: the traditional layout from low to high, the contrasts in color and flower shape, and the main flowering season of June, July, and August. New plant genera are no longer added, but improved cultivars may be introduced of plants that are already there or of plants that formerly had a place in the border.

Maintenance of the Large Border

A traditional border like the large border requires a lot of maintenance. Each species has its own spot in accordance with the planting plan. Plants that like to expand beyond their boundaries have to be held in check to protect the more modest ones. Many plants in the large border tend to fall over and therefore need support. These supports must remain unseen. For example, every *Delphinium* stalk is tied up with string to its own stick, and the weak stalks of *Alstroemeria* are kept upright by means of countless brush twigs. Flowers that have died off have to be deadheaded to prevent the plant from diverting its energy to seed forming. The stems of several plants must be cut back by about a third at the end of May or beginning of June to extend their flowering season, also known as the "Chelsea chop."

On the topic of "getting the border ready for winter" (cutting back the remains of plants that have died back in fall) Mien Ruys had a definite opinion. She wrote about it in *Borders*. She called the process of maintenance (1939) an "odious habit" and considered a pruned border to be "hopelessly dreary and bare" in winter. She found the gray and brown winter shades attractive, especially when the dead flower heads were covered in a layer of hoarfrost

or snow. "A border can be a miracle in the middle of winter," she wrote. Furthermore, the stalks provide natural protection against rotting and freezing.

Mien wrote that all perennials in a border ought to be dug up and separated once every six years, the soil should be turned over and treated with manure, and the plants then replanted. This is a tremendous amount of work when it comes to the large border, with its surface area of some 130 square meters. She did it in the early years because it "was the right thing to do." But one day, when it was the border's turn to be tackled again, it was actually looking wonderful the way it was. She decided to stop this practice and see what would happen.

At the beginning of the 1980s, the border was rather neglected. Old planting plans revealed that several plants had disappeared, and some other species had spread too far. The gardener, Dirk Jan Koning, modified the border and made sure that, in the years that followed, the plants remained more or less in their place. Nonetheless, he was not satisfied with the outcome. In November 1999, he turned over the whole border. The plants were dug up and placed in labeled crates where they would stay until spring. The soil, now considerably subsided, was topped up with soil and compost. After that, the border was replanted according to the old planting plan (for the most part) and treated with manure. Dirk Jan thought that the border could then be left for ten years, but it was another 20 years before the border was once again rigorously turned over. Starting in 2020, everything was dug up again and the soil was replenished, treated with manure, and replanted. It wasn't done all at once this time, but in three stages to spread the work. The arrangement has been slightly altered and several species have been replaced compared to the old planting plans. Nonetheless, some plants continue to be a bit sickly, and we can only guess the reason. This has actually been going on for a long time, since Mien Ruys herself said that a number of species thrived much better in the earlier years compared to recent decades. It may be because, in the early years, the borders were used as stool beds for the nursery. Cutting off the plants' young shoots and using them as cuttings caused the plants to grow more branches and become stronger. The hot, dry summers of the last few years may also help to explain the problem. We can spray plants to combat drought, but temperatures of around 40 degrees Celsius in this very sunny spot are extremes that have never occurred before. *Aconitum carmichaelii* 'Arendsii', for instance, has struggled in recent years. This monkshood, which is almost indispensable in the border due to its spiky blue flowers, prefers some shade. The plant can withstand sun, but this sunny spot with these weather conditions is too much for it. The plant thrives much better in shadier spots.

A considerable proportion of the species that used to be in the border, according to the old planting plan, are still there. Some of them are even in the same spot, such as *Eupatorium purpureum* and *Campanula lactiflora*, suffering the same problems that Mien regularly mentioned in her notes: "Make sure that the *Eupatorium* does not take over from the *Campanula*." Despite intensive maintenance and all the worries and problems, it is wondrous to see how this border develops in a single season. After the withered chaos of winter and the flat green blanket of budding plants in spring, summer brings an abundant, colorful mass of flowers that reaches higher than the fence, year after year.

Larkspur

Delphinium, or larkspur, was indispensable in the border in Mien's view. She considered it to be "a miracle of beauty, the most exquisite of all the perennials." She grew up among larkspur, as many were grown in the Moerheim Nursery. Moerheim even introduced noteworthy new hybrids into the market, such as the first white *Delphinium* 'Moerheimii' in 1909 and the lilac-pink *Delphinium ×ruysii* 'Pink Sensation' in 1938.

Larkspur's flowers may be short-lived, but their clusters of flowers on tall spikes have a commanding presence. There have been attempts to grow this plant in colors other than blue, but larkspur is mainly used for its magnificent shades of blue, ranging from very pale blue to deep, dark blue. Mien frequently used the stronger species of *Delphinium elatum* and *Delphinium* (Belladonna group) in her planting plans. She placed large numbers of larkspur in a diagonal line in bigger borders, in between later flowering perennials, so that once they finished flowering, they would be camouflaged by other plants. They are plants that need a lot of care and attention: manure, being tied up, deadheaded after they flower, regularly dug up and replanted. Besides this, they are vulnerable to slug damage, wind, and rain. As the grower Coen Jansen mentions in his catalog: "All the plagues of Egypt in one plant."

▲ Girl in amongst the *Delphinium* nursery beds in the nursery

◄ *Delphinium* 'Ouvertüre' in the large border has bright blue flowers with lilac edges.

pages 40–41: Flowering plants in harmonizing cool colors that have gray and reddish-brown foliage are used in the Mixed Border (1974).

MAKING A PLANTING PLAN

The seven commandments Mien drew up in 1939 are still very useful when making a planting plan, certainly for those new to gardening. The information below makes it easier to make a planting plan for a border of perennials.

The Place

Take account of where the border is when choosing plants. Conditions such as the type of soil, its position with respect to the sun, and the surrounding area are crucial.

Type of Soil

The type of soil provides information about its ability to hold water, the acidity of the soil, and whether the soil is rich in nutrients or lacks them. The most common types of soil in the Netherlands are sandy soil, clay soil, and peaty soil.

- Sandy soil is dry, loose, and granular. An advantage is that sandy soil is easy to work with; its disadvantages are that it is not good at retaining water and is often lacking in nutrients. You can improve its water-retaining qualities and the amount of nutrients by adding compost.
- Clay soil is very fine; it becomes sticky when wet and crusts over when dry. The soil is difficult to work, and drainage is poor. An advantage is that clay soil is usually rich in nutrients. You can improve its drainage qualities by adding compost or sand.
- Peaty soil is made up of the remains of plants and is rich in humus, but it often lacks nutrients. This soil retains water well and is easier to work with than clay soil. A disadvantage is that peaty soil is rather acidic. Its acidity can be adjusted by adding lime.

Position

The position determines how much sun the border gets each day. The amount of light plants need in summer can be defined as follows:
sun: more than six hours of sun a day
partial shade: three to six hours of sun a day
shade: fewer than three hours of sun a day
In general, south-facing gardens have the most hours of sun and north-facing gardens the fewest. An east-facing garden will have sun at the beginning of the day, while a west-facing garden will have sun at the end of the day. Most flowering plants need quite a lot of sun. Spring-flowering plants and foliage plants can be planted in shady spots.

Surroundings

A border should never be seen in isolation. Trees, hedges, shrubs, fences, and walls mark its boundaries and affect the amount of sunlight it gets. Large trees in or close to the garden may cast a lot of shade.

The Plant and the Importance of Its Scientific Name

Perennials are herbaceous plants whose visible parts—leaves, stems, and flowers—die back in fall. The roots under the ground continue to live on so that the plant can sprout again in spring. Every plant, whether natural or cultivated, has its own scientific name that comprises two or three parts. The first name is the genus, the second the species. The third part is the name of the cultivar, which applies to cultivated species. An example: *Salvia* (genus) *nemorosa* (species) 'Caradonna' (cultivar). The use of these names makes it precisely clear which plant is being referred to. Using the common name can sometimes lead to confusion. The genus *Campanula* is commonly known as bellflowers, but within the genus there are many species with different characteristics. *Campanula carpatica*, for instance, is 10 centimeters tall, while *Campanula pyramidalis* grows to 150 centimeters.

▲ The flower of *Primula japonica* 'Miller's Crimson' is much taller than its foliage.

pages 44–45: Old Experimental Garden with sundial

And the infamous *Aegopodium podagraria* has several common names: ground elder, bishop's weed, goutweed, and jump-about.

Structural, Filler, and Weaving Plants

Perennials can be classified according to their function in the border.

- Structural plants are those with a strong shape that remain visually attractive for a long time, often even in winter. Examples of structural plants are *Phlomis*, *Achillea*, *Echinacea*, and *Echinops*.
- Filler plants are those that literally fill up space. They often provide groundcover and are rather shapeless. These plants are especially useful at the front of a border. Examples of filler plants are *Geranium*, *Alchemilla*, and *Nepeta*.
- Weaving plants are transparent and rarefied, often with little foliage and tall stems. They can be used as eye-catchers in the border. Examples of meandering plants are *Verbena bonariensis*, *Thalictrum*, and *Digitalis*.

Height and Flowering Season

When choosing plants, their need for light is not the only criterion. Height and flowering season are also important. Some species are listed with two heights, since foliage and flower can differ greatly in height. The foliage of *Primula japonica* 'Miller's Crimson' grows no taller than 20 centimeters, whereas its flowers reach a height of 60 centimeters. The flowering season usually gives an indication of the period in which the plant flowers, such as May–July. This does not mean that the plant will flower from the beginning of May until the end of July, but somewhere in the period from May through July. The exact flowering is tricky to predict, because weather conditions greatly affect flowering times. A cold spring may mean late flowering, and sometimes plants spontaneously flower for a second time later in the season.

Flower Color

The choice of certain flower colors is very personal. A few general categories can serve as a guide:

- contrasting (complementary) colors: colors that reinforce each other. These are orange and blue, yellow and violet, red and green.
- harmonizing colors: colors that are related, such as blue, violet, and red-violet and yellow, orange, and red.

Combinations of contrasting colors are very striking. Harmonizing colors are more restful.

Colors can also be categorized as:

- warm colors (yellow, orange, red)
- cool colors (green, blue, violet, purple)

Green is always in abundance in a garden and provides a subduing effect. Often the color of the flower is the deciding factor when choosing a plant, but this is sometimes overestimated. A plant only flowers for a few weeks but is a feature of the border for the entire season. The shape of the plant, its height, the color and shape of its leaves and stems, and what it looks like in winter are other important aspects to consider.

Flower Shape

The shape of the flower (as shown opposite) can be categorized as:

1. spiky, such as *Salvia*
2. spherical, such as *Echinops*
3. cup-shaped, such as *Hemerocallis*
4. plumed, such as *Astilbe*
5. umbelliform, such as *Achillea*
6. radial, such as *Helenium*
7. saucer-shaped, such as *Geranium*

Combining different flower shapes makes the planting more varied. The flower shape of many perennials, particularly structural plants, remains visible in winter after the plant has died back, providing winter interest. Examples are *Achillea*, *Echinops*, and *Echinacea*.

◀ Contrasting colors of *Geum* 'Totally Tangerine' and *Geranium* 'Blue Blood'

▼ Harmonizing colors of *Monarda* 'Gewitterwolke' and *Anemone* 'Ouvertüre'

pages 46-47: Old Experimental Garden with sundial

The Plan

Having acquired all this information, it is time to make a planting plan. A step-by-step guide:

- Draw a good scale plan of the border, for example 1:50 (one centimeter on the plan is 50 centimeters in reality).
- Add an arrow showing where north is.
- Draw different sized beds in the border: about two to six square centimeters on the drawing representing half to one square meter in reality. Draw the beds organically: not too straight and not too neatly.
- Indicate the following in each bed:
  a height: for example, 0–40 cm, 40–80 cm, 80–120 cm, and taller than 120 cm
  a flowering season: for example, April–May, June–July, August–September, October–November
- Put the taller heights toward the back of the border and the lower ones at the front. Make smart combinations: most early-flowering plants are fairly short, and many late-flowering plants are a bit taller.
- Now you know the requirements the plants in each bed have in terms of soil, sun, moisture, acidity, flowering season, height, and flower color. Use this information to search websites, catalogs, or books for plants that meet these requirements. Some growers have good search engines on their websites where you can filter by different conditions and characteristics. This will give you a list of possible plants. Take note of winter interest too: evergreen, foliage color, leaf shape, flower shape, and use of ornamental grasses.
- Make a selection from the list for each bed on the plan on the basis of:
  combinations: plants that form an attractive group in terms of height, flowering time, color, and shape
  your own preferences.
- Decide on the number of square meters for each bed and calculate how many plants will have to be bought. Most growers or garden centers will tell you how many plants are needed per square meter. Lay a transparent sheet of graph paper on top of the plan to roughly determine how big each bed is.
- Look for growers who can deliver the plants.

A few more tips:

- Choose long-flowering plants for the larger beds and plants with a short flowering season for the smaller beds.
- Make sure there is variety in the shapes of flowers and foliage.
- Do not choose too many different species at first; others can always be added.
- Choose plants you know (at least for part of the border).
- Look for inspiration by visiting gardens and nurseries.
- Use the full scientific (Latin) name to be sure of getting the right plant.
- Bring the flowering season forward by planting bulbs in amongst the perennials.

A planting plan like this will ensure you have a good basis. This does not mean that all the work is done. Some plants will spread, others will disappear. Modifications will always be needed, because, as Mien Ruys used to say: "A garden is a process."

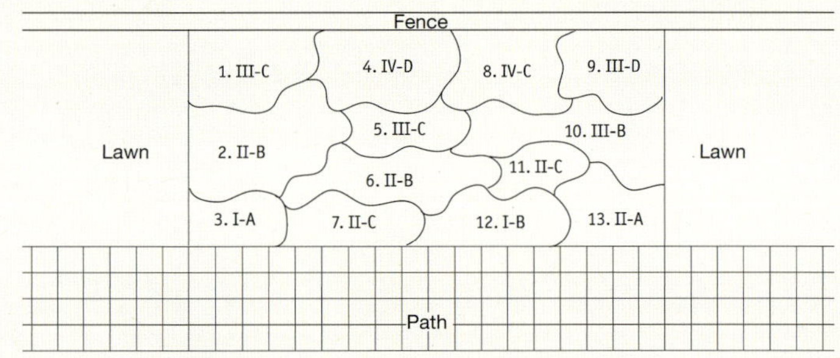

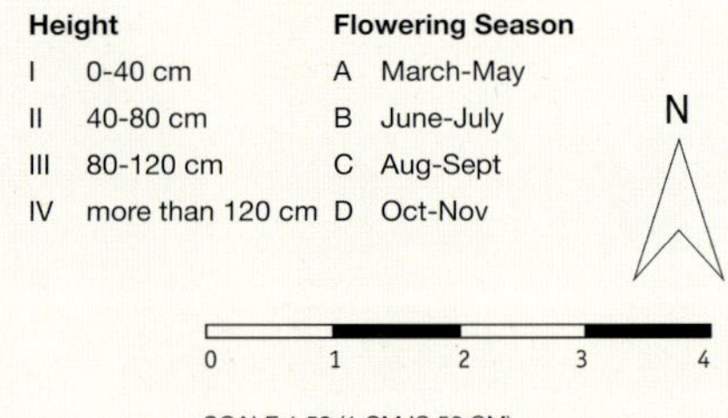

▲ An example of a plan for a border drawn to scale. Each bed contains a code for a height and a flowering season. This is a simple way of making a planting plan.

► The combination of the saucer-shaped flowers of *Anemone* and the spikes of *Persicaria* is a good example of contrast in flower shape.

1930-1940

THE NETHERLANDS DURING THE CRISIS YEARS

Plummeting share prices in the United States during the stock market crash of 1929 had an enormous snowball effect on the international economy. The crisis also reached the Netherlands. Domestic and foreign trade was reduced to a minimum. There was no money: consumers had none, businesses had none, and the banks had none. This crisis led to rocketing unemployment, and those without work were pushed into poverty by the minimum support provided by the government. The unemployed were forced to work on projects, such as planting parcels of woodland, draining and clearing peatland and heathland, and digging canals. Extreme poverty and abominable working conditions led to major unrest among the population. The economy only began to improve somewhat just before the outbreak of World War II in 1940.

A Bleak Time for Mien

The period of the economic crisis in the 1930s brought Mien Ruys little joy. She often felt dispirited and lonely in Dedemsvaart and wanted more from life. She tried to break away from the established order in her family and in Dedemsvaart. She had decidedly left-wing sympathies, which were incompatible with her parents' political convictions. She spoke of her political dilemma in a radio interview in 1987. The first time she was able to vote, probably in the early 1930s, was in the local council elections. That day, she was busy working in the nursery and did not want to go and vote. There was a bell at her parents' house that was hardly ever used. When the bell rang, she ran back to the house. Her father was waiting for her and said: "The mayor just called to say you have not voted. Go to the voting station immediately." She had no wish to vote for a right-wing candidate and had no confidence in the left-wing candidate either, " … because he was an illiterate peat digger, I couldn't do it. I knew a gentleman farmer who was right-wing, but a decent man, so I thought, 'For heaven's sake, I'll just have to vote for him'."

The Van Nelle Factory in 2017

Het Nieuwe Bouwen (Functionalism) (1920–1940)

A new, modern architectural movement developed in the Netherlands in the 1920s called *Het Nieuwe Bouwen* (also known as functionalism). It was a movement in which the function of the building or the space determined its form. Design and use of materials are functional in Het Nieuwe Bouwen; ornamental elements do not appear because they have no function. Its creed is light, air, and space, and much use was made of new building techniques with materials such as concrete, glass, and steel. Urban development, architecture, landscape gardening, and landscape architecture became intertwined, and the connection between house and garden became important. Many large projects for social housing with modern amenities were launched. Green spaces such as parks and communal gardens were thought to contribute to a healthy living environment and a feeling of solidarity. The Rotterdam group of architects *Opbouw* and its Amsterdam equivalent *De 8* both championed this architectural style. In 1927, the two groups began working together. Well-known names from these groups are Jan Brinkman and Leen van der Vlugt (who designed the Van Nelle Factory), Ben Merkelbach, Cornelis van Eesteren, Gerrit Rietveld, and Mart Stam. They challenged traditional architectural ideas, such as those of the Delftse School.

◄ An early garden design by Mien Ruys incorporating dry stack walls in the garden of a villa

> "Cosmopolitan Amsterdam and provincial Dedemsvaart was exactly the right combination."

Following an illness, Mien's mother died in 1935, which came as a great shock to Mien. The political situation in Germany, where Hitler was now in power, made her angry and depressed. She had no luck in love either. Once again, she had embarked on an uncertain relationship with a married man. Her decision to move her landscape gardening studio to Amsterdam in 1937 turned out to be a good one. Cosmopolitan Amsterdam and provincial Dedemsvaart provided exactly the right combination of art, culture, and architecture in the one, and nature, peace and quiet, and space in the other.

Working and Learning

Mien Ruys would have liked to have stayed longer in Berlin but returned to her work as a landscape designer in early 1930 when duty called her. The landscape gardening studio still had plenty of work in that first year, but as the economic crisis continued, the work diminished. In the quiet winter of 1931–1932, she attended lectures in architecture at the technical college in Delft to nurture her interest in the subject. Here, she learned how to see the connection between urban development, architecture, landscape gardening, and landscape architecture. She was taught by Professor Granpré Molière, the founder of the Delftse School, an architectural movement characterized by austerity and simplicity. It advocated the use of traditional shapes and materials, such as bricks, roof tiles, and natural stone. Mien often disagreed with Granpré Molière. After a lecture in which he said that "beauty is that which one intuitively perceives as beauty," she engaged him in debate. Mien told him that she considered the new Van Nelle Factory in Rotterdam, which she had passed on the train, to be very attractive. Granpré Molière replied that her intuition was incorrect. The Van Nelle Factory in Rotterdam was a modern building made of steel and glass and was a typical example of Het Nieuwe Bouwen. The designers, Brinkman and Van der Vlugt, were members of Opbouw, a group of architects who were diametrically opposed to Granpré Molière's Delftse School.

In the early 1930s, Mien Ruys was appointed head of the nursery's landscape gardening studio. Due to the crisis, the nursery had little income, which had forced them to dismiss workers. Mien filled the gaps in the workforce, which implied she had to work very hard and for long hours. She spent most of her time designing and making planting plans for the gardens of villas. Her designs were generally in the architectural style that was in fashion at that time: symmetric gardens with an obvious structure and height differences that were bridged by brickwork elements such as retaining walls, steps, and planters. This style of garden also included large borders of perennials, in line with the ideas of Gertrude Jekyll. Mien was able to greatly indulge herself in making planting plans for these borders due to her extensive knowledge of plants and the huge assortment available in the nursery. She was asked to write articles on this topic for various magazines, such as *Onze Tuinen* (*Our Gardens*), *De vrouw en haar Huis* (*Woman and her Home*) and *Het Landhuis* (*The Country House*). In 1939, she published her first book, *Borders. Hoe men ze maakt en onderhoudt* (*Borders: How to Make and Maintain Them*), in which she talked about design, choosing plants, and the layout and maintenance of gardens as a way of sharing her own knowledge and experience of gardens and gardening with garden owners. The Old Experimental Garden is clearly recognizable as a source of inspiration for the text and the photos.

Borders. Hoe men ze maakt en onderhoudt, Mien's first book

She also began designing communal gardens for various housing projects that emerged from Het Nieuwe Bouwen in the 1930s. Mien was an advocate of having communal gardens close to large apartment buildings. She felt that the countless private gardens in the city, with all their fences, sheds, henhouses, and laden washing lines, made an untidy impression. Despite the shadows cast by the high buildings, the advantages of communal gardens lay in the space that they created: space in which residents could be outside and children could play safely in the busy, crowded city. The design for the communal garden for the Geuzenhof I apartment building in Amsterdam in 1933 was probably her first project. This almost symmetrical design features hedges, groups of shrubs, groups of perennials, a pond, an aviary, sandpits, and a playground for children with benches where mothers could sit and knit while keeping an eye on their children, as Mien later described.

▼ The large border in the Old Experimental Garden in the 1930s

THE EXPERIMENTAL GARDENS AFTER 1927

▲ The now-lost Blue Garden in the 1930s

◀ Queen Juliana of the Netherlands and Mien Ruys in the Pink Border in 1950

▶ The Avenue of *Hostas* in 1934 (above)

▶ The Double Border in 1934 (below left)

▶ Design drawing for the Blue Garden for the BNT exhibition in 1941 (below right)

page 56: The Pink Border in the 1930s. Several groups of *Phlox*, a plant Mien Ruys frequently planted in her borders, can be seen in the photo.

page 57: The pale pink *Phlox* 'Utopia', grown by Coen Jansen, is a strong cultivar and resistant to mildew. It is seen here in combination with *Anemone* 'Ouvertüre'. *Persicaria amplexicaulis* 'Blackfield' and *Veronicastrum virginicum* 'Roseum' can be seen in the background.

Blue Garden and Other Lost Gardens

The Old Experimental Garden from 1927 is the last of Mien Ruys's experiments from before the war to still be in existence. Old photos reveal that she conducted several experiments in those days, such as the Avenue of *Hostas*, the Double Border, and the Pink Border, which used to be where the current Herb Garden is. Somewhere between 1927 and 1939 there was an experiment with planting in the primary color blue. The design for this Blue Garden, which she used for the exhibition organized by the *Bond van Nederlandse Tuinarchitecten* (Federation of Dutch Landscape Gardeners, aka BNT), still exists. It can be seen from the drawing that the Blue Garden was in the spot occupied by the later Water Garden in 1954. The little bridges, the birch, and the hedge of *Chamaecyparis lawsoniana* 'Triomf van Boskoop' in the drawing are elements that were retained in the Water Garden. Her first book, *Borders. Hoe men ze maakt en onderhoudt*, published in 1939, contains photos of the garden and Mien's descriptions of her findings. Experimenting with planting in a single color does not produce attractive results, she felt. "It all becomes rather static due to the lack of contrast and lack of variety." One can read that she made many attempts to improve the color combinations by separating blue and purple with gray and some white and by using pale blue and lilac. Eventually, she did consider the blue border to be a success. "A blue border

is not cheerful, luminous, or radiant. But once one has immersed oneself in the strange atmosphere, it never lets one go; one is driven to observe this wonder at all times of the day, in all lights."

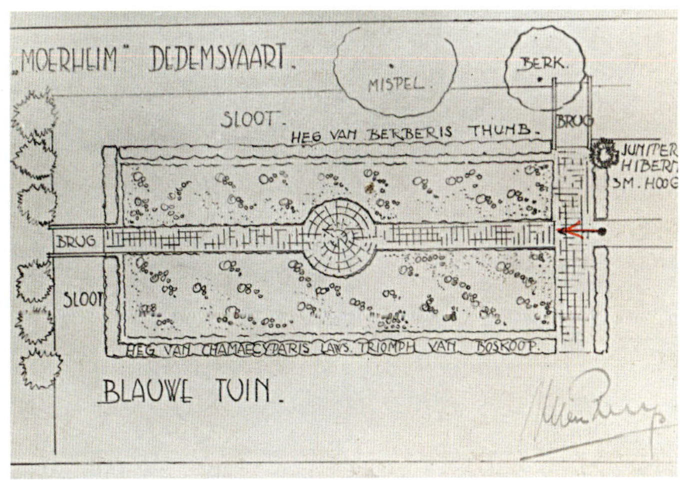

1940-1945

THE NETHERLANDS DURING THE WAR

On May 10, 1940, the German army invaded the Netherlands, and, after the bombing of Rotterdam on May 14, the Netherlands surrendered. The first few months of the occupation were relatively quiet, but as the war progressed, the German occupying forces began imposing more and more restrictions and the atmosphere became grim. The deportation of Jews was stepped up, and the *Arbeitseinsatz* made it compulsory for young Dutchmen to go and work in Germany.

In 1942, artists, entertainers, architects, musicians, and other groups of professionals working in art and culture were obliged to join the *Kultuurkamer.* Its main aim was to spread the National Socialist message. Refusal meant that you could not practice your profession. In the winter of 1944–1945, food shortages and extreme cold led to a severe famine, especially in the west of the country. The south of the Netherlands was liberated in the fall of 1944, and on May 5, 1945, Germany's capitulation was officially signed.

Between Amsterdam and Dedemsvaart

During the war years, Mien Ruys's feelings lurched back and forth between anger, hate, fear, guilt, and resignation, but sometimes also optimism about a good outcome and gratitude that she was still able to work. She was now living in Amsterdam but returned to Dedemsvaart shortly after the outbreak of war. There, she "went crazy because nothing happened there," as she said later, and returned to Amsterdam. She regularly traveled back and forth by train and a bike with wooden wheels. When she was in Dedemsvaart, she wanted to be in Amsterdam and vice versa. She no longer knew where home was and felt uprooted and despairing. In the end, she decided to continue her work in the studio in Amsterdam. She received a lot of help from her sister Lotte, who also lived in Amsterdam with her partner, Guus.

> "Will you make sure that someone is on the bus at such and such a time, because a bag of baby roses is coming?"

In 1941, Mien moved to the house at 157 Amstel in Amsterdam, where she would continue to live and work for the rest of her life when she wasn't in Dedemsvaart. More or less by accident, as the war went on, she became a contact between Jews in Amsterdam who were looking for a place to hide and Jo Scholten, a nurse in Dedemsvaart who arranged safe houses. They kept in touch by telephone, using a code language. Mien and Jo recounted that time in an interview with Koos Postema in 1983. Mien would say something like "I have a large standard rose I'm prepared to part with; can you look for a garden for it?" and "Will you make sure that someone is on the bus at such and such a time, because a bag of baby roses is coming?" Or Jo would phone Mien and say, "I have a little garden on the Zwarte Pad where there is room for some plants, will you send a few?" By doing so, she helped many Jews to find safe houses in the last period of the war.

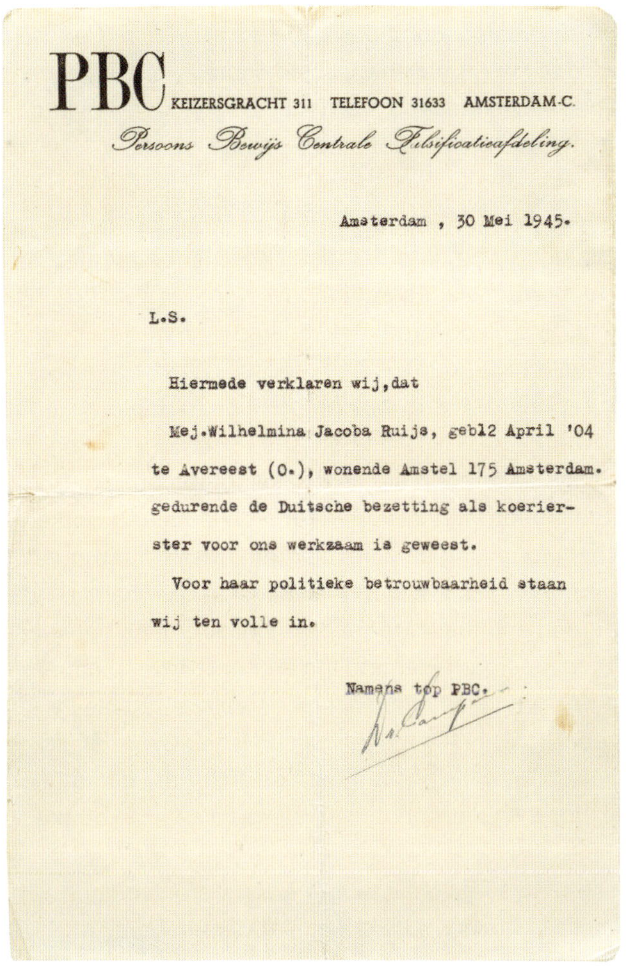

PBC KEIZERSGRACHT 311 TELEFOON 31633 AMSTERDAM-C.

Persoons Bewijs Centrale Falsificatieafdeling.

Amsterdam , 30 Mei 1945.

L.S.

Hiermede verklaren wij,dat

Mej.Wilhelmina Jacoba Ruijs, geb12 April '04 te Avereest (O.), wonende Amstel 175 Amsterdam. gedurende de Duitsche bezetting als koerierster voor ons werkzaam is geweest.

Voor haar politieke betrouwbaarheid staan wij ten volle in.

Namens tòp PBC.

Letter from *Persoonsbewijzencentrale* (Dutch resistance group that provided forged identity documents) stating that Mien Ruys had worked for the Resistance during the war

Working During the War

In September 1940, Bonne Ruys decided to retire as director of the nursery and was succeeded by Mien. She and her brothers, Jan Daniël and Theo, became co-directors of Moerheim. International trade again came to a halt during the war, but the work for the landscape gardening studio continued, particularly in the early years of the war. The workload was heavy, but Mien was glad to be able to continue working. It was a distraction and gave her satisfaction in this gloomy period. She wrote various articles for newspapers and magazines about gardens and, in 1941, her second book, *Vijvers in de tuin* (*Ponds in the Garden*), was published. In the same year, the garden designer and landscape architect Jan Bijhouwer invited her to attend a meeting of architects in Doorn.

Mien noticed that the architects there were split into groups, each with different ideas about architecture. Architects from De 8 and Opbouw were also at the meeting. She discovered that she had a great deal of affinity with this group's range of ideas. What appealed to her in particular was their proposition for the functional use of materials. This was how she used her planting, too: not as decoration but as a basis for the design. She became friends with this group of architects and worked with them for a long time. In their turn, the group thought highly of her ideas about the relationship between house and garden and the importance of collaboration between the landscape gardener and the architect/town planner in the design phase of a plan. She wrote an article in 1942 about this in the magazine published by De 8 and Opbouw, in which she cited her design for the communal garden for the Geuzenhof in Amsterdam as an example.

From 1942 to 1943, Mien taught *Tuinkunstoefeningen* (exercises in the art of gardening) at the Academy of Architecture in Amsterdam, where she was able to pass on her vision of the connection between house and garden to aspiring architects. She enjoyed the work; it challenged her and distracted her from the grim period of the war. Mien had joined the BNT (*Bond van Nederlandse Tuinarchitecten*, or Association of Dutch Landscape Architects) before the war and had now become a committee member. During the occupation, Mien was worried that members of the association would be obliged to join the *Nederlandsche Kultuurkamer* and come under the control of the occupying forces. To avoid this happening, she proposed that the association be disbanded. The chairman, Jan Bijhouwer, would not hear of it. Mien then decided to resign from the BNT to avoid being forced to join the *Nederlandsche Kultuurkamer.* Despite this, she was able to continue her work as a landscape gardener during the war, provided she had assignments.

THE EXPERIMENTAL GARDENS

As far as is known, no experimental gardens were laid out during the war and even the existing gardens were neglected. In all likelihood, it was difficult to find gardeners and materials, certainly in the second half of the war.

The alder at Wiekend in winter

1945-1955

THE NETHERLANDS DURING POST-WAR RECONSTRUCTION

Following liberation in 1945, people acted swiftly to repair the war damage to buildings and infrastructure and to build new homes. An enormous feeling of solidarity arose among the population, and within a few years, the economy had recovered and prosperity increased. Nonetheless, there was a huge shortage of housing. Many residential properties had been damaged during the war and few had been built since the crisis years. Many people lived in old, poorly maintained houses or were forced to move in with other people. Furthermore, the war was immediately followed by a baby boom. The housing shortage was dubbed "public enemy number one" and lasted until the 1960s.

Dutch society underwent enormous changes. The differences between the social classes began to fade, but the church and the traditional family still played important roles. The family, headed by the father, was seen as the cornerstone of society.

Better Times

Shortly after the war, Mien Ruys began a relationship with the publisher Theo Moussault. She had written a few articles in 1940 for the magazine *De Groene Amsterdammer*, for which Theo was executive director. In wasn't until years later, in 1947, that they actually met in person. "We finally noticed each other," as Mien wrote in her diary. They soon began living together in her house in Amsterdam, and they were married in 1950. Theo was keen to marry, but Mien didn't really see the need. She was 46; it was her first and only marriage. He was 62 and had already been married twice before. Theo was a *bon vivant* who brought a light and cheerful note into her strict Calvinist attitude to life. She spoke of this later: "He ridiculed me if I was too fanatical." Theo encouraged her in her work, especially when it came to sharing her knowledge and experience with others, and through his own pleasure-seeking lifestyle, he taught her to enjoy life more. He cooked regularly and took her out to dinner. Before they lived together, she had warned him of her terrible domestic skills. One day, when Theo brought a business associate home and asked if there was something to eat, Mien replied that she had told him she couldn't cook. Theo replied: "But I didn't know it was that bad!" Despite their differences, they were a happy couple whose marriage was harmonious.

Mien and Theo married in 1950

New Opportunities

Work in the design studio gained momentum again quite quickly after the war. Changes in society meant that the nature of the assignments also changed. There was less demand for designs for large villa gardens because it was almost impossible to find gardeners to maintain these types of gardens, with their lawns and large borders. As a socialist, Mien Ruys wanted to focus more on green spaces close to social housing and less on assignments for private gardens. She abandoned the architectural style with little walls and height differences that she had used before the war. Increasingly, she chose a plain, streamlined design incorporating straight lines and geometric shapes, obviously where appropriate for the building and its surroundings.

Initiated by Jan Bijhouwer and Mien Ruys, the BNT (association of Dutch landscape gardeners) was resurrected in 1945. Jan Bijhouwer became a board member while Mien Ruys became an ordinary member, without an executive position. The architects of De 8 and Opbouw had also reunited after the war. Because Mien felt more at home with this modernist group of architects than with the landscape gardeners and landscape architects at that time, her focus shifted away from her colleagues in the BNT. She only felt a connection with a few of them, such as Wim Boer and Hans Warnau. The collaboration with De 8 and Opbouw that had begun during the war developed further and led to many projects in which Mien Ruys played an important role as a landscape gardener and landscape architect. She made countless designs for communal gardens for housing projects and for gardens of institutions and factories in this period.

Mien's father, Bonne Ruys, died in 1950 at the age of 84. Since she had moved to Amsterdam in 1937, Mien generally lived and worked in Dedemsvaart during summer. After her father's death, the family home was sold. New accommodation had to be found, and Mien enlisted the help of Ben Merkelbach, one of the architects in De 8 and Opbouw who had become a good friend. He felt that the pigsty on the nursery site was the only suitable place to turn into a house. He designed a conversion to make a summer house, where Mien spent every summer. In her latter years, she lived there permanently, until her death in 1999.

The Garden City Movement

The garden city movement has been around since the beginning of the twentieth century. The idea of the urban garden emerged from the desire to improve the poor conditions in which workers then lived by combining the best of the city and the countryside to create a single "urban garden." Every village or neighborhood is an independent entity with its own facilities, plenty of green spaces, and playgrounds. Even before World War II, neighborhoods and villages in the Netherlands were built in accordance with this concept. Initially, building took place according to the artisan architecture of movements such as the Amsterdam School, using traditional materials like bricks. Later, the garden city movement was woven into the functionalist ideas of Het Nieuwe Bouwen. It encompassed various types of residential property, from villas to mid-rise apartment buildings with no more than four floors. Taking the creed of "light, air, and space" as its basis, the residential properties were situated such that a maximum amount of light would enter. Main roads were separated from the residential areas; shops were situated on these main roads. The village of Nagele is an example of building according to these principles, as were the apartment buildings of Geuzenhof, Frankendael, and Patrimonium in Amsterdam, which are examples of projects built in line with the garden city movement.

Mien Ruys with drawing board in 1954

Sharing Knowledge

Theo Moussault encouraged Mien to share her knowledge and experience of gardens with the large group of people who had now been given gardens but knew little of gardening. This led to the publication of *Het vaste planten boek* (*Perennials*) in 1950, containing examples of garden designs and planting for flower gardens and dark urban gardens. She also gave tips for maintaining a garden, lists of plants for specific conditions, even for roof gardens, and an alphabetical list with extensive information about each plant. Her brothers, Jan Daniël and Theo, and her sister Miekie also collaborated on the book, but Mien Ruys was probably responsible for most of its contents. At that time, there was no practical standard work available on perennials, whose range had undergone enormous development in the previous 50 years. In the words of Jan Bijhouwer, who wrote the foreword, this book "... met a long-felt need." German and Swedish translations of the book followed swiftly. *Het vaste planten boek* was reprinted at regular intervals until the end of the 1970s and, for many people in the world of green spaces, it is the definitive handbook for information and inspiration.

Mien Ruys gave lectures on landscape gardening, landscape architecture, and the art of gardening at the Universities of Wageningen and Delft in this period. Initially, she substituted for Jan Bijhouwer, who had gone to the United States as a guest lecturer. When he returned, Mien was asked to continue her lectures, and she lectured on urban greenery at the Faculty of Architecture. When she asked for more attention to be paid to landscape gardening and landscape architecture as part of this class and the university refused to comply, she resigned.

Mien in the nursery in 1954

Mien in the Old Experimental Garden in 1954

▲ The garden at Wiekend in the spring of 2023

▶ Mien with a drawing board on the patio at Wiekend in the 1950s (above)

▶ Mien painting at Wiekend in the 1950s/1960s (center)

▶ Mien with her sister Miekie in 1955 (below)

pages 68-69: The Square Garden, Autumn Garden, and City Garden

Wiekend (1950)

The summerhouse that had been built by converting the old pigsty in 1950 and given the name *Wiekend* obviously needed a garden. A diagonal line, which Mien Ruys frequently used in her designs, still divides the space into a patio, lawn, and beds with plants. The design brings the lawn and the plants close to the living room, which affords a view of the garden through French windows. This means that you look out onto the green of the garden rather than the patio with its garden chairs. The garden borders on the Wiek, one of the old, reclaimed ditches that were known as *wijken* or *wiek* in the local dialect. Once some of the reeds in the ditch were removed, the other side of the garden came into view. Opening up this view created a connection between the surroundings and the garden, making it appear bigger than it is. The triangular bed contains strong, long-flowering "typical Mien Ruys" plants in bright colors, such as *Achillea filipendulina* 'Cloth of Gold', *Aconitum carmichaelii* 'Arendsii', *Solidago* [Golden Gate] ('Dansolgold'), *Lychnis chalcedonica*, *Geranium* ×*magnificum*, and *Salvia nemorosa* 'Blauhügel'. Hedges and palisades provide boundaries for the garden. After Mien Ruys's death in 1999, the house had various functions and, until 2016, did not form part of the tour of the Gardens. Wiekend was radically altered in 2013. The internal walls were removed, and the roof was lifted half a meter. The half meter between the façade and the roof was filled in with glass and now provides light, air, and space—entirely in line with the modern building style popular in the post-war reconstruction period. The space is now used as a knowledge center and area for workshops and exhibitions. New grion tiles (see page 248 in the chapter "Typical Mien Ruys") were handmade and laid during the restoration of the garden.

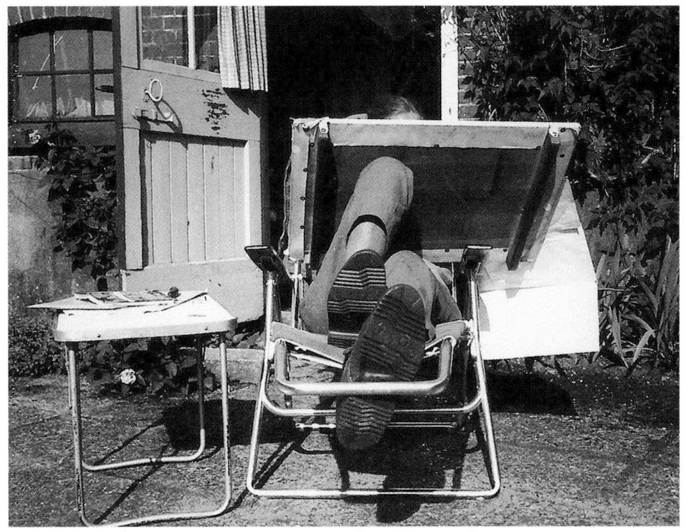

Water Garden (1954)

Mien Ruys's first experiment in her gardens after World War II was the Water Garden in 1954. A little bridge across the existing ditch connected the Old Experimental Garden with this part of the garden and the nursery behind it. This is probably where the Blue Garden was. It was now time for a new experiment: a design for a smaller garden in response to the fact that more people had a garden attached to their house. It had to be low-maintenance so that there was no need to employ a gardener. The aim of this experiment was not just to find a type of design that met these new circumstances, but also to establish which plants were suitable for dry or wet conditions. The weeping birch and the conifer hedge were included in the design.

The design for the Water Garden is still in its original form and comprises beds for plants, a place to sit, and a pond. The garden is surrounded by hedges. The impression is of an enclosed space, helped by the small difference in height of about 10 centimeters. There is a definite contrast between the high, dry, and sunny south-facing section and the low, damp, and shady section to the north of the garden. The L-shaped pond continues a little into the dry, sunny part and thus connects the two areas. The

south-facing section comprises two raised levels, and its planting makes it look like a rock garden. Its lines are clear-cut and straight, however, and "not a naturalistic pile of haphazard rocks looking like a disoriented imitation of mountainous scenery in our flat country," as Mien later described it in her magazine *Onze Eigen Tuin* (*Our Own Garden*). The planting consists of miniature conifers combined with gray and fine-leaved plants to reinforce the dry, sunny impression. The dry-stack walls are made from blocks of natural stone. At the northern end of the garden, large-leaved, linear plants in combination with the water plants in the pond provide a green, fresh, and damp look. Grion tiles laid in a staggered pattern a few centimeters apart were used for the paving. Moss and grass are allowed to grow in between the tiles. The effect is to make the garden look softer, and the structure of the paving pattern is clearly visible. During the renovation of this garden in 2002, a mirror image of an imprint of the newspaper the *Dedemvaartse Courant* from 1954 was found on one of the old grion tiles. The newspaper had been used to line the templates for the tiles.

In its time, the garden was designated low-maintenance due to the absence of large borders and a lawn, which required a lot of time to maintain. At a time when there were no robot lawnmowers, maintaining a lawn was particularly intensive. Nevertheless, this garden, with its gaps between the tiles that regularly have to be trimmed, a pond, and the planting of over a hundred species, is not what would be called low-maintenance nowadays.

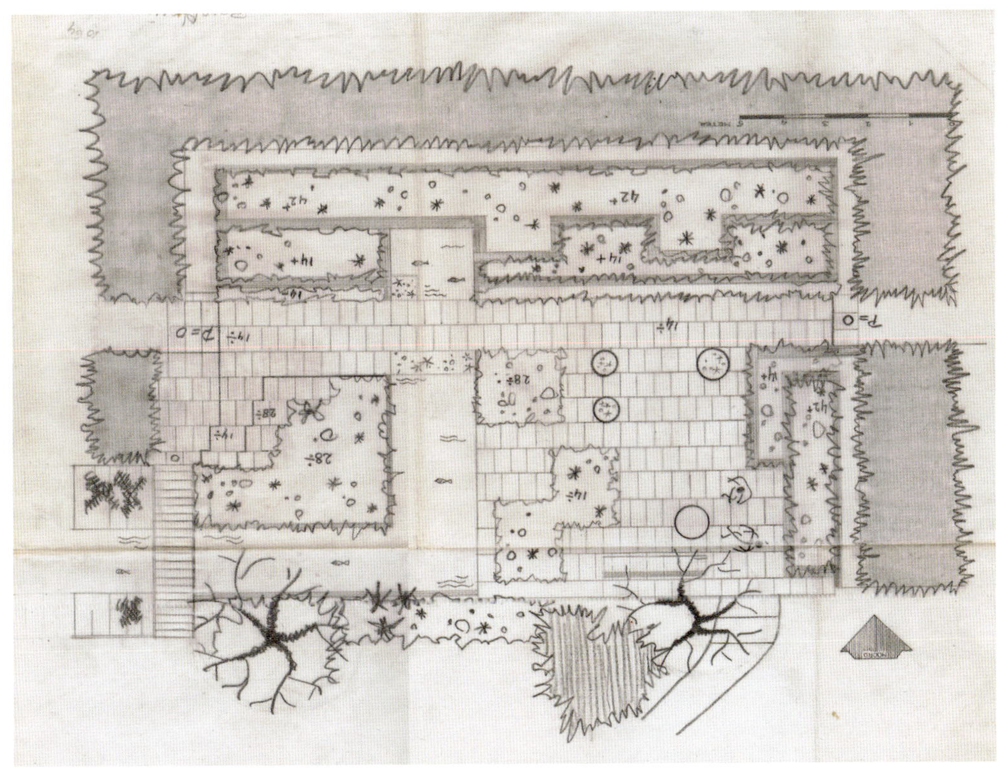

◀ The rock garden part of the Water Garden with little walls made from natural stone (above left)

◀ The lions head is a built-in water ornament in the Water Garden (above right)

◀ Laying the Water Garden in 1954. Mien is on the right helping to set out the plants. (below left)

◀ Mien and Theo on the patio at the Water Garden in the 1950s (below right)

▶ Design for the Water Garden by Mien Ruys in 1954

1945–1955

The New Village of Nagele

After the war, a completely new village was built in the Northeast Polder that was reclaimed in 1942. The group of architects united in De 8 and Opbouw designed the village. Town planners, architects, landscape gardeners, and landscape architects, some of whom worked under the banner of De 8 and Opbouw, collaborated closely to invent a village on the drawing board. It was a unique opportunity to turn the functionalist ideas of Het Nieuwe Bouwen into a reality.

A broad, wooded green strip surrounds the village of Nagele, which lies in an open polder landscape. The layout of the village consists of horizontal and vertical straight lines and sections at right angles to each other. Facilities are clustered in the center of the village among green surroundings. Various residential nuclei with their own green spaces surround the center. Arterial roads run around the edge of the village, which means there is no through traffic in the village. Concrete and glass were used in abundance for the buildings. The houses—designed by Gerrit Rietveld and others—were placed such that as much light as possible can enter; each has only two floors and a flat roof. None of them have attics, because it was felt that they would become dusty, musty spaces where unnecessary junk would be stored, going against the creed of "light, air, and space." Mien Ruys worked on this project as its landscape gardener and landscape architect. She worked on the green structure of the village. The various green elements all had a specific function: to provide shelter, as partitions, for emphasis, to divide the space, or to guide the eye. The cemetery has the same layout as the village, with straight lines and sections, and its planting is rather exuberant with plenty of flowers and color. Her design included a beech archway as the entrance to the cemetery. Her idea was that everyone eventually goes the same way, regardless of religion. To Mien's disappointment, the archway was initially not included. In a letter written in 1974, she insisted that it should still be created. It wasn't until 2010 that a group of volunteers from Nagele ensured that the archway was finally erected.

Frankendael

Frankendael in Amsterdam is an example of post-war expansion in line with the garden city movement. The project comprised eight courtyard complexes, each of which has two L-shaped apartment buildings surrounding a communal inner garden. The properties were designed by Merkelbach and Karsten, architects associated with De 8 and Opbouw. They were known as duplex apartments, an idea that arose from the housing crisis: single-family dwellings on two floors, each with its own entrance. This meant that two families could temporarily live one above the other. Once the housing crisis had abated, the two

apartments could be combined into a single home. The apartments each had their own front yard and backyard, with the communal garden being bordered by the backyards of one L-shaped block and the front yards of the other. Mien Ruys designed the inner gardens. She made several designs because she considered it important that the communal garden in each block be different. The groups of buildings, which looked the same architecturally, would thus be given their own identities so that the residents would recognize their own gardens. To prevent the rectangular inner gardens from being divided into long, narrow strips, she employed the diagonal. Playgrounds for children were not to be forgotten in the inner gardens. She worked closely with the architect Aldo van Eyck on these; he had designed many children's playgrounds in Amsterdam. His tumble bars and climbing domes are particularly well-known.

Van Nelle Factory

Back in 1942, Mien Ruys had drawn up a design for the site surrounding the Van Nelle Factory she so admired. The war was probably the reason why it was not laid out until the early 1950s. The factory garden comprised a large lawn, colorful borders, flowering shrubs, and a pond. No tall trees, because she did not feel they were appropriate considering the scale of the tall building, but rather small trees that grow horizontally and large groups of strong shrubs and perennials. Entirely in line with the ideas at that time, it was important to her to improve the working conditions of the factory workers by giving them green and colorful surroundings. She wrote about this in her book on perennials, *Het vaste planten boek*, published in 1950: "Working in the factory was, for many, monotonous and stultifying enough but, until recently, they even had to spend their breaks and lunch hours in the same cheerless surroundings or ambling around the streets. Their aversion often began as they approached the factory. If the aim is to increase production, the first thing to do is arouse interest in the work in pleasant surroundings. Not only should the factory itself be a place where people are willing to work; not only are bright canteens necessary, the surrounding area must be nurtured too. […] Would it not be wonderful, after a long day standing at machines, to feel the damp soil beneath one's feet, to smell the scent of earth and grass?"

◀ Nagele at the end of the 1950s with homes designed by Gerrit Rietveld (left)

◀ One of the Frankendael courtyard complexes with the communal inner garden on the left and the backyards of the ground-floor apartments on the right (right)

▲ The Van Nelle factory with Mien Ruys's borders of perennials in the 1950s

1955-1965

THE NETHERLANDS: INCREASING PROSPERITY

Prosperity increased rapidly in the second half of the 1950s and the first half of the 1960s. Rising wages meant people had more to spend, and the introduction of the five-day work week gave them more time for recreation and vacations. Women began to challenge their role of housewife, and feminists fought for equal rights. Rock and roll reached the Netherlands and "greasers"—youths with greased quiffs who dressed in denim jeans and leather jackets and hung around the streets, many with motor scooters—rebelled against their parents and society.

Happy Times

This period was a happy one for Mien Ruys. Her marriage to Theo brought her the happiness she had missed in her younger years. They spent the springs and summers together in Dedemsvaart. For Mien, this was an ideal combination of working and being outside: she drew designs for her assignments and was busy in her experimental gardens. When a journalist from the *Volkskrant* newspaper rang the nursery to get information for an article, the answer was: "Miss Mien can't be found. She is probably in the garden, but we don't know where." The same article reported: "Ms. Ruys's work in the nursery—'I feel my hands itching in May and then I have to feel the soil'—and in her studio in Amsterdam provide her with an excellent synthesis for her assignment. In Dedemsvaart—her house there is a converted pigsty—she can grow the plants and flowers she expects to need for a particular assignment if, that is, she is asked to plant the garden as well as design it." Family and friends were frequent visitors. Theo cooked for them, and Mien was responsible for the flowers for the table. Her contribution to keeping house was still minimal. She said later in an interview: "Creating order out of chaos was what I did in gardens, but I was hopeless when it came to housekeeping. I was completely worthless domestically." They traveled to several places together, including to Denmark, the south of France, and the United States. They stayed in the Caribbean with Theo's daughter for a month. Mien loved it there and suggested to Theo that they should remain for longer. She wanted to sit on a boulder, stare at the sea, and see how long it took before she had had enough of it. Theo didn't think it was a good idea; he wanted to smell the asphalt in Amsterdam again. When they got back, Mien concluded that she too was delighted to be home again. When interviewed for the TV program *Laat ze maar praten* for the Dutch broadcaster NOS, she said: "This is what I want. I don't want to sit on a boulder; I want to make gardens until I die."

▲ Mien and Theo looking at a design

◄ Mien and Theo on one of their vacations

Large Projects and Small Gardens

Many of the newly built houses came with either a private garden or a green space for communal use. This brought an increasing amount of work for the design studio in Amsterdam, and it grew steadily. Mien poured love and passion into her work because designing gardens was her life. She was delighted to be given a leading role in designing green spaces for new housing estates with communal gardens, whose social aspect greatly appealed to her. Organization was not her greatest talent, and she had no patience for working out her designs in detail. She took on staff to do this kind of work for her. Her sister Miekie also came to work in the studio. She had looked after her father until she was 38 and, through living next to the nursery for all these years, had acquired a great deal of knowledge about plants. Mien coached her for a while, but soon Miekie was able to start making her own planting designs. Although the two sisters did not always work harmoniously together, they continued to do so for 30 years.

Onze Eigen Tuin

The idea for a magazine about gardens and gardening came from Theo Moussault. *Onze Eigen Tuin* (*Our Own Garden*) was launched in 1955. It was to be an affordable, simple, and accessible magazine about gardens and garden maintenance that both academics and laypeople could enjoy reading. It was a clever move by Theo the businessman as a means of putting the whole company in the spotlight. It forged a symbiosis between the design studio, the nursery, and the magazine. The magazine frequently ran advertisements for the nursery, both directly and indirectly. The studio's designs were often the topic of articles. The various experimental gardens in Dedemsvaart were singled out too, such as the Water Garden, Wiekend, and the City Garden, often combined with the Ready-to-make Borders, which were praised in passing as convenient and cheap. Several authors, including Jan Bijhouwer, provided practical and in-depth articles on gardens. Mien herself wrote a regular column entitled "Mien Ruys describes what needs to be done in the garden now." She wrote about garden plants, layouts, and maintenance. There were also regular offers of garden tours, for which Mien was the guide. *Onze Eigen Tuin*, "the gardener's favorite magazine to read," still publishes four times a year.

◂ Cover of *Onze Eigen Tuin*, winter edition 2022

▸ *Onze Eigen Tuin*, spring edition 1960, with the regular column "Mien Ruys describes what needs to be done in the garden now." Here, she explains how to plant trees, shrubs, and roses.

100 TUINEN
6e JAARGANG Nr 1 MAART
OPLAGE 100.000 EXEMPLAREN
ADMINISTRATIE POSTBUS 1
DEDEMSVAART TEL. 05230-2345 en 2346
ABONNEMENT f 1.90 PER JAAR
BIJ VOORUITBET. - GIRO 809821

DIRECTIE EN REDACTIE TE
AMSTERDAM, AMSTEL 157
TELEFOON 0 2 0 no 51973

1960

Onze eigen tuin

DRIEMAANDELIJKS TIJDSCHRIFT VOOR HEN DIE VAN BLOEMEN HOUDEN
EEN UITGAVE VAN DE UITGEVERSMAATSCHAPPIJ LINNAEUS
IN SAMENWERKING MET DE KONINKLIJKE KWEKERIJ MOERHEIM TE DEDEMSVAART

BIJ HET EERSTE LUSTRUM

Het is nu 5 jaar geleden dat „Onze eigen tuin" voor het eerst verscheen. ■ Wij wisten dat er bij bezit(s)ters van tuinen en tuintjes behoefte aan dergelijke voorlichting bestond. Daarom stelden wij alles in het werk, de beste vaklieden aan te trekken, die bereid en in staat waren hun kennis op boeiende wijze aan de leek over te dragen. ■ Thans, na 5 jaar, weten wij dat we met „Onze eigen tuin" midden in de roos geschoten hebben.

5555555555555

Het geweldige aantal abonnees en de uitgebreide correspondentie met hen zegt ons dit. ■ Hoe groter echter het aantal abonnees is, hoe beter we ons blad kunnen maken. Daarom vragen we vriendelijk aan hen, die „Onze eigen tuin" regelmatig lezen, hun nummers na lezing aan tuinbezitters en bloemenliefhebbers te geven en ze op te wekken tot het nemen van een abonnement. ■ Op aanvrage zenden we aan onze abonnees gaarne een stel gratis nummers, ter verspreiding voor dit doel. ■ De prijs f 1.90 per jaar bij vooruitbetaling, kan voor niemand bezwaarlijk zijn. ■ Postgironummer 809821 ten name van „Uitgeverij Linnaeus" te Dedemsvaart, waar ook de gratis verspreidingsnummers door onze abonnees kunnen worden aangevraagd.

MIEN RUYS VERTELT WAT ER NU IN DE TUIN MOET GEBEUREN

MAART
APRIL
MEI

. . . Te planten bomen nemen we eerst goed onder de loupe . . .

Inplaats van de eerste warme voorjaarsdag te begroeten met jubeltonen en opgestroopte mouwen om aan de slag te gaan, doen we wijs te streven naar zelfbeheersing en ons af te vragen: zullen we of zullen we niet? Zullen we het dekmateriaal verwijderen of een week wachten, zullen we de rozen snoeien of straks eerst naar het landbouwpraatje in de radio luisteren? Wikken en wegen, wachten maar ook weer niet uitstellen, dat is de moeilijke eerste voorjaarstaak van de tuinbezitter.

Wie een nieuwe beplanting heeft uitgedacht en die nu wil aanbrengen moet met bomen, heesters of rozen vooral niet wachten, tenzij de grond hard bevroren is. Nachtvorst doet hier weinig of geen kwaad, terwijl laat planten veel gevaarlijker is met het oog op een eventueel droog en warm voorjaar. Te planten bomen nemen we eerst goed onder de loupe; van takken die langs elkaar schuiven kan er één worden verwijderd, waar veel dunne takken bijeen zitten vooral in het midden van de kroon nemen we ze grotendeels weg ten behoeve van een enkele krachtige, die de boom een goede contour moet geven. Wij streven ernaar het hart van de kroon open te houden zodat de takken van het midden uit onbelemmerd kunnen uitgroeien om zo een stevige basis te vormen voor de toekomst. Vooral bij meidoorn en sierappel mogen de takken niet willekeurig worden ingekort omdat zich dan veelal juist in het hart jong loot ontwikkelt ten koste van een goed en regelmatig gevormde kroon. Op de kwekerijen snoeit men gewoonlijk niet voor de verzending met het oog op de eventuele beschadiging onderweg; men kan de beste vorm beter overzien als de boom ter plaatse is.

Wie een boom plant moet eerst zorgen voor een ruim plantgat, zodat de wortels niet in een koker behoeven te worden geperst. Men plant de boom even diep als hij vroeger heeft gestaan, iets wat op de stam zichtbaar is.

Als de grond niet tevoren was gemest doet men goed er oude verteerde koe- of paardemest uit te strooien, echter niet direct op de wortels maar vrijwel bovenin het plantgat, alvorens de laatste laag grond aan te vullen. Tegelijkertijd met het planten wordt een stevige boompaal gezet aan die zijde waar vandaan de meeste wind komt en men bevestigt paal en stam aaneen door boomband, zodanig dat de paal de stam niet kan beschadigen doordat deze er langs schuurt, maar toch zo stevig dat de boom met de wind niet heen en weer beweegt waardoor de jonge haarwortels telkens breken.

Heesters kunnen bij het planten voor 1/3 deel worden teruggesnoeid om gemakkelijker aanslaan te bevorderen. Ze vragen eveneens een ruim plantgat, een goede bemesting en ze moeten stevig met de voet worden vastgedrukt als het plantgat is aangevuld. Etiketten worden losgedraaid om later takbreuk te voorkomen. Komt de nieuwe aanplant in een windhoek dan is een tijdelijk scherm van b.v. rietmat aan te bevelen totdat de beplanting goed aan de groei is.

Rozen vragen bij het planten ook de volle aandacht. Men zet ze in aaneengesloten vak op een onderlinge afstand van 40 cm. Zeer lange wortels kunnen worden ingekort. Snoeien doen we ze gewoonlijk tegen half maart, mits het niet vriest. Wie weten wil hoe vindt op blz. 7 een tekening.

Elke nieuwe aanplant eist de eerste maanden extra verzorging om de kansen van aanslaan — na de ingrijpende operatie van het overplanten — zo groot mogelijk te maken. Geef water niet alleen bij het planten maar ook daarna bij droogte b.v. 2 × per week een flinke hoeveelheid Coniferen kunnen we binnen in het groen tot op de stam nat maken met een dun straaltje of een verneveling. We doen dit echter bij voorkeur niet overdag als de zon schijnt.

Ook houden we onkruid weg en we hakken van tijd tot tijd de aarde los tussen de struiken of rondom boom of conifeer, zodat lucht in de bodem kan toetreden.

Op zeer droge, arme grond kunnen we deze boven de wortels afdekken met natgemaakte turfstrooisel of met ruigte als blad of riet om sterk verdampen te voorkomen. Vooral rhododendrons en azalea's die dicht aan de oppervlakte wortelen reageren hier gunstig op. In oudere tuinen waar we het blad onder de struiken jaarlijks laten liggen ontstaat ge-

▶ pagina 2

Hoewel vergelijkingen steeds min of meer mank gaan, kan men, wanneer men de sterrenwereld met de wereld der plantkundigen vergelijkt, wellicht zeggen dat Pierre Magnol dan onze zon voorstelt, een ster zoals vele andere, maar ons veel vertrouwder dan alle overige. Zo ook was Pierre Magnol, een botanicus, niet belangrijker dan verschillende andere „voorgangers van Linnaeus", omdat min of meer toevallig, het bijzonder opvallende geslacht sierheester Magnolia zijn naam draagt. Welke plantenliefhebber immers kent de Magnolia's niet? Wie echter is even vertrouwd met Bauhinia, Caesalpinia, Thunbergia en Vaillantia, genoemd naar de niet minder verdienstelijke Bauhin, Caesalpinus, Thunberg en Vaillant, om er slechts enkele te noemen?

Maar ook al is dan de naam Magnol vertrouwd, zijn persoon zal vrijwel onbekend zijn. Hij leefde van 1638—1715 in Montpellier (Zuid-Frankrijk). De plantengroei van zijn omgeving kende hij al vroeg en beschreef hij later in een Flora van Montpellier. Van de beroemde plantentuin was hij lange tijd directeur. Hij onderhield een levendige ruil van planten en zaden met instituten en apothekers over de gehele wereld en zijn roem was alom verbreid. Zijn belangrijkste verdienste was wel het samenstellen van een plantensysteem (1689) met tien klassen waarbij hij de bloembouw en de groeiwijze van de planten vooral gebruikte en als eerste een scherp onderscheid tussen kelk en kroon van de bloem maakte.

Zijn systeem was evenwel niet het eerste; Bauhin had reeds in 1620 zijn „Pinax" geschreven, waarin hij evenals Magnol, de planten indeelde naar de habitus (algemeen voorkomen) en door een studie van alle synoniemen en het invoeren van korte, scherpe beschrijvingen, ter vervanging van de stilaan gebruikelijk geworden wijdlopige zinnen, bijzonder verdienstelijk werk deed.

Andere botanici wilden echter een enkel kenmerk voor een systeem uitkiezen en zo was het systeem van Caesalpinus (1583) vooral gebaseerd op de vruchten en dat van Ray (1690) op de knoppen. Tournefort, leerling van Magnol, maakte gebruik van de door deze gepreciseerde kelk en kroon en kwam rond 1700 tot een systeem met de los- of vergroeidbladige bloemkroon als basis. Evenals Ray maakte hij duidelijk onderscheid tussen bomen, struiken en kruiden. In al deze systemen vindt men details van het als overkoepelend, later algemeen aanvaarde, systeem van Linnaeus, die als eerste een combinatie van de goede elementen van de verschillende plantensystemen gaf. Linnaeus gebruikte het aantal en de plaatsing van de meeldraden als hoofdindelingsmotief (1738). Van het belang van deze organen, die overwegend als onbelangrijk beschouwd werden, was hij overtuigd geraakt door een lezing van Vaillant, ruim twintig jaar ervoor. Niettemin onderschatte hij de werkelijke betekenis ervan schromelijk en we kunnen ons nu nauwelijks voorstellen dat eerst honderd jaar later daaromtrent een goed inzicht algemeen verbreid begon te worden. Linnaeus had echter aan vorm, aantal en plaatsing van de meeldraden voor zijn indeling genoeg en zijn systeem was dus in dit opzicht even kunstmatig als de andere. Daarnaast laste hij echter gedeeltelijk een natuurlijk systeem in, gegrondvest op vele kenmerken. Hiervoor putte hij uit de werken van de genoemde voorgangers en men kan niet zeggen dat hij veel originele elementen toevoegde. Zijn scherpe diagnosen zijn te prijzen, maar Caesalpinus en Bauhin waren hem daarin met succes voorgegaan en de binaire nomenclatuur (naamgeving met geslachts- en soortnaam), die hij aanvankelijk achteloos invoerde (de naam was de korte beschrijving), vinden we al bij Rivinus en Bauhin. Ray had in 1690 al een goed soortsbegrip en beschreef toen al niet minder dan ruim 18500 planten, waarvan Linnaeus er maar 7000 overhield. Tournefort onderscheidde reeds scherp klassen, orden, geslachten, soorten en variëteiten hetgeen Linnaeus overnam. Eert men hem, dan dus ook zijn voorgangers, die de bouwstenen voor zijn systeem reeds alle aandroegen.

Evenwel blijft het de onsterfelijke verdienste van Linnaeus, dat hij het wezenlijk goede en blijvende van de verschillende (vele!) systemen uitkoos en daarvan een hecht geheel wist te maken met geniale visie.

Men kan het met zijn eigen, niet van zelfoverschatting getuigende woorden weergeven en „Deus creavit, Linnaeus disposuit", God schiep, Linnaeus ordende. Hoewel deze slotzin door zijn kortheid imponeert, ware het zoals aangetoond juister in te lassen; maar Ray, Bauhin, Tournefort, Magnol en anderen beten de spits af!

LOSSE NUMMERS 50 CT

Herb Garden (1957)

After the Water Garden was laid out in 1954, there was still an unused corner of her parents' kitchen garden bordering the nursery, measuring 9 × 14 meters. The space was surrounded by the fence of the Old Experimental Garden and the hedge of the Water Garden, making it suitable for "something small-scale." By erecting a rush matting fence on the nursery side, Mien created an enclosed space that reminded her of walled medieval cloister gardens. This gave her the idea of creating an herb garden here. Because only a limited quantity of herbs are needed for use in the kitchen, small rectangular beds were laid, each with one or two species of herb. The little herb beds required a more substantial focal point in the form of blocks of *Buxus* and a circle of shells in the middle. At its heart was a witch ball, which in the Middle Ages was thought to ward off witches, devils, and birds of prey hunting for chickens. A turf bench was not to be forgotten either: another medieval element, made of grass and herbs and intended as a seat for courting couples. In those days, the function of the scented herbs was to disguise the lovers' own unpleasant bodily smells. A well was dug in a corner of the Herb Garden so that the plants could be watered with rainwater. Bricks were laid to form a path between the herb plots. The rush matting was replaced by a brick wall in 1983. This made it possible to plant a fig tree and a mulberry tree against the warm south-facing wall. The

Herb Garden, after several renovations, is still almost completely intact. It is the only experimental garden with a historical character, which sets it apart from Mien Ruys's modernist style, in which minimalist, straight shapes are softened by lush vegetation.

◂ The well in the Herb Garden in the 1960s (above)

◂ Spring 2023: the infested *Buxus* has just been replaced by privet (below left)

◂ The Herb Garden in the morning sun (below right)

▴ The Herb Garden from above, clearly showing its functional, formal layout

pages 84–85: Design with planting plan for the Herb Garden in 1965, drawn by Miekie Ruys

pages 86–87: The Herb Garden in the winter of 2017. The blocks of *Buxus* had not yet been infested.

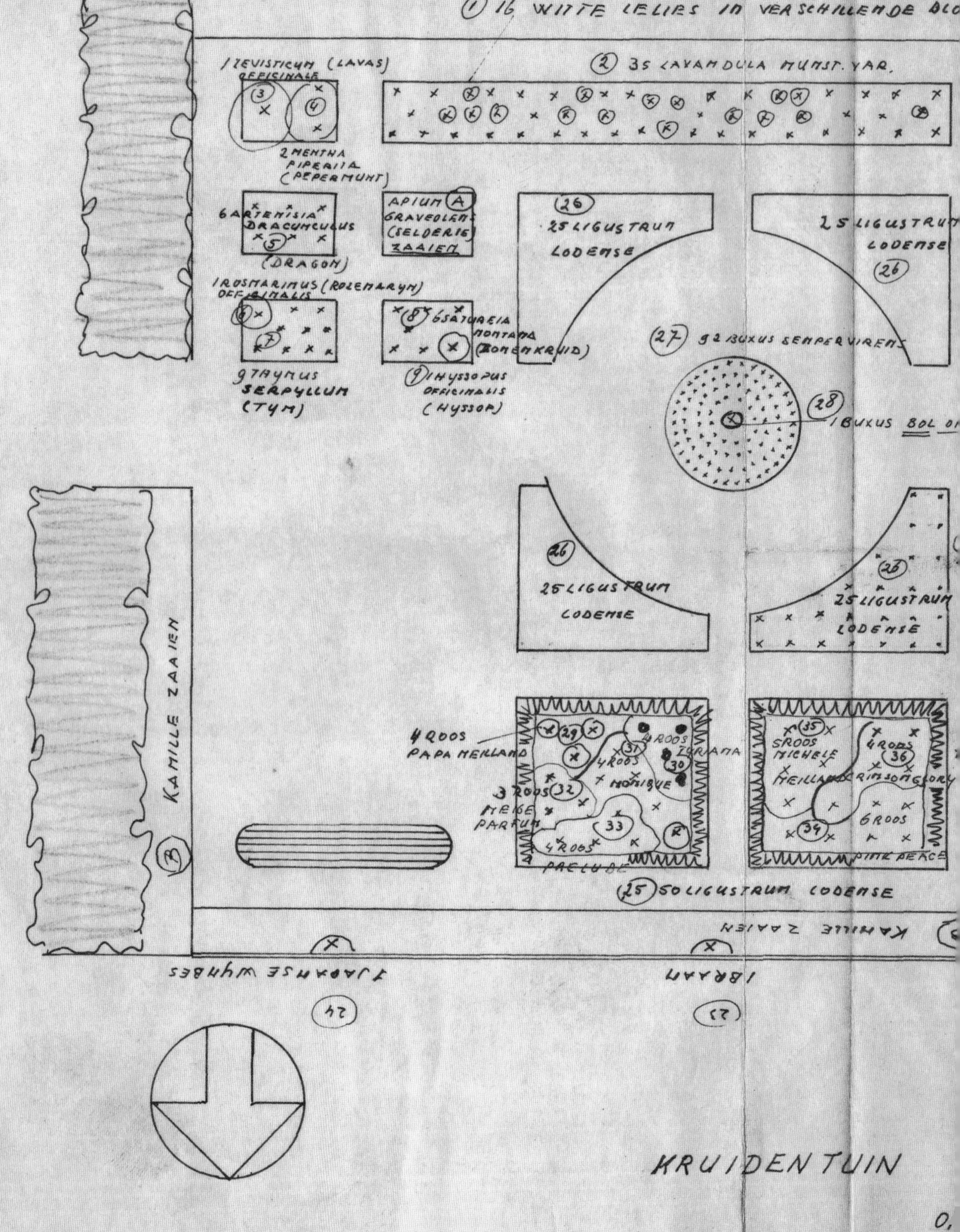

(1) 16 WITTE LELIES IN VERSCHILLENDE
(2) 35 LAVANDULA MUNST. VAR.
1 LEVISTICUM (LAVAS) OFFICINALE
2 MENTHA PIPERITA (PEPERMUNT)
6 ARTEMISIA DRACUNCULUS (DRAGON)
APIUM GRAVEOLENS (SELDERIE) ZAAIEN
1 ROSMARINUS (ROZEMARYN) OFFICINALIS
6 SATUREIA MONTANA (BONENKRUID)
9 THYMUS SERPYLLUM (TYM)
1 HYSSOPUS OFFICINALIS (HYSSOP)
25 LIGUSTRUM LODENSE
92 BUXUS SEMPERVIRENS
1 BUXUS BOL
4 ROOS PAPA MEILLAND
4 ROOS ZORIANA
4 ROOS MONIQUE
3 ROOS MEIGE PARFUM
4 ROOS PRELUDE
5 ROOS MICHELE MEILLAND
4 ROOS CRIMSON GLORY
6 ROOS PINK PEACE
50 LIGUSTRUM LODENSE
KAMILLE ZAAIEN
1 JAPANSE WYNBES
1 BRAAM
KRUIDENTUIN

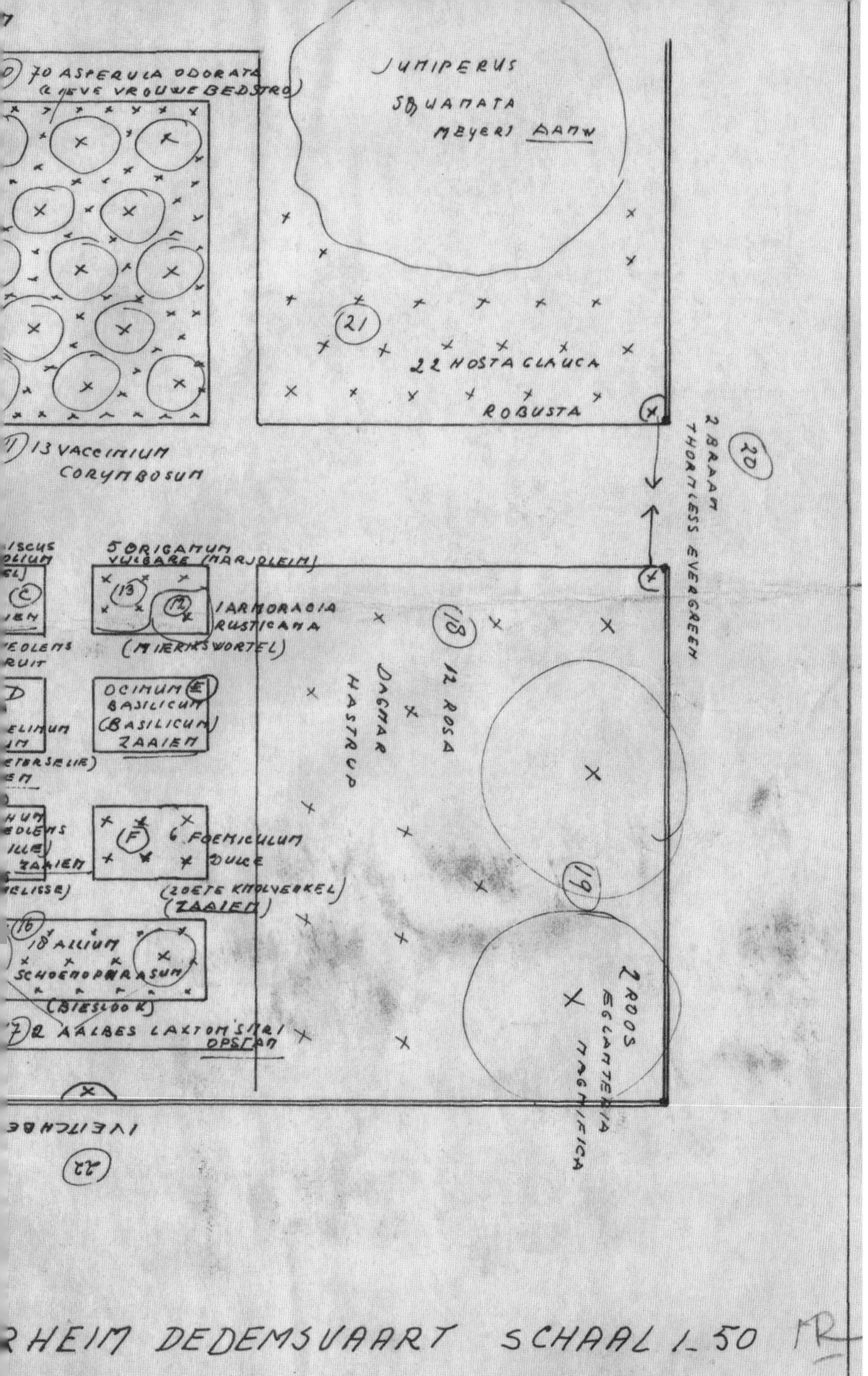

70 ASPERULA ODORATA
(LIEVE VROUWE BEDSTRO)
JUNIPERUS
SQUAMATA
MEYERI AANW
21
22 HOSTA GLAUCA
ROBUSTA
13 VACCINIUM
CORYMBOSUM
20
2 BRAAM
THORNLESS EVERGREEN
5 ORIGANUM
VULGARE (MARJOLEIN)
13
12
ARMORACIA
RUSTICANA
(MIERIKSWORTEL)
OCIMUM E
BASILICUM
(BASILICUM)
ZAAIEN
F
6 FOENICULUM
DULCE
(ZOETE KNOLVENKEL)
(ZAAIEN)
16
18 ALLIUM
SCHOENOPRASUM
(BIESLOOK)
2 AALBES LAXTON'S NR 1
OPSLAN
18
12 ROSA
DAGMAR
HASTRUP
19
2 ROOS
EGLANTERIA
MAGNIFICA
22
RHEIM DEDEMSVAART SCHAAL 1_50
C.H.R. TEK. NR. 1/36 EN A/6
19 JANUARI 1965

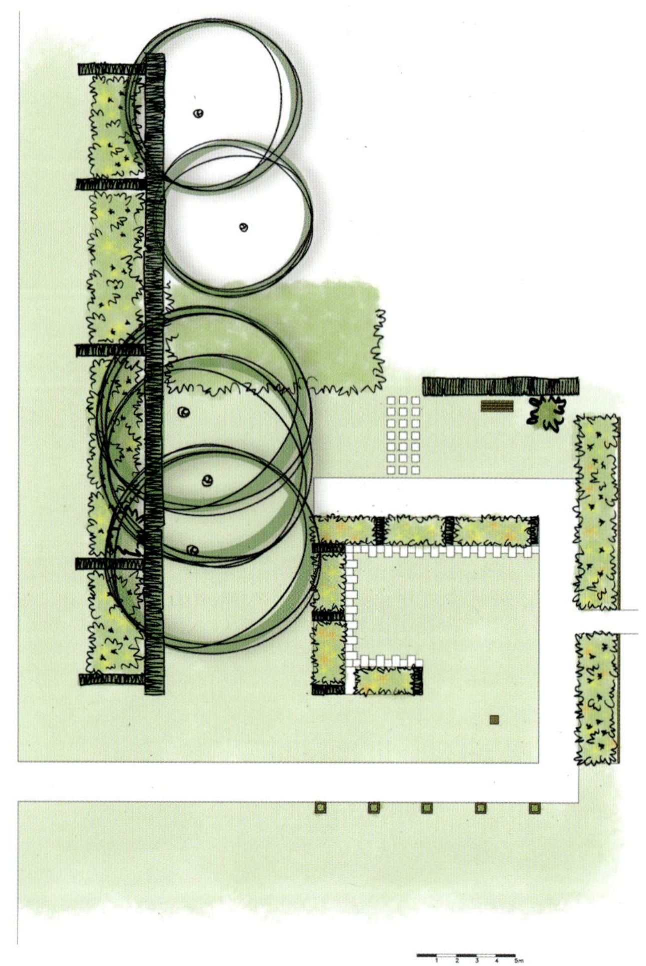

EXPANSION BEYOND THE WOODS

Plans were made around 1960 to extend the experimental gardens. The old kitchen garden was now full, and there was an increasing interest in perennials. While Mien Ruys was working on communal gardens during this period, she was also involved in designs for the many new private gardens in the city. She needed space to experiment and to have examples of layouts and plantings to show people. A suitable strip of land was found at the north end of the oak woods, which served as a windbreak for the nursery. She drew designs and planting plans for several smaller gardens. To try things out and learn from them, various standard borders were planted on this strip of land, each with a background of different sorts of hedges.

Railway-Sleeper Bench and Ready-to-make Borders (1960)

The newly acquired plot of land provided space to experiment with the railway sleepers (called "railroad ties" in the United States) that Mien had recently discovered (see page 253). She quickly recognized that this material required its own design. By sawing the sleepers into different lengths, quirky lines and little variations in height could be achieved. She made seating from railway sleepers: piled up, the sleepers created a sort of bench around an open space. This would provide room for a sandpit or somewhere to pot plants. A *Prunus*, a species Mien used frequently in her work at that time, was planted in a raised bed.

Several Ready-to-make Borders of different sizes, colors, soil types, and light needs were laid around the railway-sleepers project. The smallest borders were separated by low hedges of *Symphoricarpos ×chenaultii* and *Spiraea ×arguta* 'Compacta'. Their fine leaves make them very "strokable." As you pass them, you just have to touch them.

When the *Prunus* within the Railway-Sleeper Bench died in 1987, it offered an ideal opportunity to clear out this experiment with sleepers and alter the Ready-to-make Borders. The *Metasequoia* trees had grown tremendously in the meantime, casting too much shade onto the borders designed for sun. Mien Ruys drew a new design for borders around a lawn, a few meters further away from the *Metasequoia* than the previous borders. A hedge of *Spiraea ×arguta* ‘Compacta’ was again planted between the new borders: a compact little shrub with fine foliage that can withstand pruning well. Their top edges have been trimmed in a curve for many years, which makes them a very striking element in the Ready-to-make Borders. When at an exhibition, Mien Ruys had seen a sculpture of a reclining female figure that had made a big impression on her. This sculpture by Thijl Wijdeveld was subsequently bought and given a prominent position on the lawn.

◀ The Railway-Sleeper Bench with *Prunus*, one of the experiments with railway sleepers in the Gardens.

▶ View from the Ready-to-make Borders to the Sunken Garden, with one of the “strokable” spirea hedges in the foreground

▼ Planting plan for Mien Ruys’s Ready-to-make Borders in the 1960s

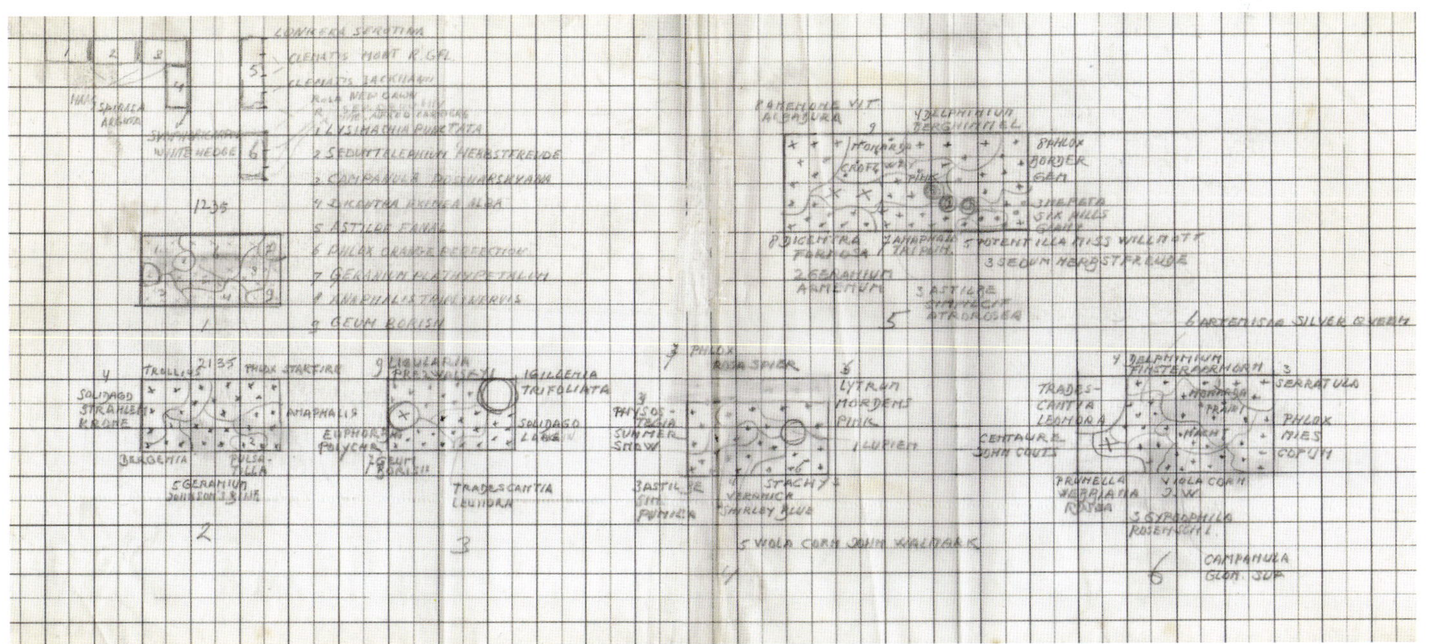

Metasequoia glyptostroboides

Before the 1940s, the millions-of-years-old *Metasequoia glyptostroboides*, or dawn redwood, was only known as a fossil; it was thought that it was extinct. But in the 1940s, a rumor emerged that living examples had been found in central China. An expedition was dispatched, and the living fossils were indeed found; seeds and cuttings were taken that were eventually distributed to countries in Europe. Moerheim Nursery received a few seeds, only one of which germinated successfully. Nonetheless, this one sample was enough from which to grow many offspring. Moerheim sold many of them, and some of them were planted on the nursery site. One specimen was planted near the house, one near the summerhouse of Wiekend, two on the west side, and three in the expansion strip in the 1960s. The tree at Wiekend had to be felled due to root rot, which this species is susceptible to; the others are still standing. Mien Ruys planted the three samples as "a group," and they are so close together that their stem bases almost touch each other. In all likelihood, she did not realize that the trees—now some 25 meters high—would grow so tall. A visitor to the Gardens recounts how Mien had advised him personally to plant a *Metasequoia* in his front garden, and he had followed her advice. To his great sorrow, the tree had to be felled a few years ago, also due to root rot. Whether his neighbors were as upset is questionable. During a severe storm in January 2018, the center tree of the trio broke in half and came down. The tree has since sprouted again, but the sight of the entwined tree crowns has been lost forever. When the *Metasequoia* loses its needles in winter, it is particularly noticeable that the three trunks have been reduced to two and a half. Luckily, this is not visible at eye level, and these sturdy, muscular trunks stand next to each other like brothers.

Because the *Metasequoia* has only been in Europe for a relatively short time, we don't know how the tree will develop further in terms of height and lifespan. *Metasequoia glyptostroboides* is occasionally confused with the *Sequoiadendron giganteum*, or giant redwood, which has a soft trunk you can punch with your fist, giving it the nickname of "the boxing tree." The *Metasequoia* does not have a soft trunk, and boxing it with your fist is not recommended.

▾ The middle *Metasequoia* broke in half during a severe storm in January 2018 (left)

▾ The sculpture by Thijl Wijdeveld in the Ready-to-make Borders, with the *Metasequioa* in the background

▸ The three *Metasequoia* trees in the winter of January 2017

Sunken Garden (1960)

The Sunken Garden was another experiment with railway sleepers. A sunken, enclosed garden was created by digging up part of the garden and using the soil to raise another part. The railway sleepers were used as a retaining wall and as steps to bridge the height differences with the surrounding gardens. Mien did not feel that the grion tiles she frequently used in those days were suitable for the little terrace. She went in search of a material that would match the scale of the garden better and decided on natural stone cobbles. This was an expensive but sustainable investment, as the cobbles are still there today.

▲ Theo sitting on the railway sleepers around the Sunken Garden in 1963

▶ View from the Sunken Garden toward the Sun Borders, with *Chamaecyparis obtusa* 'Nana Gracilis' at the corner, in the 1970s

▶ When the old *Chamaecyparis obtusa* 'Nana Gracilis' had become far too big, it was replaced with a new specimen during the renovation in 2016 (opposite, above)

▶ A line of sight runs from the Sunken Garden across the lawn in the middle to the Mixed Border (1974) (opposite, below)

Sun Borders

Shady Borders

Sun Borders (1960)

The Sun Borders proceeded naturally from the Sunken Garden: two standard borders opposite each other in the sun, with a path through the middle serving as the line of sight from the Sunken Garden. The path was originally grass but was later paved. The borders had a hedge on two sides, the evergreen yew on one side and the deciduous hornbeam on the other. Two holes were cut out of the hornbeam at eye level so that you could peep through to the adjoining garden. Here, too, the surrounding trees cast a good deal of shade, leading to the planting being altered over the years. A path of grion tiles was laid in a strip of grass to mark the transition between the Ready-to-make Borders to the Railway-Sleeper Bench and the Sunken Garden. The tiles were laid about 15 centimeters apart, giving the effect of the lawn continuing between the tiles and making the transition much softer and more natural than a solid path.

Shady Borders (1960)

The strip of land bordering the woods with their tall oak trees was an ideal place to try out a few borders for partial shade. To separate these borders from the other gardens, shrubs, small trees, and various conifers were planted, including the three *Metasequoia* trees. The borders in partial shade were given a background of *Ligustrum vulgare* 'Atrovirens', which only loses its leaves in very cold winters. Low privet hedges were planted between the various borders and continued into the grass border in front of them. As such, they served to break up the long strip and create an intriguing rhythm.

The City Garden was also given a place in this strip. This garden is still a good example of how a small garden can be designed. The City Garden is discussed extensively on page 102.

Rose Garden (1960)

Moerheim Nursery had many roses in its assortment at that time, making them interesting material to experiment with. A rose garden was planted in the westernmost corner of the new strip. Beds of varying sizes were dug at random among grion tiles and planted with roses. Some of the beds were surrounded by a hedge of *Ligustrum vulgare* 'Lodense', while others were highlighted by a block of *Buxus sempervirens*. The combination of roses and the acidic peaty soil of Dedemsvaart was never a happy one, and the increasing shade to the south of the garden contributed to part of the garden being altered in 1969. After that, the garden went through various reincarnations: from Heath Garden to Bee Garden and, ultimately, to the Autumn Garden in 2002.

Autumn Garden (was Rose Garden)

Pond with Reeds

Pond with Reeds (early 1960s)

The first ponds Mien Ruys dug in the Wilderness Garden and the Water Garden were made of concrete. In the early 1960s, ready-made plastic ponds in various shapes and sizes came onto the market. This material offered new opportunities. Mien wanted to try one of these ponds, but they were too deep for marsh plants. She asked the pond manufacturer to add a 30-centimeter-deep edge to the pond so that she could grow marsh plants. She called it a sort of "windowsill." This enabled her to grow both marsh plants and water plants. She created a new experimental garden containing a plastic, rectangular pond "with a windowsill" in the line of sight from the Sunken Garden. A terrace with a bench was built next to the 2 × 3-meter pond. One problem was how to disguise the pond's edges, which she did not want to be able to see. The tiles on the terrace side were laid so that they extended over the edge of the pond. The other edges of the pond were disguised by allowing grass sods to extend right to the edge. Ornamental grasses were starting to be used more and more, but Mien was amazed that most people chose *Cortaderia selloana*, or pampas grass. In her view, pampas grass was difficult to combine because of its exotic nature, and furthermore, this grass was not completely hardy. It was better to look at prevailing conditions and choose an appropriate ornamental grass to suit them. For her pond, therefore, she chose a bed of *Miscanthus ×giganteus*, or giant miscanthus. It is an ornamental grass that can easily grow to a height of three meters and can therefore form a back wall for a small garden. She called her project Pond with Reeds. It is a uniting element in this part of the Gardens. A line of sight runs from the bench near the pond through the Sun Borders, under the crown of the *Amelanchier laevis* 'Ballerina' to the Square Garden, and up to the boundary wall at the side. Another long line of sight runs from the Sunken Garden across the pond, between the reeds and a small willow, and under the tree crown via the Yellow Garden and the Mixed Border (1974) to the boundary at the back of the Gardens.

The Moerheim Nursery catalogs had attractive covers and titles

KONINKLIJKE KWEEKERIJ 'MOERHEIM' VH B. RUYS NV DEDEMSVAART
RAPSODIE IN KLEUR

N.V. KONINKLIJKE KWEEKERIJ MOERHEIM DEDEMSVAART
typisch Moerheim

N.V. KONINKLIJKE KWEEKERIJ MOERHEIM DEDEMSVAART
wat de zon ons schonk
Azalea japonica (A.mollis)

N.V. KONINKLIJKE KWEEKERIJ MOERHEIM DEDEMSVAART
wij strooien rozen op uw pad
SARABANDE

KONINKLIJKE KWEEKERIJ 'MOERHEIM' VH B. RUYS NV DEDEMSVAART
70 jaar Heesters

KONINKLIJKE KWEEKERIJ 'MOERHEIM' V.H. B. RUYS NV DEDEMSVAART.
als kleurige sterren
Prunus serrulata Shidare-zakura

The City Garden (around 1960)

The new houses built in the 1950s and 1960s routinely had backyards measuring about 6 × 10 meters. Mien Ruys called these backyards "city gardens" and was fascinated by their small size. She wanted to demonstrate that more was possible than the usual layout: narrow borders against the wooden fences at each side and a hard, straight path through the lawn from the kitchen door to the path along the back. She drew various designs for this size of garden, some of which appeared in *Onze Eigen Tuin*. The city gardens had to be cheap to lay out and easy to maintain. Her Ready-to-make Borders, available from Moerheim for an affordable price (along with a planting plan and a booklet containing information about layout and maintenance), were in keeping with these requirements. The standard borders were often used in her design models. Mien felt it was important not to build high fences or walls in small backyards so that their surroundings could be incorporated into the garden. People's pleasure in their gardens could be augmented by their neighbors' gardens, in her opinion; they could enjoy each other's plants and chat over the low fences.

A city garden was also laid out in Dedemsvaart with a lawn, a hedge, a simple palisade, and a horizontal wooden fence. She laid the patio and the path to the end of the garden in a diagonal line. For the paving, she used standard paving stones measuring 30 × 30 centimeters, laid upside down. The tiles for the path through the lawn were laid about 10 centimeters apart, so that the grass could grow between them. A blue spruce and a lollipop tree were planted in the lawn. A standard border measuring 5 × 2 meters gave the garden color and natural beauty.

◀ The City Garden in the early years after planting. The low fence meant it was possible to have a chat with the neighbors.

▲ The City Garden in 2023. The *Koelreuteria paniculata* now provides considerable shade in the garden (left).

▲ The palisade from the original design is still a feature of the City Garden. Mien Ruys used concrete U-shaped blocks for various purposes, such as seating elements (right).

pages 104–105: The City Garden from above in early spring. The different layout principles used in the garden are clearly visible through the crown of the *Koelreuteria paniculata*.

DESIGNING A SMALL BACKYARD

The City Garden was laid out when the Gardens were expanded around 1960. This garden served as a model for the layout of a backyard in the standard measurements of the time. The application of a few simple design principles makes the yard appear larger than it is. Even though the City Garden is over 60 years old, these principles are still applicable and relevant today. The simplicity and clarity of Mien Ruys's design gives it a timeless quality.

The City Garden through the Years

The layout of the City Garden has remained practically the same throughout the years. A sandpit was added on the patio, the low fence was replaced by a field maple hedge, and the blue spruce was felled. The lollipop tree was replaced by a *Koelreuteria paniculata*. A chat over the fence is no longer possible, but two holes have been cut in one of the hedges at eye level, giving a view into the next garden. Circumstances have changed, however, because the garden now gets more shade from the tall conifers in the strip of land at the back. The standard border for a sunny spot that was in the original design has been altered through the years to include species that can withstand more shade but are still in keeping with the character of the 1960s.

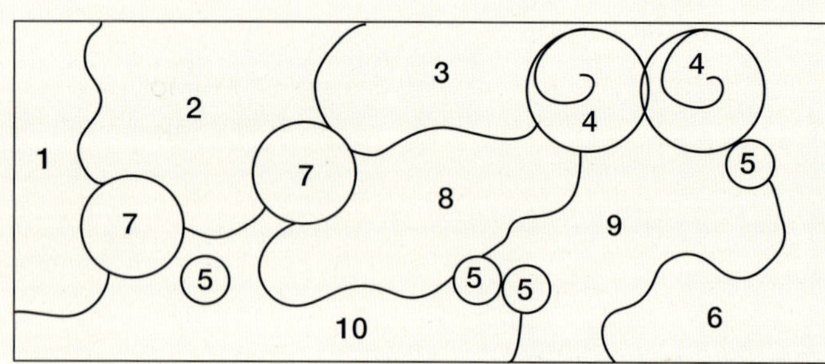

Border 1 for a sunny spot

Measurements:	2.5 × 6 m
Theme:	bees and butterflies
Flower color:	lilac, blue, purple
Foliage color:	gray
Layout:	from high to low

1. *Brunnera macrophylla* 'Jack Frost' × 5
2. *Phlox* 'Purpermantel' × 5
3. *upatorium rugosum* 'Chocolate' × 2
4. *Miscanthus sinensis* 'Morning Light' 2 × 1
5. *Verbena bonariensis* 4 × 1
6. *Hylotelephium spectabile* (Brilliant Group) 'Brilliant' × 8
7. *Aster lateriflorus* 'Horizontalis' 2 × 1
8. *Echinacea purpurea* × 6
9. *Salvia nemorosa* 'Caradonna' × 8
10. *Nepeta* 'Grol' × 10

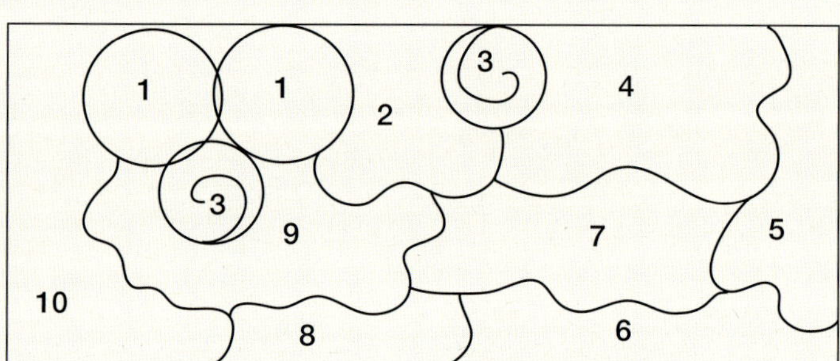

Border 2 for a sunny spot

Measurements:	2.5 × 6 m
Theme:	winter interest and evergreen
Flower color:	bright colors
Layout:	from high to low

1. *Sarcococca hookeriana* var. *humilis* 2 × 1
2. *Achillea filipendulina* 'Coronation Gold' × 3
3. *Calamagrostis* 'Karl Foerster' 2 × 1
4. *Kalimeris incisa* 'Madiva' × 8
5. *Bergenia* 'Silberlicht' × 6
6. *Campanula poscharskyana* × 10
7. *Hemerocallis citrina* × 9
8. *Geum coccineum* 'Borisii' × 4
9. *Geranium* 'Rozanne' × 7
10. *Liriope muscari* 'Moneymaker' × 13

Small Backyards Nowadays

The average backyard has become smaller in the last 70 years. Compared to 1950, the total surface area of a new residential plot has reduced by about one third, while the houses built on these plots have increased in size. Another factor is that existing houses have often been extended. All this means that there is less room for the backyard. Often it is therefore little more than a tiled courtyard with few or no plants, surrounded by fencing. In an age in which paying heed to heat stress and biodiversity is becoming ever more important, a backyard like the one described certainly does not help. Applying Mien Ruys's layout principles will not only make the backyard appear bigger, but will also be future-proof. The combination of a lawn, plants, a small tree, and hedges is cooling in hot summers, prevents water damage in the event of heavy downpours (since there is minimal paving), provides seasonal and natural beauty close to home, and is attractive to insects, birds, and small animals.

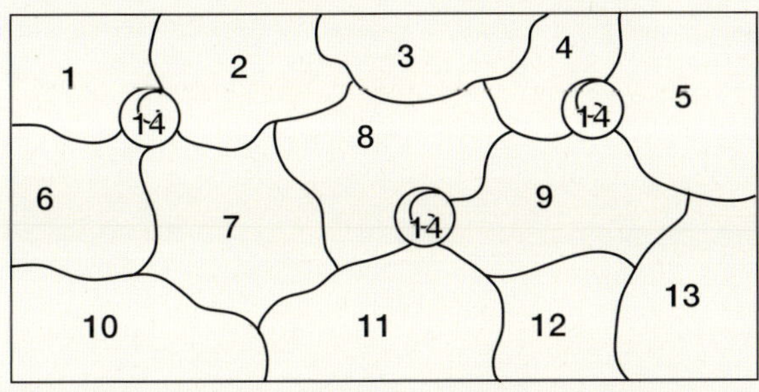

Border 3 for partial shade/shade

Measurements:	2.5 × 5 m
Theme:	foliage shape and foliage color
Layout:	toward the center

1. *Lamiastrum galeobdolon* 'Florentinum' × 5
2. *Hakonechloa macra* 'All Gold' × 5
3. *Asarum europaeum* × 11
4. *Astilbe* 'Deutschland' × 5
5. *Ajuga reptans* 'Atropurpurea' × 13
6. *Hosta* 'Halcyon' × 7
7. *Anemone ×hybrida* 'Königin Charlotte' × 6
8. *Actaea simplex* 'Brunette' × 8
9. *Dryopteris filix-mas* × 5
10. *Brunnera macrophylla* 'Sea Heart' × 8
11. *Heuchera* 'Citronelle' × 11
12. *Heuchera micrantha* 'Palace Purple' × 8
13. *Pulmonaria longifolia* × 13
14. *Briza media* 'Tinkerbell' 3 × 1

Tips for Designing a Small Backyard

- Use a diagonal line. This is the longest line in a rectangle. Lay the patio and the path to the boundary at the back along this line. It will make the garden appear bigger. Don't place this line at a 45-degree angle, because that would create sharp, unusable corners, but rather at an angle of about 60 degrees. A diagonal line will enable plants in some places to be close to the house, which means you will be able to see them better from inside.
- Don't lay the tiles for the path too close together; leave about 10 centimeters between the tiles. It will look softer and produce a more spacious effect. The grass will then grow in between the tiles, preventing the path from cutting the yard in two. Simple 30 × 30-cm tiles, possibly laid upside down, are practical and cheap; often you can even get hold of used tiles for free. Remember that the paving is not an important part of the garden; the focus should be on the plants.
- Make a decent-sized border measuring a few square meters. This will have more effect than two narrow strips. The lawn can then run from one side boundary to the other, making the yard look bigger. Make sure that your line of sight is along the border and not straight at it so that any gaps are less visible. Don't place the border against the boundary at the back, either, because that would make the yard look shorter.
- Plant a small tree in the yard. It will create depth, provide a canopy over the yard, limit your neighbors' view of the yard, allow you to experience the seasons, and, most important, provide shade in hot summers.
- Make the partitions around the yard from different materials and at different heights, such as a hedge at each side from two different species and a palisade at the back.

New Standard Borders for Small Backyards

To provide inspiration, Mien Ruys Landscape Architectural Firm (in Dutch, Buro Mien Ruys for short) has produced three new standard borders suitable for small backyards. The choice of plants is based on what is currently available in the Netherlands. Borders 1 and 2 have been designed by Anet Scholma, while Border 3 came from Ward Maaswinkel.

Patrimonium

The residential properties that were part of the post-war expansion of Amsterdam into Geuzenveld and Slotermeer were also built in line with the ideas of the garden city movement. Mien Ruys carried out a lot of work for the Patrimonium housing association in the period between 1954 and 1956. Four housing projects were built according to the urban-development principle of parallel strips. These included single family dwellings, apartments, and communal gardens. Just as for the Frankendael apartment buildings, she wanted to give each building its own courtyard garden. The communal gardens were laid out with trees in the lawn, shrubberies, beds of roses, and perennial borders. The use of flowering perennials made these gardens particularly colorful and differentiated Mien Ruys from her fellow landscape gardeners. It was here that she first made use of her "Repeat Borders." And, of course, she didn't forget the children's playgrounds, with sandpits and Aldo van Eyck's playground equipment. Her idealistic vision of mothers sitting knitting on benches in the playground as they watched their children began to disintegrate somewhat as the years went on. Groups of youths caused a nuisance and destroyed the plants. Because of this, barbed wire was later erected around the inner courtyards, and thorny shrubs were planted as a means of preventing such damage. We would call this "jerk-proof" nowadays.

Weverij De Ploeg

Weverij De Ploeg was a weaving mill in the village of Bergeijk in the south of the Netherlands, founded by an idealistic agricultural community that wanted everyone to be able to live and work comfortably. When a new building for the factory was needed, the furniture maker and architect Gerrit Rietveld was commissioned to design the building and Mien Ruys was asked to design its surroundings. Their ideas were in keeping with the idealistic nature of De Ploeg. The board of directors considered harmony between industry and nature to be important. A building in a green environment would benefit the workers' well-being. Gerrit Rietveld designed an eye-catching building for the factory, entirely in line with the principles of Het Nieuwe Bouwen, incorporating light, air, and space. The concrete sawtooth roofs gave the building its characteristic shape, and the windows on the north side ensured that daylight, but not direct sunlight, would enter. The geometric division of the surface with touches of bright colors and black-and-white is characteristic of Gerrit Rietveld's designs. The executive director, Piet Blijenburg, had envisioned a garden for the outdoor space in an English landscape style, but Mien Ruys preferred to leave the original landscape of woods and fields intact as far as possible. In the end, they reached a compromise: Mien Ruys's minimalist, straight style can be seen close to the building as represented by the trees, blocks of hedges, borders with repeat plantings, and the lawn. Further away, toward the entrance to the site, the garden is in the English landscape style. Gerrit Rietveld also designed two directors' houses, one of which included a garden design by Mien Ruys. This house and its garden are still virtually in their original state. It is a well-preserved example of the collaboration between the architect Gerrit Rietveld and the landscape gardener Mien Ruys. The factory closed in 2007, and its activities were moved elsewhere. The complex now has a new owner who has extensively renovated the building and the park. Weverij de Ploeg and the Ploeg Park have the status of a national monument.

page 108: The Mix Border (2018) with *Veronicastrum virginicum*, *Lythrum salicaria*, and *Phlomis russeliana*

page 109: *Dahlia* in the Changeover Border

◂ One of the communal gardens of the Patrimonium complex, featuring Aldo van Eyck's playground and climbing frame

▴ Mill and surroundings of Weverij De Ploeg with its sawtooth roofs. The compact blocks of hedges, so typical of Mien Ruys's style, can be seen on the left.

1965-1980

THE NETHERLANDS: FOCUS ON THE INDIVIDUAL

The collective solidarity that dominated the years after the war made way for individualism in the second half of the 1960s. The greasers were followed by the hippies of the flower-power movement. They rebelled against capitalism, the middle-class mentality, and polarization, instead advocating freedom, peace, equality, and love. More and more women no longer wanted to just look after their children and do housework, preferring to have paid jobs. The first feminist wave of the 1920s was now followed by a second: the Dutch activist group known as the *Dolle Mina* was set up in 1969. Their aim was to fight for women's rights, especially when it came to work and education, childcare, and abortion.

Prosperity continued to increase. Car ownership became more common, leading to an upsurge in road traffic, which had major consequences for infrastructure in the Netherlands. People began to worry about the negative consequences of economic growth: air pollution, the use of pesticides, and the discharging of hazardous substances by industry. Environmental movements gained momentum; organizations such as Greenpeace and the Dutch *Milieudefensie* were founded. A report published in 1972 by the Club of Rome, "The Limits of Growth," warned that, if the world were to continue along the same lines, population growth, food production, industrialization, depletion of natural resources, and pollution would lead to enormous problems within 100 years.

Work Less, Enjoy More Free Time

By then, Mien was over 60 and Theo was about 80. She had no intention of stopping work, but she did slow down somewhat. Gradually, she made more time for her private life. She and Theo often spent time in Dedemsvaart, and she made various trips abroad, sometimes with Theo, sometimes on a garden tour arranged through *Onze Eigen Tuin*, and sometimes with friends and acquaintances. Around 1970, Mien and Theo got to know the town planner Fred Zandvoort and his wife Rosette through a project they were working on, and they became firm friends. Theo died in October 1974, just before his 86th birthday. Having to continue without Theo affected Mien greatly. Their years together had made her milder and less opinionated. She had not felt the need to write in her diary during their time together because she could discuss everything with him. After his death, she returned to writing, and a few years later, she wrote in her diary: "Theo taught me how to give and receive warmth."

▲ Mien in the nursery, 1970s

▶ Mien and Theo in 1974

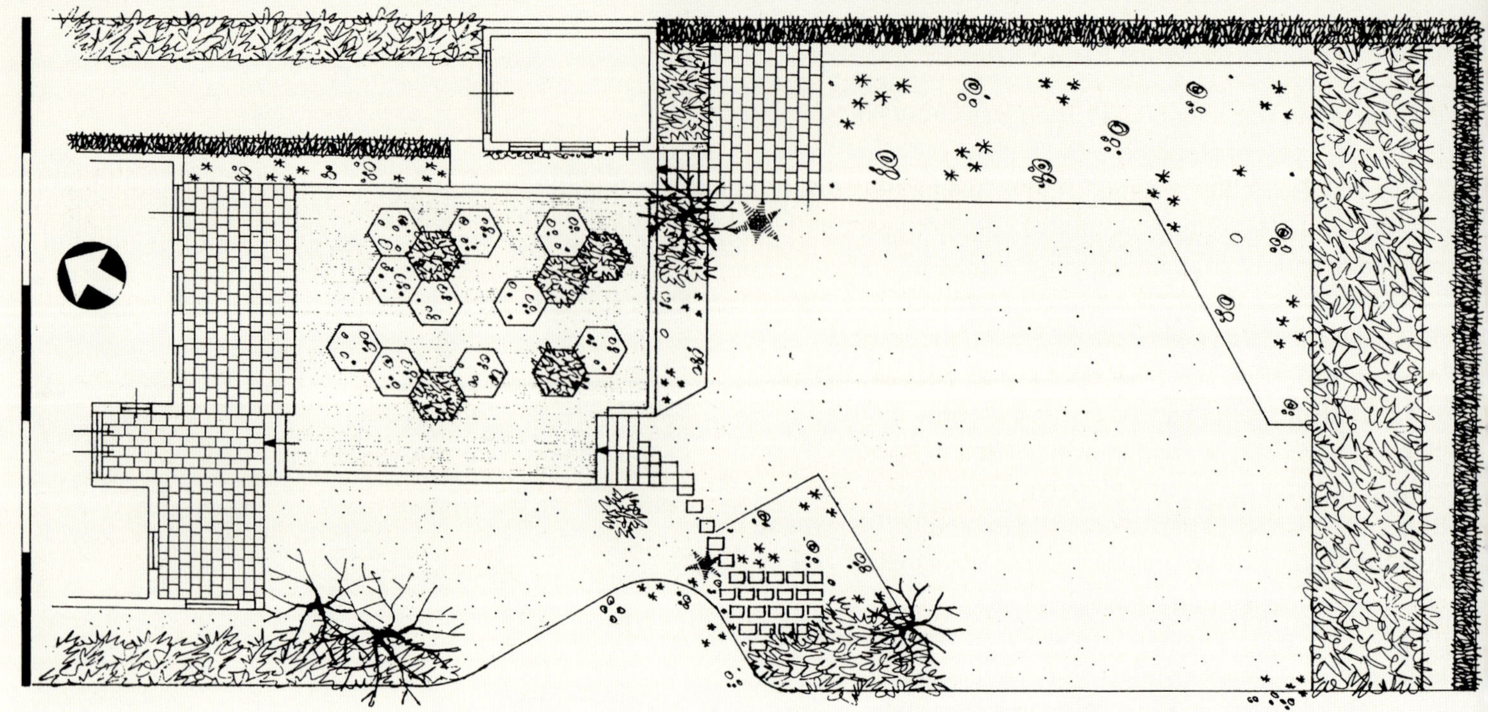

Focus on the Environment and the Natural Garden

The concerns about the growing economy and its detrimental effect on the natural world and the wider environment led to a greater focus on wild, natural planting. It became all the rage to include natural features in gardens, parks, and public green spaces. One of the advocates of this was Louis le Roy. He started his first "Eco Cathedral" in Mildam, near Heerenveen, in 1965. He created a space where nature and culture could come together, using building debris and wild plants but without a preconceived plan. Mien Ruys also considered the focus on natural planting to be important, given that she had loved nature since she was young. She greatly admired Louis le Roy's work, which she felt had significantly influenced architects and town planners. "The concept of 'green spaces' gained much more significance and substance for them; he demonstrated that 'green' is more than grass and roses," something she had been doing for the last 50 years. The difference was that he took no interest in form; he was only interested in naturalizing. According to le Roy, nature arranges itself, while for Mien Ruys, design was always the basis—even in her wilderness garden, intervention was always necessary to keep things under control. Later, in a radio interview in 1987, she said: "One of the essential things in my designs is creating order out of chaos [. . .] Imitating nature fills me with horror, because to me, this is truly phony. There are an awful lot of people nowadays who think you must bring nature into your garden and that you just have to let everything take its course, so actually do nothing. And then they think they'll get a lovely wild garden, when in fact, all they'll get is chaos."

Structuralism and "Cauliflower Estates"

In reaction to the large-scale commercial urban development of the years of post-war reconstruction, a new architectural period based on structuralism dawned after 1965. It was a derivative of modernism, but small-scale this time and with a focus on the human dimension. The architect Aldo van Eyck was the engine driving this movement. Structures of small units in geometric shapes, such as circles, triangles, squares, and hexagons, formed a cohesive entity without any hierarchy. A new type of residential area emerged, incorporating pedestrian-friendly cul-de-sacs. Green spaces and water were used as structural elements. Viewed from above, the various residential areas looked like cauliflower rosettes. This gave them the name "cauliflower estates," *bloemkoolwijken* in Dutch. In response to this, landscape gardeners incorporated these geometric shapes into their garden designs. There was an increasing interest in making the garden an extension of the home, with barbecues and sunken areas in which to sit. Planting was given a minor role: low-maintenance borders of perennials made way for groundcovers, creeping perennials, and low shrubs.

◂ Diagram of a design for a private garden by Mien Ruys's landscape gardening studio, *Tuinarchitectenbureau* Mien Ruys. The hexagonal beds of roses and *Buxus* are a typical example of structuralism in the 1960s.

▴ An example of the use of hexagonal tiles (above)

▴ View of the garden created from the design on the left-hand page (below)

Support of Colleagues

When Mien Ruys decided to take things a little easier, she took on two landscape gardeners: Hans Veldhoen in 1968 and Arend Jan van der Horst in 1969. Prior to this, she had always done all the design work herself; she only had help when specifying the details. She had little contact with other landscape gardeners. In an interview later, she spoke about this: "Prior to this period, I had little engagement with others. I always worked alone: quite a lonely existence. I found that engagement with Hans Veldhoen." Both men started making more and more designs, always in consultation with Mien, and they regularly wrote articles for *Onze Eigen Tuin*. Bit by bit, Mien began restricting her work to a few specific projects and to making planting plans. Fewer commissions for new-build projects came in, as municipalities often had their own departments for designing green spaces. The studio's assignments focused mainly on gardens around factories, offices, and healthcare institutions, and for private individuals. Many landscape gardeners were less interested in private gardens, but they remained Mien Ruys's core business: the link between humans and nature. She also continued to be committed to the role of the landscape gardener and landscape architect in urban development. She felt that urbanization and the expansion of infrastructure was distancing people from nature. A well-planned garden could compensate for this absence.

Sharing Knowledge

Mien Ruys continued to write books regularly in this period as a means of sharing her knowledge, making it feasible for everyone to lay out and maintain a garden. Zo beplanten we onze tuin (How We Plant Our Garden) appeared in 1965: a compact book about the position of the garden, soil types, the use of different groups of plants in the garden (from trees to bulbs and annuals), and handy lists of plants for specific spots or with particular characteristics. The foreword contained a summary of her vision of gardens in two sentences: "A garden without plants is not a garden. Likewise, a garden full of plants, but without line or form, without space, is not a garden either." She included a dedication to Theo at the front of the book: "To my husband Theo Moussault, who enjoys the garden without working in it, who enabled this book to appear without writing it himself."

When *Het vaste planten boek* (*Perennials*) went out of print in 1950, no reprint appeared due to a lack of interest in perennials. As interest increased again, there were calls for the book to be reprinted. Because the range of available plants, names of perennials, and opinions on landscape gardening had changed, she decided to write a new edition. She also wanted to make use of the 50 years' experience she had gained in working with perennials for the new book. The first edition of *Het nieuwe vaste planten boek* (*The New Perennials Book*) was published in 1973. Several reprints appeared up to 1979.

◀ Planting in the Mix Border (2018) including *Phlomis russeliana*, *Veronicastrum virginicum*, and *Lythrum salicaria* (opposite)

◀ Third edition of *Zo beplanten we onze tuin* (*How We Plant Our Garden*) from 1969

Stichting Tuinen Mien Ruys (1976)

In the early years, Mien maintained her experimental gardens herself for the most part, with some help from workers in the nursery. As the Gardens expanded, a permanent employee was taken on via the nursery to handle maintenance: Henk Verweg. When the work became too much for one person, the board of management at Moerheim felt that the maintenance costs were too high. Soon after Theo died in 1974, Mien broke her hip. All these factors—her limited mobility, her grief at the loss of her husband, and the conflict about the deployment of staff—were probably the reason why she began to doubt whether she wanted to keep the experimental gardens going. A solution was found by separating the experimental gardens from the nursery and incorporating them in a foundation. The *Stichting Tuinen Mien Ruys* (Mien Ruys Garden Foundation) was founded in 1976 with the aim of "maintaining the gardens and possibly extending them, while keeping a close watch on the essence of the gardens—experimenting and advising," as Mien Ruys later described in *Mijn Tuinen* (*My Gardens*) in 1987. The land was acquired on a long lease from the nursery, and several interested parties were prepared to invest in the foundation. As such, the experimental gardens became an independent organization. Responsibility shifted to the board of the foundation, with the mayor of Dedemsvaart as its chair, thus relieving Mien of a lot of work. Dirk Jan Koning was taken on as a gardener, and he helped and supported her in all matters relating to the gardens for many years. He asked "why" questions about decisions on the use of plants and materials, which kept Mien sharp.

The experimental gardens grew to become visitors' gardens with a signposted route throughout. Attention was paid to organizing activities and giving advice on gardening, planting, and maintenance. Money for visitors' entrance tickets and contributions from donors provided the foundation with income. The foundation is now almost 50 years old, and its objectives are largely still the same. A team of motivated, expert employees and a large group of enthusiastic volunteers ensure that Mien Ruys Gardens can continue to exist.

Onderhoud
Tot ± half juni was het onderhoud voortreffelijk. Daarna en vooral na ½ juli zakt de animo. Dat komt tendele door slecht weer en ook veel bezoek maar mag geen blijvende invloed hebben. Er moet eerder zwaarder rijshout worden gezet en eerder en voortdurend uitgebloeide bloemen worden uitgeplukt. Doordat dingen te laat gebeuren doet het door de border lopen om achterom te komen teveel schade. Ook blijft dan de tweede bloei achterwege.
Klimplanten moeten meer gesnoeid en geleid. Als zwaar rijshout problemen geeft moet vooral in de achtergrond (Echinops, Ligularia, Helenium, Aconitum) met stokken worden opgebonden maar dan zorgvuldiger zodat zelfs al zie je er in het begin iets van dit niet storend hoeft te zijn. Als hiervoor geen tijd is moet extra hulp voor 3 à 4 zomermaanden worden aangetrokken. Die moet dan òf het routine-werk overnemen zoals gras maaien, hagen knippen, randen bijwerken, zodat er tijd overblijft voor de borders, òf juist omgekeerd het fijnere werk doen wat ik vroeger deed. Wordt voor het laatste gekozen dan is een vrouwehand gewenst die begeleid moet worden.
Al in de winter nagaan of dit financieel uitvoerbaar is en dan maatregelen nemen.

Snoeien Gleditsia   Moraine.

Tussen narcissen tegen Thuyahaag het fluitekruid weghalen.

Gaten in haagbeuk wat groter en rechter als echte ramen.

Bemesting
Ik vraag me af of we nog niet eens iets extra moeten toevoegen als zeewier of/en gesteentemeel waarmee we jaren geleden veel succes hadden o.a. intensere kleuren.
De beste oplossing zou zijn als Anet Lambers vanuit Zwolle b.v. 2 dagen per week zou komen van ½ juni tot ½ september om het fijnere werk te doen als bloemen uitplukken enz. Daarmee zou zij beter inzicht krijgen in de beplanting en de tuinen zouden geholpen zijn. Hans Veldhoen denkt dat dit financieel te regelen is.

Playing with Plants

After more than 50 years of experiments, the first book about the Mien Ruys Gardens—the booklet *Spelen met planten* (*Playing with Plants*)—was published in 1977. The 18 experimental gardens then in existence were presented as models for people's own gardens, with a brief description of each garden and a diagram of the planting. It also included some designs for city gardens, maintenance tips, and descriptions of various plants. This booklet now provides a treasure trove of information about which gardens there were at the time and what the planting looked like.

▲ Mien Ruys's note about maintaining the Gardens in August 1983. She felt that a woman's hand was needed for the more delicate work. She suggested getting Anet Lamberts (later Scholma) to do this.

▶ Artwork POSE#02 by Zus van Zand on the central lawn in the Yellow Garden, with the larch hedge on the left

Drawing of the Gardens site and part of the nursery, made by Henk Gerritsen in 1979. The three comma-shaped hedges and the rose-circle "bubbles" (see page 256) can be seen on the left.

Square Garden (1969)

A new, sunnier spot was needed for the experiments with roses, and so the garden was extended in 1969, and the Stone Garden—now the Square Garden—was laid out. It became a typical example of Mien's "throwing dice" design method, which she used frequently in this period: placing square beds at random. The beds were filled with strong roses and *Buxus*. There was a need for a clearly defined boundary with the nursery at the northern end. She was in contact with the concrete manufacturer Bredero through her work, and they suggested building an L-shaped wall with a mixture of solid and openwork elements. These elements, known as patio blocks and interlocking B2 blocks, were used extensively during the structuralism period.

B2 blocks were used at the corner of the wall to create a background for a raised, partially covered terrace. A square pond was dug close to the terrace. The paving comprised—unsurprisingly—square tiles. Here, too, several centimeters were left between each tile, just as in the Water Garden. Mosses could grow in between the tiles, thus emphasizing their pattern. A brick path formed the link with the rest of the site. Where the path met the lawn, the bricks were laid in a "fanned out" pattern so that the transition to the lawn would not end too abruptly. The openwork and solid blocks were placed alternately further along the wall. Climbing plants could grow through the patio blocks, but Mien soon discovered that the haphazard growth competed too much with the open blocks, making it all look rather untidy. Later, the wall was demolished and replaced with only solid blocks, as designed by

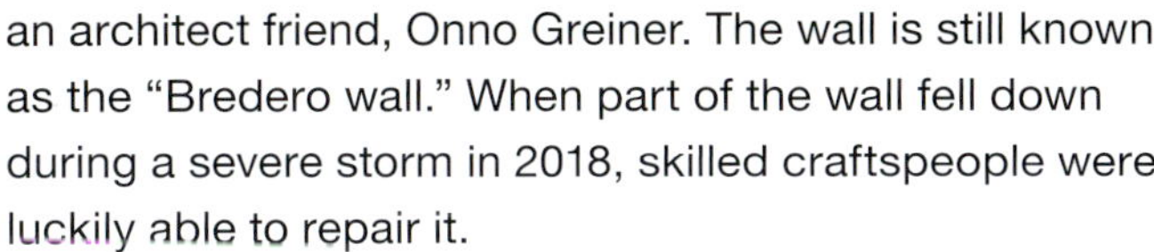

an architect friend, Onno Greiner. The wall is still known as the "Bredero wall." When part of the wall fell down during a severe storm in 2018, skilled craftspeople were luckily able to repair it.

Things did not go well with the roses. The wall and all the paving proved to be the wrong surroundings for growing roses. Some of the roses were preserved; the other beds were filled with one or two species of perennial in each bed. By 1984, the design required some modifications. The number of visitors had substantially increased, and the space between the terrace and the pond had become too small. The arrangement of the beds was changed, the pond was made bigger, and a new planting plan was conceived. The *Buxus* beds remained, but the roses increasingly had to give way to perennials. However, the square theme has always remained the basis for this garden.

The composition that emerged through the use of staggered beds is reminiscent of paintings by Mondrian. The impression is reinforced by the use of the primary colors yellow, red, and blue for the plants. Whether Mien Ruys was really inspired by Mondrian for her compositions and use of color is unclear; what is known is that her earlier planting plans did not always incorporate primary colors.

◄ The Square Garden with wooden canopy in the 1970s (above)

▲ The Square Garden in 2022 with red, yellow, and blue flowers (left)

▲ The "fan" helped to create a seamless transition from path to lawn (right)

pages 124–125: The Square Garden from above: the randomly laid square beds can be clearly seen.

Bench by the Water Ball (1970)

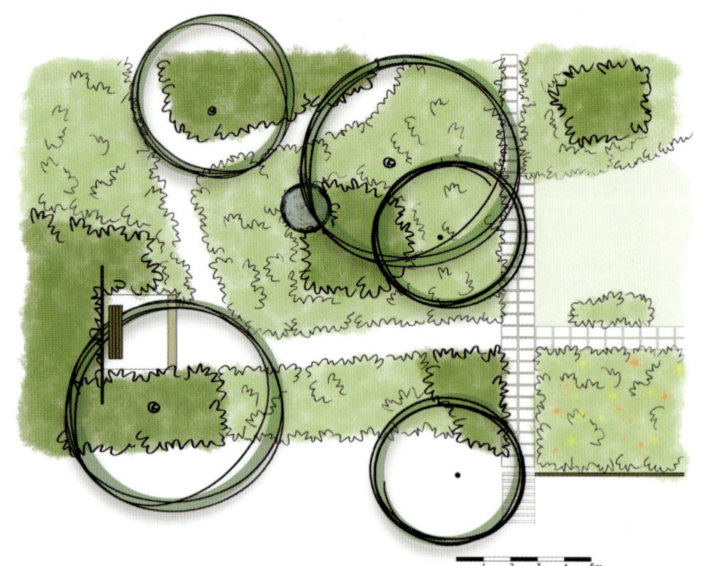

In the oldest part of the experimental gardens, there was an enormous contrast between the Old Experimental Garden and the shady Wilderness Garden. This contrast was most visible at the corner between the two gardens. Theo once pointed out to Mien that, although this was the most beautiful part of the gardens, he had nowhere to sit to enjoy it. This led her to create a raised platform in this "in-between world" with a bench hidden behind a large hazelnut tree; she called it "my throne for Theo." Theo had the idea of placing a large water-ball feature—designed by the artist Auk Fock van Coppenaal—at an angle with the hazelnut tree. It is a simple construction of chicken wire covered in several layers of concrete. Water bubbles up through a tube in the ball and flows along the surface of the ball into the ground. The ravages of time have since left their marks on the mossy ball. The concrete has been worn away by the water in some places, and the wire is now visible. As you sit on the bench, you look directly at the colorful, sunny border of the Old Experimental Garden, encircled by the bent branches of the hazelnut tree. On the left is the quiet, shady green oasis of the Wilderness Garden. Theo was right: the Bench by the Water Ball is one of the most beautiful places in the Gardens.

▼ The hazelnut tree draws your eye from the shady spot of "Theo's throne" to the sunny Old Experimental Garden.

▶ The water ball in early spring. In the foreground is the pale green foliage of *Trachystemon orientalis*.

pages 128–129: An artwork of the quote from Mien's diary "*heden mijn loopbaan begonnen*" (today my career has begun) has been placed along the path to the Wilderness Garden.

heden
loopbaan

A NEW EXTENSION

The gardens were extended once again. The plot from the 1960s had already been extended previously with a strip at the northern end and, in 1974, the nursery relinquished another substantial plot of land. The new site offered unprecedented opportunities for new experiments. Various design solutions that Mien Ruys often used around this time were applied here and they can clearly be seen in her work from this period.

Rose circles and the Kitsch Mound in the 1970s

Blowing Bubbles with Roses (1974)

Mien felt unable to give up on the roses and wanted to do another experiment in the newly acquired plot. She wrote in her booklet *Mijn Tuinen* (*My Gardens*) in 1987: "I went and stood on the new field and metaphorically blew soap bubbles. The bubbles descended as large colorful circles, and these became the rose beds." The circles were of various sizes, and each one was filled with a different species of rose. To keep clashing colors of roses away from each other, the beds were separated by three comma-shaped hedges of *Larix kaempferi*. One of the circles became the "Kitsch Mound," one of Mien's jokes. It was a reference to the old-fashioned, romantic circular mounds seen abroad, surrounded by annuals planted in a circle with a clock in the center. She presented her own interpretation of these "odd sugary cakes" by planting lilac, blue, and violet annuals in the circle.

Despite all the compost and loving care they were given, the roses again failed to thrive. Mien blamed it on the acidic, damp soil in the gardens and her aversion to using chemicals. The roses were removed in the early 1980s. By then the larch hedges were fully grown; they were allowed to remain and were given an alternative function in new experiments. Later, in 1984, another rose garden was planted in the corner of the site. The garden was raised to ensure that the soil would be drier, but this experiment with roses also failed.

◄ The Mixed Border (1974) in 2022 with shrubs, roses, and perennials

► Rose circles and larch hedges in the central lawn in 1978

Shrub Border and Mixed Border (1974)

The boundary of the experimental gardens was now definite and had to be enclosed. There was a large gold-leaved maple tree, *Acer cappadocicum* 'Aureum', on the western side. Mien actually hated these types of trees, but she could not bring herself to have it removed. Instead, the tree became an independent, visually prominent element by being placed literally on a pedestal with a little gravel square around its trunk. Borders of shrubs that flowered consecutively from early spring to winter were planted on both sides. This experiment taught her a lot about the use of shrubs, about their flowers, foliage color, and berries, and how to combine them. A great deal of the Shrub Border has now been removed and replaced by other experimental gardens.

The Mixed Border (1974) formed the boundary at the northern end of the site. It was an experiment involving combining shrubs and—once again—roses, supplemented by perennials. Mien chose reddish-brown and silver-gray as the foliage colors. She limited flower colors to pastel shades of lilac, pink, carmine red, purple, blue, gray, and a small amount of white. A brown-leaved beech hedge was planted to form a background. In terms of position, shape, and size, this border is similar to the large border in the Old Experimental Garden, but that is where the similarities end.

The feel and impact of this border are completely different due to the dark background of the beech hedge, the combination of roses, shrubs, and perennials, and the colors of the foliage and flowers. This is not an easy border to maintain. The shrubs grow bigger and bigger and bend toward the light, forcing the perennials in front of them to do the same. The site of the nursery behind the border was sold in the 1990s and a new housing estate built on it. To retain the green character of the gardens, the brown beech hedge was raised half a meter, and a green buffer of woodland wall was planted. The hedge, now several meters high, forms the background to the Mixed Border (1974). The combination of the high, dark-leaved beech hedge and the shrubs has a tendency to become too solid. The border is kept light by regularly pruning and occasionally replacing some of the shrubs with smaller or gray-leaved shrubs.

◂ The Mixed Border (1974) in the 1970s (above) and in 2023 (below) clearly showing the difference in growth behind the border

▸ Alterations to the planting plan for the Mixed Border (1974) in 1979, drawn by Mien Ruys (above)

▸ View of the central lawn and the grasses from under the *Acer cappadocicum* 'Aureum' (below)

pages 134–135: The foliage of *Acer cappadocicum* 'Aureum' turns golden yellow in fall.

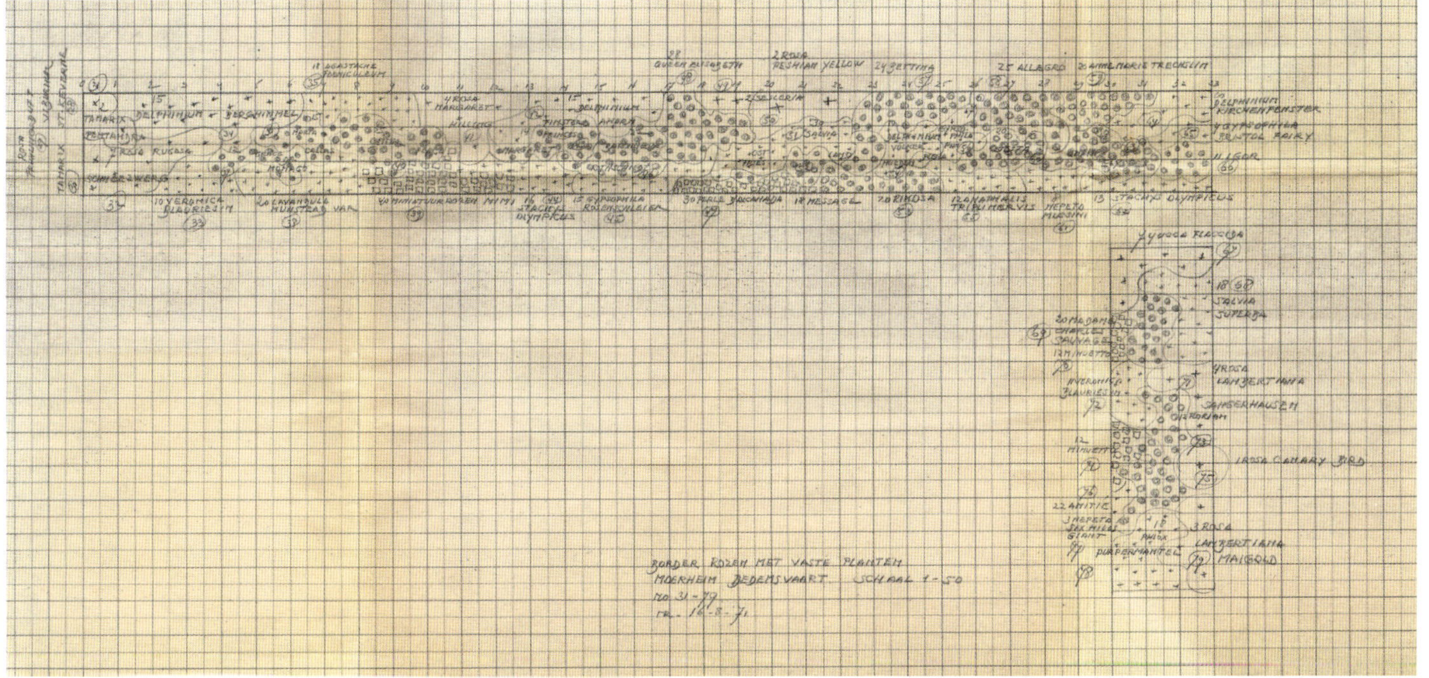
BORDER ROZEN MET VASTE PLANTEN
MOERHEIM DEDEMSVAART SCHAAL 1-50
NO. 31-79
16-8-71
SALVIA SUPERBA
STACHYS OLYMPICUS

Experiments with Flower-Meadow Mixtures (1974)

Mien Ruys

bloemenweidemengsels of..???

wie wil er nog een kamerplant?

12

Onze Eigen Tuin, jaargang 21, voorjaar

Interest in wildflowers in the 1970s led to a demand for verges and meadows with a more natural look than regularly mown grass. Various seed merchants responded to this demand by bringing "flower-meadow mixtures" onto the market. Her curiosity aroused, Mien ordered several of these mixtures to try out in the new part of her experimental gardens. She called the result "fascinating, exciting, and alarming at the same time." Most of the mixtures were explosions of color from annual flowers that originated much further south. A mixture like this was ideal for making pretty bouquets throughout summer, but it had little in common with native flora, was no use for naturalizing, and certainly did not produce the natural look that was wanted.

Furthermore, because it had to be resown every year, it was a lot of work to keep the meadows weed-free. Experiments with the various mixtures were done for many years until it was decided to create a kitchen garden here.

◄ Article by Mien Ruys on flower-meadow mixtures in *Onze Eigen Tuin* in March 1975

▼ The kitchen garden in 1981. It was maintained by Pien van der Stadt (below left and right).

► One of the flower-meadow mixtures used in an experiment

Heath Garden (around 1975)

Heath gardens were hugely popular in the 1970s. Visitors to the Gardens started asking about this type of garden. Mien Ruys could not understand the sudden interest, and she even found the word a contradiction in terms. She wrote the following in *Onze Eigen Tuin* and *Mijn Tuinen*: "Heather infers nature and limitlessness; garden infers a limited space with something inside which is emphatically not shaped by nature but by human hands" and "It is usually even embellished with conifers in yellow and blue. To make matters worse, growers have been marketing different colored heathers for years. It's difficult to imagine anything more unnatural. Another reason I don't like heath gardens is that they are so static, the same all year round." She thought that the interest might have something to do with the need for a natural garden, as this was also in vogue at the time. Or the idea that a heath garden would need little maintenance, something she believed would only work if the conditions were right. Heather needs soil that is not too dry and a bit acidic, which isn't always the case, but the soil in Dedemsvaart largely met these conditions. It was probably this fact and her opinion of heath gardens that challenged her to create one. It was an attempt to "reconcile naturalness and artificiality."

The original rose garden had been moved in the meantime. There were still several beds of strong roses, perennials, and the blocks of *Buxus*. The design for the Heath Garden was completely different, but a clearly defined

shape remained the basis. Mien created a slightly sunken circular space with curved paths and used the soil that was dug out to create some differences in height. The existing blocks of *Buxus* did not really belong in the Heath Garden but were allowed to stay as a contrast with the nature-inspired heather. She looked for plants that were consistent with the look and feel of heather and came up with the idea of planting two sections. In one section, she combined various species of heather with lilac, carmine red flowers, and gray-leaved ornamental grasses and perennials. Miniature conifers separated it from the other section, where species of yellow heather were combined with golden shrubs and yellow-flowering perennials.

Espaliered golden alder, *Alnus incana* 'Aurea', was planted to separate the organic shapes of the Heath Garden from the minimalist squares of the Square Garden (still the Stone Garden at that time). The trees were pruned in the shape of hedges. Mien called them "a hedge on legs."

◂ Mien at work among the heather in 1980 (left)

◂ The lilac and carmine section of the Heath Garden in 1978 (below)

▾ The gold and yellow section of the Heath Garden in 1980

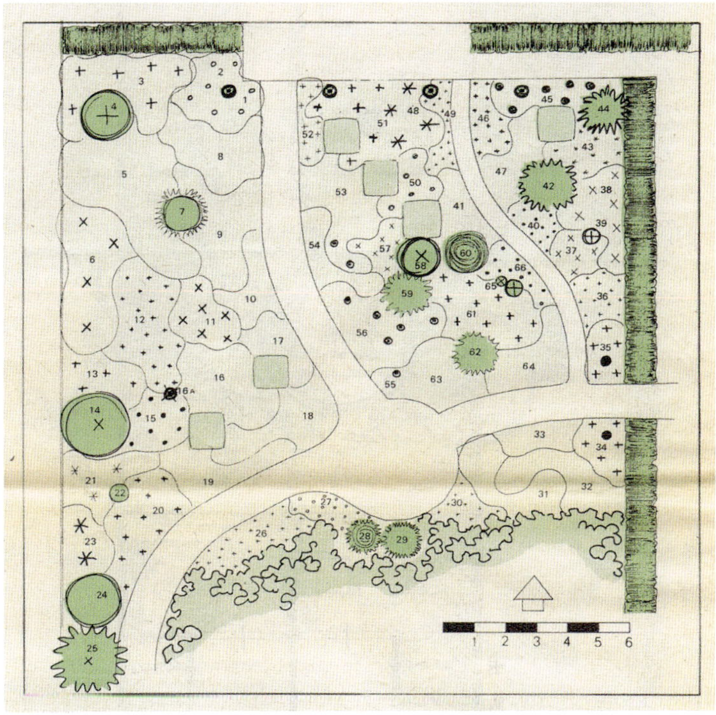

PLANTENLIJST

nr	aantal	soort
1	4	Alnus incana 'Aurea' op stam
2	7	Andromeda taiwanensis
3	16	Cytisus 'Allgold'
4	1	Rosa rubiginosa 'Eos'
5	15	Azalea gemengd
6	4	Cotoneaster wardii
7	1	Thuya globosa
8	20	Erica cineria 'Velvet Knight'
9	30	Calluna vulgaris 'Mrs. H. E. Beale'
10	15	Calluna vulgaris 'Alba Plena'
11	·6	Rhododendron praecox
12	20	Lythrum 'Dropmore Purple'
13	4	Lavatera olbia 'Rosea'
14	1	Salix irrorata
15	8	Andromeda japonica 'Variegata'
16	16	Polyantharozen 'Betty Prior'
16a	1	Lonicera henryi
17	15	Erica tetralix
18	25	Calluna vulgaris 'Long White'
19	22	Calluna vulgaris 'Alportii'
20	11	Euonymus fortunei 'Colorata'
21	3	Vaccinium corymbosum
22	1	Betula youngii op stam
23	2	Salix wehrhahnii
24	1	Osmarea burkwoodii
25	1	Tsuga canadensis
26	25	Geranium 'Johnson's Blue'
27	15	Anaphalis triplinervis
28	1	Chamaecyparis recurvii 'Nana'
29	1	Picea albertiana 'Conica'
30	10	Centaurea 'John Couts'
31	22	Erica carnea 'Pink Spangles'
32	16	Erica darleyensis 'Silberschmelze'
33	12	Erica carnea 'Vivellii'
34	11	Rhododendron repens 'Baden-Baden'
35	2	Gleditschia 'Moraine' op stam
36	15	Salvia 'Mainacht'
37	5	Euphorbia polychroma
38	6	Rosa 'Canary Bird'
39	2	Acer campestre 'Elsrijk' op stam
40	12	Berberis thunbergii 'Aurea'
41	20	Erica carnea 'Aurea'
42	1	Chamaecyparis kelleris 'Aurea'
43	10	Ligularia przewalskyi
44	1	Torreya californica
45	6	Verbascum nigrum
46	15	Buphthalmum salicifolium
47	25	Calluna 'Orange Queen'
48	4	Aucuba japonica
49	18	Erica cineria 'Golden Drop'
50	5	Spartina pectinata 'Aurea-marginata'
51	6	Symphoricarpus 'Hancock'
52	10	Andromeda compacta 'Grandiflora'
53	25	Erica vagans 'Lyonesse'
54	18	Calluna vulgaris J. H. Hamilton'
55	8	Helictotrichon sempervirens
56	30	Calluna vulgaris 'Elsie Purnell'
57	7	Cirsium rivulare 'Atropurpureum'
58	11	Cytisus scoparius 'Andreanus'
59	1	Taxus baccata 'Adpressa'
60	1	Ligustrum 'Vicaryi'
61	10	Berberis 'Carminea'
62	1	Picea omorika 'Nana'
63	20	Erica carnea 'Arthur Johnson'
64	18	Erica carnea 'King George'
65	1	Lonicera serotina
66	10	Euonymus fortunei 'Vegeta'

▴ The planting plan and the list of plants for the Heath Garden, published in *Onze Eigen Tuin* in March 1976

pages 140–141: The "hedge on legs" of golden alder in between the Heath Garden and the Square Garden in 1986

Millstone Garden (1976)

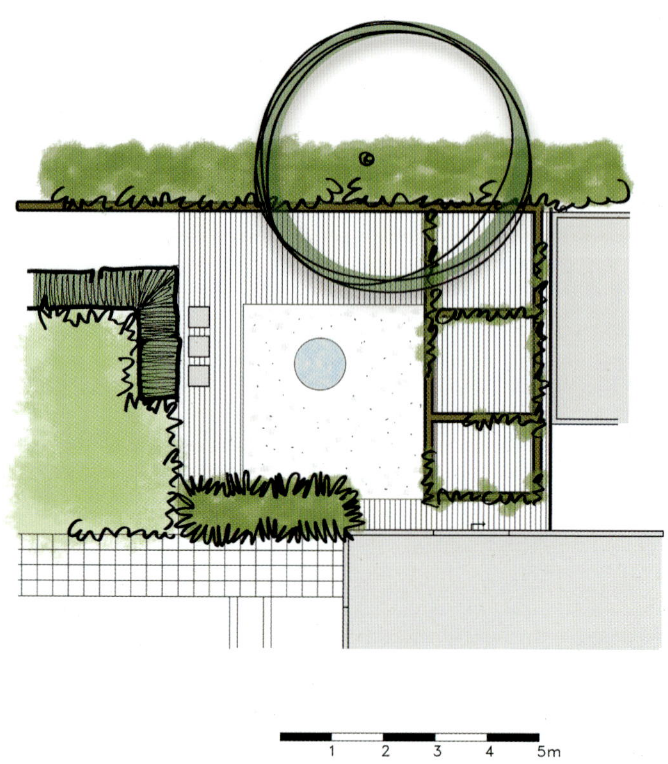

As the experimental garden evolved into a visitors' garden, a new entrance was required. A former greenhouse beside the Old Experimental Garden became the official visitors' entrance and a new garden, designed by Arend Jan van der Horst, was created as a starting point for the tour. Curved, red brick paths led visitors to the entrance to the Old Experimental Garden. A large millstone was transformed into a water feature. A plastic tank was placed beneath the stone and camouflaged by rocks and gravel. Water was pumped up through a hole in the stone such that it flowed over the stone back into the tank. The curved lines were later removed to make way for straight lines. The millstone was given a new home in a square spot in the shade of an old corkscrew willow. A substantial bed of butterbur, *Petasites hybridus*, consolidates the setting for the bubbling water. A few years later, the corkscrew willow died. Because a green foliage roof was indispensable in this garden, a new tree was needed. A *Cercidiphyllum japonicum* was planted in 1994, and a pergola was built with a *Wisteria* at its foot. Both soon created a new green roof for the garden. A large group of bamboo, *Phyllostachys nigra*, was planted where the corkscrew willow had been. The entrance to the Gardens was moved in 2008, making it necessary to alter the Millstone Garden again. By this time, the *Cercidiphyllum* had grown to become a sizeable tree, causing problems for the *Wisteria*. When the pergola's posts were found to be rotten a few years ago, the whole thing was demolished. In any case, the *Cercidiphyllum* was quite able to create a green roof on its own.

◂ The millstone in the garden with curved lines in 1978

▸ The millstone in the fall of 2023 covered with leaves from the *Cercidiphyllum japonicum* (above)

▸ Sketch of the Millstone Garden with curved lines from 1975 (below)

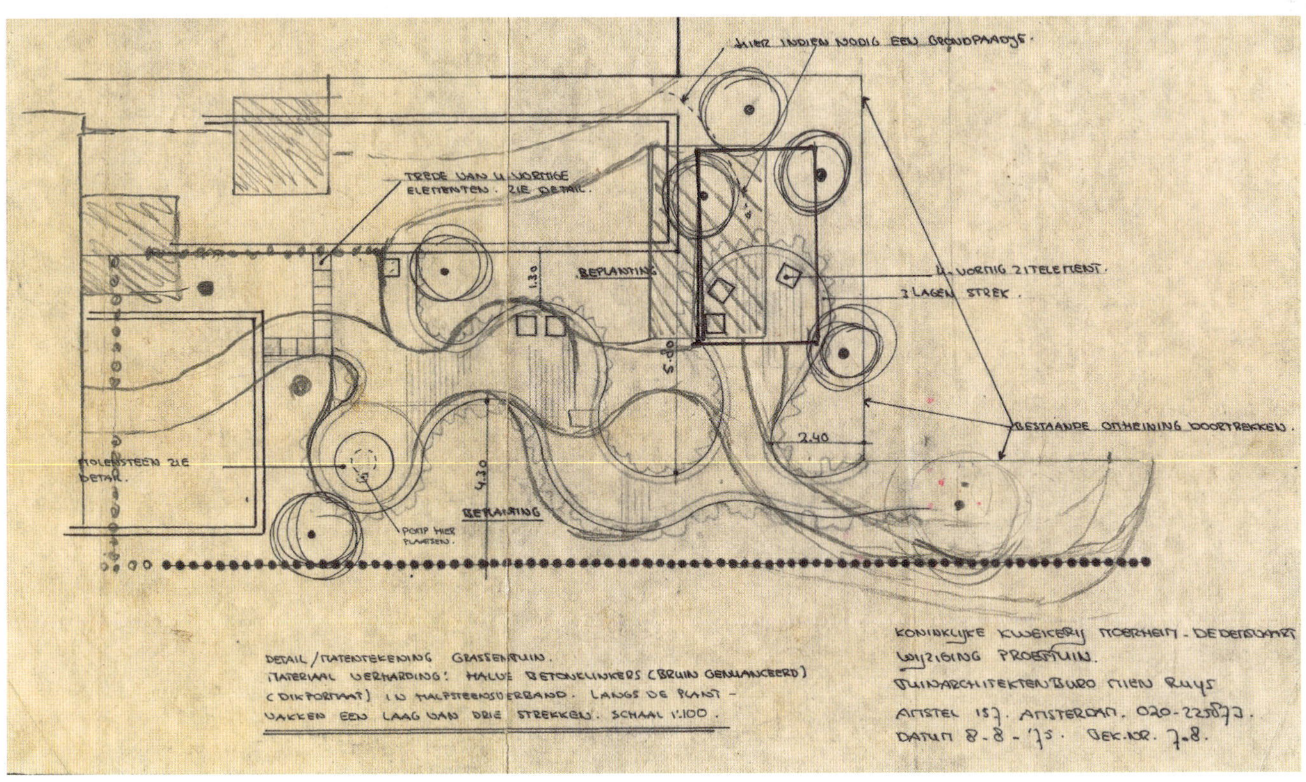
HIER INDIEN NODIG EEN GRONDPAADJE.
TREDE VAN U-VORMIGE ELEMENTEN. ZIE DETAIL.
1.30
BEPLANTING
U-VORMIG ZITELEMENT.
3 LAGEN STREK.
5.00
2.40
BESTAANDE OMHEINING DOORTREKKEN.
MOLENSTEEN ZIE DETAIL.
4.30
POMP HIER PLAATSEN.
BEPLANTING
DETAIL/MATENTEKENING GRASSENTUIN.
MATERIAAL VERHARDING: HALVE BETONKLINKERS (BRUIN GENUANCEERD) (DIKFORMAAT) IN HALFSTEENSVERBAND. LANGS DE PLANT-VAKKEN EEN LAAG VAN DRIE STREKKEN. SCHAAL 1:100.
KONINKLIJKE KWEKERIJ MOERHEIM - DEDEMSVAART
WIJZIGING PROEFTUIN.
TUINARCHITEKTENBURO MIEN RUYS
AMSTEL 157. AMSTERDAM. 020-225873.
DATUM 8-8-'75. TEK.NR. 7-8.

Gardening on the Roof (1979)

A square, wooden construction with decking, planters, a fence, and a pergola was part of an exhibition of roof gardens in Amstel Park. After the exhibition finished, the entire construction was transported to Dedemsvaart to experiment on plants for the planters. There was space for the roof terrace between the rock garden and the flower meadow mixtures. Mien Ruys felt that "the colossus stood there all alone like an ugly obstacle." To make the construction fit in better, two terraces were added alongside and plants positioned to screen it off from the rest of the gardens. Various lightweight materials were tested for planters in which plants could grow. Many experiments were conducted with plants and materials for the Roof Garden.

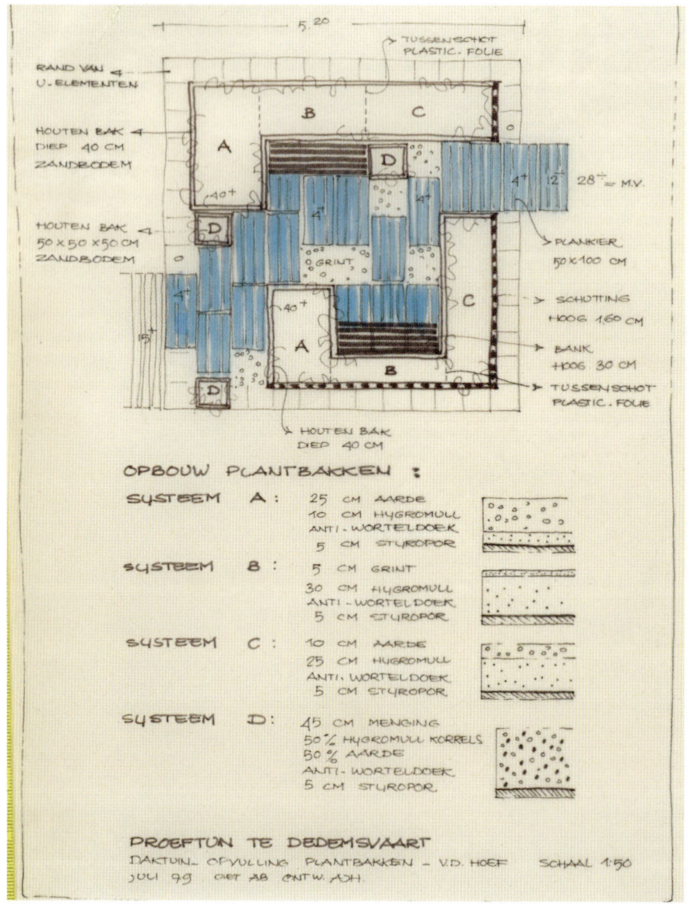

▲▶ The Roof Garden in the early 1980s

◀ Design for part of the Roof Garden by Arend Jan van der Horst in 1979, with details of the layers in each planter

pages 146–147: The seedbed for the Roof Garden in 2012 with vegetables, herbs, and flowers

ABOUT ROOF GARDENS

Conditions are different in a roof garden compared to those in a garden on the ground. The available space is often limited and there is no natural soil. Ordinary garden soil is usually too heavy for the construction of the roof, certainly if the soil becomes too wet. Plants have to grow in a nutrient medium of other lighter materials (substrate) and within the enclosed surrounds of planters and pots. The substrate in which the plants grow must drain well but not dry out too much. Roof gardens are usually exposed to more wind and more sun than ordinary gardens. All this means that planting conditions are not exactly ideal. When choosing material for planters, fences, pergolas, and furniture, weight is an important factor to take into account. All these limiting factors make designing a roof garden quite a challenge and perfect for experiments.

▲▼ Various parts of the Roof Garden in the early 1980s

▶ Design for part of the Roof Garden by Arend Jan van der Horst in 1979 showing a cross section of the fence

The Roof Garden over the Years

From the first experiment in 1979, all sorts of different experiments were conducted with materials and planting in the place where the Roof Garden was situated. Various drainage materials, combinations of substrates, and soil in different layer depths were tried out with bulbs, annuals, perennials, ornamental grasses, shrubs, and miniature conifers. Conclusions were drawn on the basis of the results: which combinations of substrates and plants worked, and which did not. The Roof Garden remained largely the same until the early 1980s.

PLATTEGROND

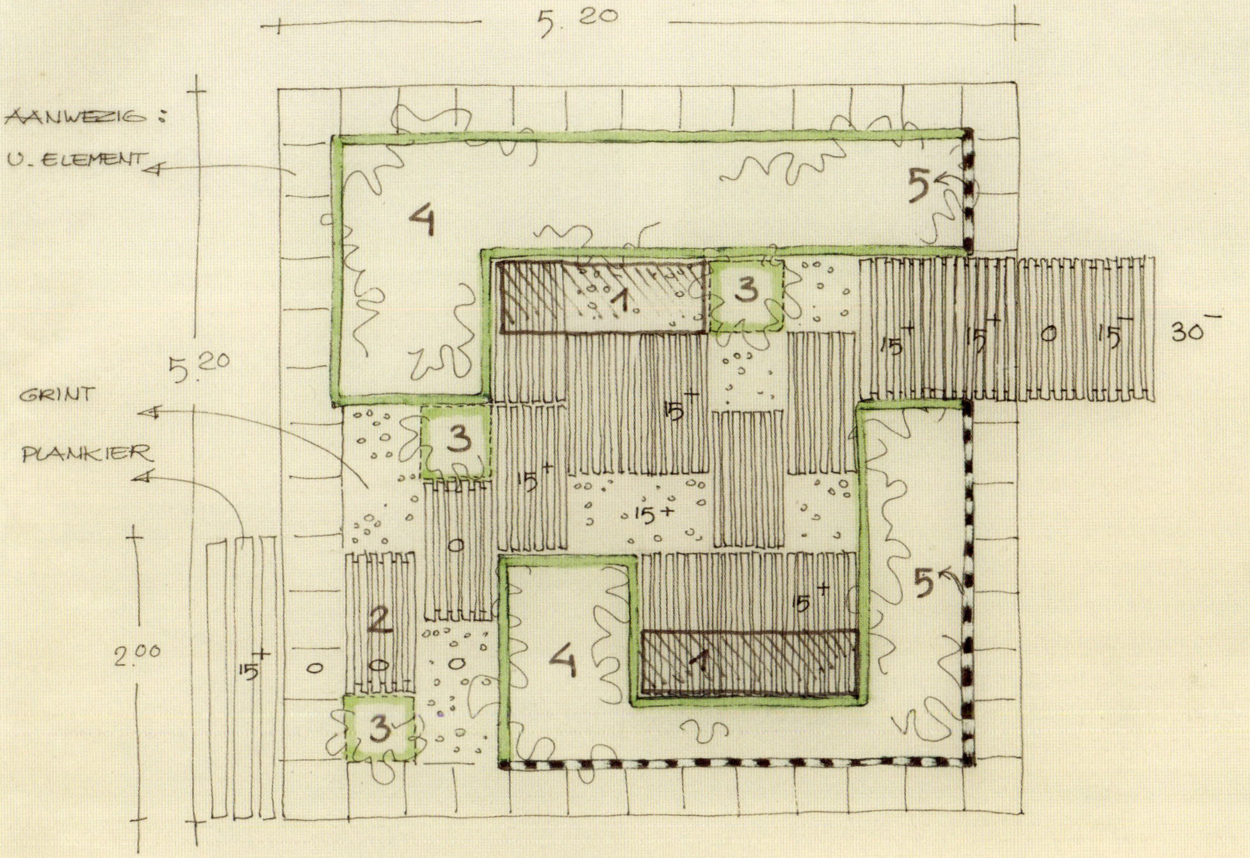

5.20

AANWEZIG:
U-ELEMENT
GRINT
PLANKIER
5.20
2.00

1 BANKJE ZIE BIJGAAND DETAIL
2 BUITENPARKET 50 X 100 CM
3 PLANTENBAK VAN BUITENPARKET 50X50X50 CM
4 PLANTENBAK VAN VERTIKALE DELEN 40 CM IN DEKBALK
5 SCHUTTING VAN VERTIKALE DELEN AFWISSELEND 1.60 m EN 0.40 m IN DEKBALK, (EINDIGEN MET 1.60 OP HOEK)
DE DEKBALK AAN BUITENZIJDE PLANTENBAK RUST GEHEEL OP DE RAND VAN U-ELEMENTEN.

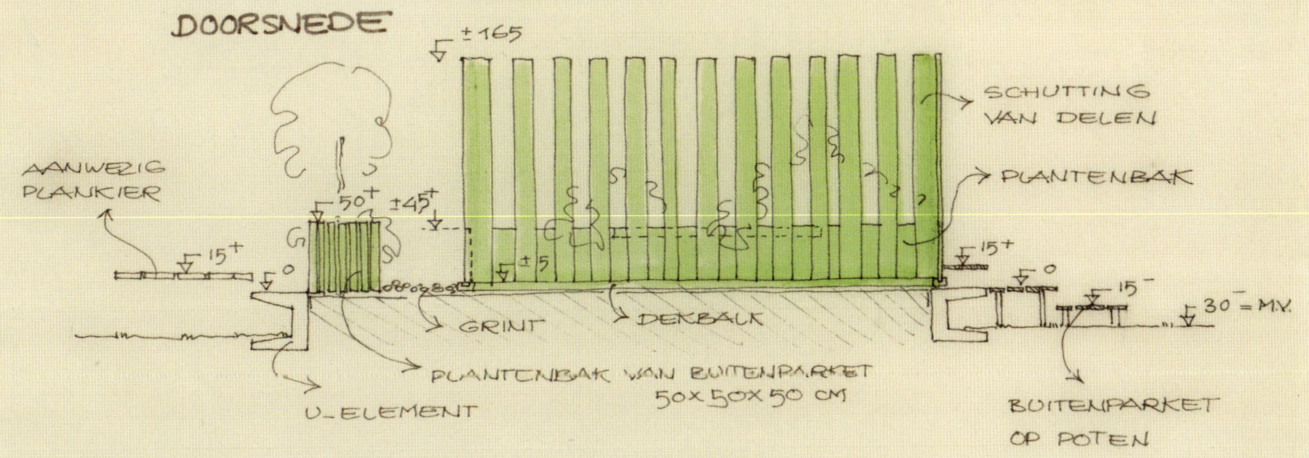

PROEFTUIN TE DEDEMSVAART
DAKTUIN TE MAKEN DOOR HOUTCREATIEF
SCHAAL 1:50
JULI 79 GET. AB ONTW. ADH

After ten years or more, some of the wood was rotten and it was time for a new experiment. Buro Mien Ruys was increasingly being asked to design roof gardens, sometimes on roofs that could bear very little weight. An experiment with plants that can grow in a thin layer—only a few centimeters—of substrate followed in the early 1990s. Low-growing plants, such as *Sedum*, *Waldsteinia,* and *Saxifraga*, were placed in square beds with different types of substrate. The plants had to be able to survive with little maintenance and no extra water in dry periods.

Experiment in the Roof Garden with various combinations of substrate in square beds in 1992

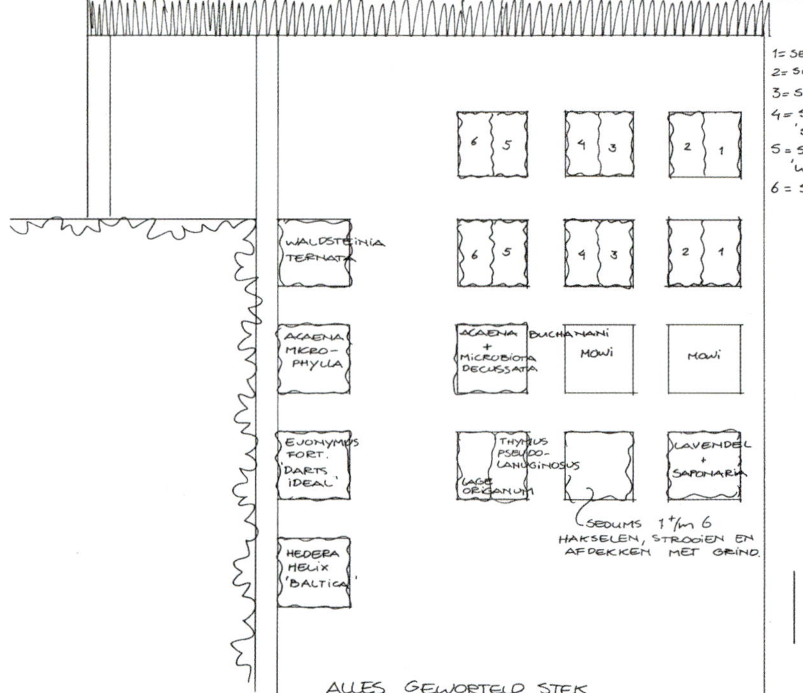

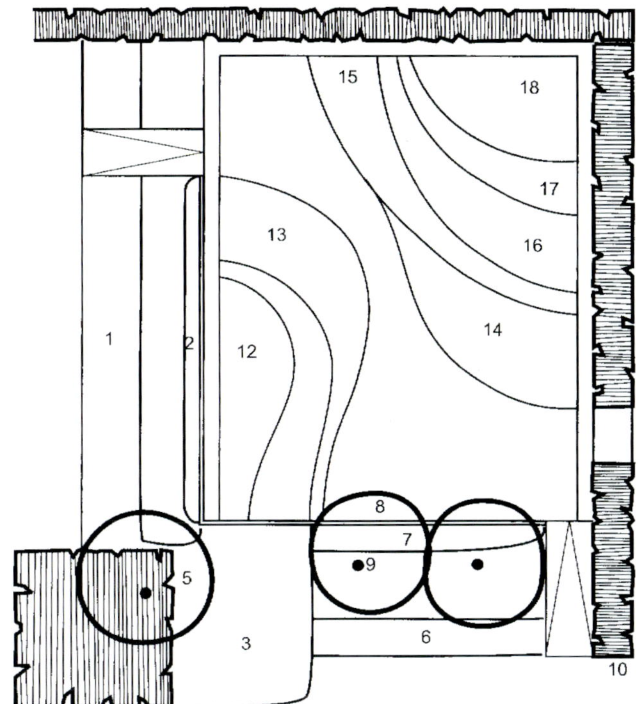

Roof Terrace

1 *Potentilla fruticosa* 'Abbotswood'
2 *Ligustrum vulgare* 'Atrovirens'
3 *Symphoricarpos* ×*chenaultii*
4 *Ilex* ×*meserveae* 'Blue Prince'
5 *Pyrus salicifolia* 'Pendula'
6 *Lonicera syringantha* var. *wolfii*
7 *Lonicera nitida* 'Elegant'
8 *Cornus alba* 'Sibirica'
9 *Salix alba* 'Tristis'
10 *Acer campestre*
11 *Thuja*
12 *Waldsteinia ternata*
13 *Sedum acre* 'Aureum'
14 *Sedum* 'Robustum'
15 *Silene maritima* 'Weisskehlchen'
16 *Sedum spurium* 'Schobuser Blut'
17 *Gypsophila repens*
18 *Geranium sanguineum*

▲ Planting plan for the Roof Garden from the 1999 planting plan booklet (above left)

▲ The Roof Garden around 2008, featuring strips with different substrates and plants that crisscrossed each other (above right)

It is clear from what Mien Ruys said about this experiment that she never intended her experimental gardens to be gardens for visitors, but a place in which she could conduct experiments: "I can't explain to everyone who comes here that I do really ugly things too, but I just want to try things out; will it work or won't it?" In the anniversary year of 1999, the Roof Garden was given a makeover. The square beds looked a bit shabby, and many species were failing to thrive. The strongest species were used in a new design of meandering strips, leading along the diagonal route through the Roof Garden. Different substrates were put in large beds so that all the strips combined all the types of substrates. After a few years, it transpired that no difference in growth could be seen between the various substrates.

In the winter of 2008–2009, the whole Roof Garden was dug over for an experiment with a new material: timber that has been made sustainable by heating. Fast-growing timber—such as poplar and whitewood, originating in responsibly managed forests in Europe—is given this treatment, after which its sustainability is comparable to tropical hardwood. No chemicals are used in this process to make it more sustainable, and less transportation is needed compared to certified tropical hardwood. Furthermore, this timber is ideal for roof gardens because it becomes much lighter after the treatment. Buro Mien Ruys came up with a completely new design with a fence, a large seedbed, movable planters in two heights, and seating elements made from this new timber. The planters and the seating elements, exactly the same size as the

60 × 60-centimeter tiles, were easy to move around, making it possible to change their arrangement according to requirements. Three different substrates were experimented with in the planters: two ready-made products, each from a different supplier, and a mixture made in the Gardens from 50 percent potting compost and 50 percent perlite. Perlite is an organic, natural material that is very lightweight and can retain moisture well—ideal for use in a roof garden. Special provision was made for draining water through overflow pipes in the soil in a buffer layer of perlite. Vegetables, fruit, herbs, and cut flowers were grown in the large L-shaped seedbed, in a 15- to 20-centimeter-thick layer of the potting compost and perlite mixture. This planter was also given a buffer layer of perlite and overflow pipes to drain off excess water. Little hatches were made in the unused space under the planter to create storage space for garden tools. During winter, when the Gardens were closed to the public, the timber was sawn, holes were drilled, and the planters were screwed together. It was time-consuming work, since all the holes for the screws had to be pre-drilled to ensure that the relatively fragile timber was not damaged. But the result was wonderful, and the large vegetable seedbed was a particular success, not just in terms of yield, but also in terms of beauty. The Gardens' own mixture produced the best results in the movable planters. After a while, the overflow pipes became blocked, causing the planters to stay too wet. Even the use of drainage pipes could not solve this shortcoming. And, of course, damp is eventually disastrous for garden timber, as happened here too. The large

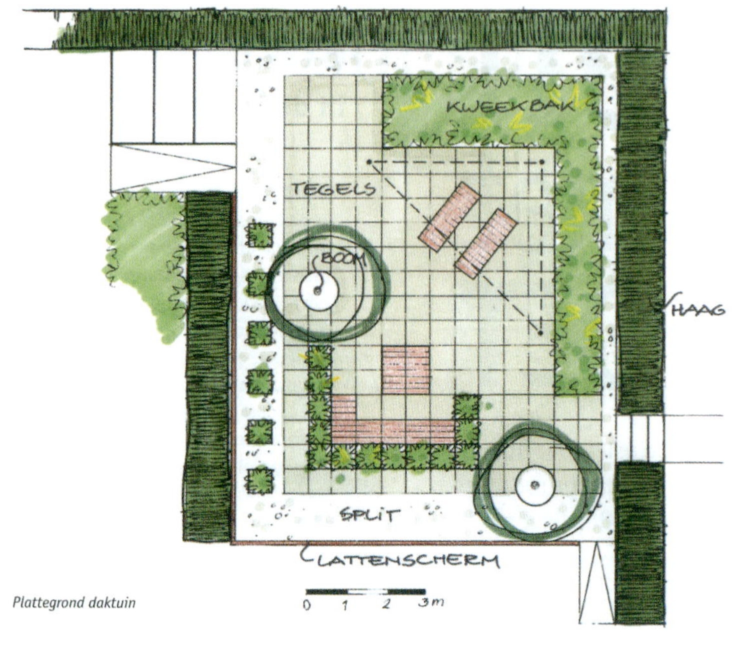

Plattegrond daktuin

▲ Design for the Roof Garden in 2008

▼ The Roof Garden from various angles in the summer of 2009. The fence, the seedbed, the movable planters, and the seating elements were all made from Platowood.

seedbed was dismantled after a few years. The movable planters and the seating elements survived for quite a few years but have now perished too.

Two large, round stainless-steel planters filled with a mixture of mineral wool and clay granules held fruit trees that never thrived successfully. The trees were planted in the ground, and two medlars were planted in the planters that had previously been in the large vegetable seedbed, but these trees were unable to thrive in the planters either. One of the two is now in the Herb Garden.

Growing plants in high planters was found to be a very pleasant way of working, as there is no need to bend over. They are ideal for older people who have become stiffer but still want to continue gardening. Furthermore, it is easier to keep on top of the work when plants are in planters, and substrate is often lighter to handle than soil.

One part of the experiment involved a fence with a wooden frame, posts, and slats. Black geotextile fabric with narrow horizontal slats attached to it was stretched across one side of the frame. The same story of rotting wood applied to the posts: the point at which they went into the ground rotted right through after about ten years. A severe storm did the rest, and one ill-fated day, part of the construction was blown down. The fence was kept going for a while thereafter, helped by a makeshift solution until, in August 2020, a substantial part of the weeping willow close to the Roof Garden broke off, wreaking havoc. The horizontal slats hardly suffered at all over the years, which meant that most of them could be reused for a fence in another part of the garden.

By this time, there was little left of the original plan from 2008. In 2017, the movable planters and the seating elements were moved to make way for an experiment involving planting in two low planters with a roughly 10-centimeter layer of substrate. The results were somewhat disappointing. Such a thin layer turned out to be too little to achieve the same effect as when the plants were planted in the ground. It all looked rather pathetic. It was time for a new Roof Garden.

During the winter of 2020–2021, Anet Scholma drew a design for a new layout of the entire area around the New Experimental Garden, the Roof Garden, and the Middle Garden. One of the reasons for this was that the Roof Garden's entrance and exit were diagonally opposite each other. The walking route therefore ran diagonally through the area and limited the layout. By moving the passageways so that they were opposite each other, a pleasing line of sight was created from the Middle Garden to the old white willow in the Marsh Garden, and it also increased the options for the layout of the Roof Garden. Existing hedges were dug up and partly replanted. The *Dakdokters*, a company from Amsterdam that specializes in green roofs, proposed a new layout for the Roof Garden. They started with a simple, functional design to match Mien Ruys's style, with lots of greenery and materials that were reused or sustainable as far as possible. The tiles, grit, gravel boards, aluminum profiles,

drainage mats, and substrate were reused, for example. The round stainless-steel planters were also given a place in the new Roof Garden. A new fence—with evenly spaced-out vertical slats so that the wind could blow between them—was made from untreated Douglas-fir timber and erected on two sides of the Roof Garden. To prevent them from rotting, the fence posts were placed in fence post supports. The sustainable material olivine was used as gravel to add a broad edging to the tiles.

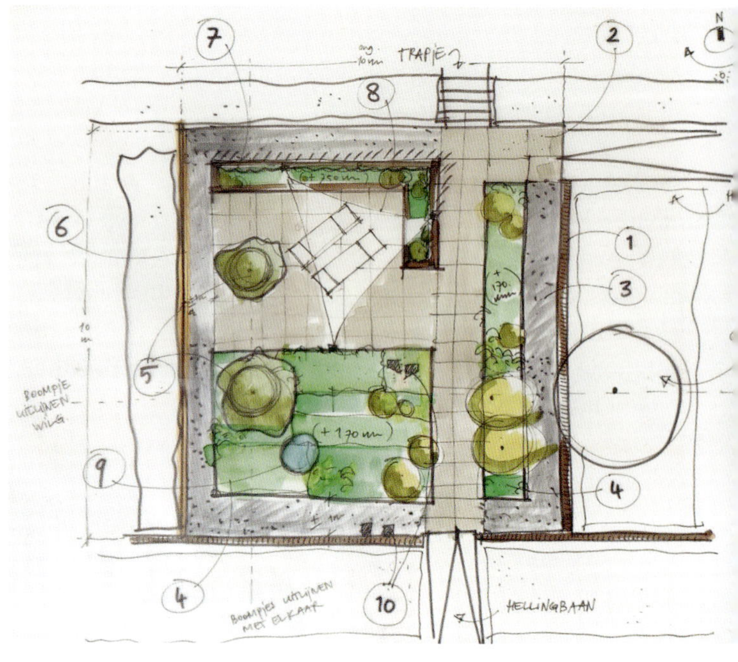

▲ Sketch for the layout of the Roof Garden in 2021

◀ Plants for the large planter ready to be planted in the layer of substrate in April 2022

▼ The Roof Garden and its surrounding area was dug up in the winter of 2021–2022 (below left).

▼ Experiments with various mixtures of bulbs in planters were conducted using substrate from Verver Export. *Tulipa clusiana* 'Peppermint Stick' (below right and opposite below) is suitable for naturalizing.

▶ *Sedum* 'José Aubergine' and *Echinacea purpurea* 'White Swan' (opposite above)

Olivine

Olivine is a rock-forming mineral that can be found in various parts of the world, including the Eifel in Germany. It is now regarded as a very promising new material that can capture carbon from the air through a chemical reaction, helping to reduce it. It is available in various granule sizes: as sand, grit, or gravel. Grit and gravel can be incorporated into semi-hard surfaces, while the sand can improve the soil. Olivine can be used as lime to increase the acidity of soil and, as it weathers, it emits magnesium, a nutrient that plants need.

▲ The Roof Garden in the summer of 2023, with the recently planted *Buddleja davidii* 'Black Knight' in the round stainless-steel planters. On the left is a strip of olivine.

Two planters that fit exactly on top of the 60 × 60-centimeter tiles form the basis for the garden: a long, narrow planter measuring 7.80 × 1.20 meters and a large planter measuring 6.60 × 3 meters. The edge of the planter is an L-shaped aluminum profile. A drainage mat was placed on top of the tiles within this aluminum edge, followed by a filter cloth and a layer of substrate.

The reused substrate in the shallow planter contains very little organic material and is about 12 centimeters thick. A limited number of species were planted at random in it. Several of the plants from the original planting plan did not survive, but others are thriving and spontaneously self-seeding. New species have been added to see how they develop.

The large planter has a layer of about 22 centimeters of substrate. This substrate contains more organic material, making it suitable for perennials.

The composition and thickness of this layer provide far more possibilities in plant choice than is the case for the shallow planter, but it is heavier. Many different species of plants have been tried out to discover which will survive and which will not. The advantage of growing plants in substrate is that the conditions are different from those in the soil in the gardens: drier and probably richer in lime than the moisture-retaining, rather acidic soil in Dedemsvaart. Lime-loving and drought-tolerant plants that often do not thrive well in the ground do well in the planters. The plants are given organic nutrients in the form of granules in spring to provide them with sufficient nutrients.

Not only are perennials tested for their suitability for planters with substrate, hundreds of bulbs are also dug in to try out. Verver Export supplied packets of botanical tulips, crocuses, narcissus, and other naturalizing bulbs. The idea is to test whether the bulbs can hold their own in the substrate. Up to now, most of them have appeared again every spring, and some are even in a better state than before. As such, the flowering season can be brought forward by several months, not just in the garden but also in roof gardens.

The alteration of the Roof Garden and its surroundings is being done in phases. A high planter, a shade sail, and garden furniture will be added soon. It will be a few years before the newly planted privet hedges have grown to the right height to give the Roof Garden sufficient privacy.

A Few Tips When Making a Roof Garden

- If you are adding a hard surface, make sure it drains well—for instance, by putting lightweight tiles on pedestals so that rainwater can run underneath them to the drainpipe. Or use lightweight composite decking, incorporating a thin, water-permeable layer of gravel so that the material stays in place well. The finer the material, the thinner the layer can be.
- Make walls and fences slatted so that the wind can blow through them. Take account of safety requirements and any local bylaws when deciding on their height.
- Use lightweight materials for planters, such as hydrothermally modified timber, COR-TEN® steel, aluminum, or plastic.
- Leave an empty space under high planters to limit their weight. This space could be used as storage.
- Use a special substrate to fill planters; it is lighter and more permeable than ordinary garden soil.
- Choose plants that can withstand the intense weather conditions of a roof.

▶ The Roof Garden is still visible from the central lawn. The privet hedge will eventually screen off the Roof Garden from the rest.

Gardens for Architects

All her life, Mien Ruys had more affinity with architects than with landscape gardeners. Her collaborations with many of them often led to friendships. Abe Bonnema and Onno Greiner were particular friends in the 1960s and 1970s. In the early 1960s, Bonnema asked her to design a garden for the modernist house/annex/office he had designed for himself. In exchange for a design, which he was unable to pay for, he promised her that she could collaborate on all his future projects. Mien agreed, and Abe Bonnema kept his promise. Her design for his garden was one with many contrasts: clean and loose, open and closed, architectural and natural. She used characteristic elements from the period in this garden, such as the clear, defined division of a surface with a flower terrace, square beds of roses, grion tiles in the lawn, and railway sleepers to bridge differences in height. The house and garden are still largely intact and owned by *Hendrick de Keyser Monumenten*. In 1967, she designed a garden for Onno Greiner's bungalow with a patio that he had designed himself.

▲ Abe Bonnema's garden with a flower terrace, railway sleepers, and grion tiles

▼ The patio garden of Onno Greiner's home

▶ The park around the town hall, *Stadthalle* Biberach, Germany, in the 1970s, featuring curved lines (above and below)

Stadthalle Biberach (1973–1978)

One example of the collaboration between Mien Ruys and Onno Greiner was the proposed new town hall and theater in an existing park in Biberach, Germany. Onno asked Mien to design the outdoor areas for his structuralist design of the building. The dominant building on a small plot, various prerequisites, and a difference in height of 20 meters made this assignment pretty challenging. With the help of Hans Veldhoen and Arend Jan van der Horst, she came up with a design in which she sought to create a contrast with the austere, rectangular building by making use of ovals, curved lines, and a round pond.

1980-1990

THE NETHERLANDS: A GLOOMY PERIOD

The first half of the 1980s was defined by an economic downturn. One of the reasons for this was unrest in the Middle East, which caused a sharp rise in the price of oil. The government in the Netherlands decided to impose sweeping austerity measures to solve the budget deficits that had arisen in the 1970s. Unemployment was high, and the shortage of affordable housing and speculation on the housing market led to a housing crisis. The environment was under threat due to pollution, nuclear waste, and what was then known as “acid rain” caused by the increase in road traffic and intensive stock farming. Tensions between East and West mounted, and the threat of a nuclear war grew. The squatters’ movement and punk subculture were a reaction to the feeling of hopelessness and social discontent among the younger generation.

Changes in the division of roles between men and women continued to advance. More and more women went outside the home to work, often part-time, and girls from all sections of society embarked on professional and vocational training. Even their mothers were given the chance to resume the secondary schooling they had missed out on by studying for the *moedermavo* (secondary education for adults, especially women).

The Years Begin to Tell

By now, Mien was approaching her 80s. Stopping work was still not an option, but physical ailments, such as back problems, meant she was no longer as mobile as before. Domestic work was never her forte, and this did not improve as she got older. She once said: "The only things I can do are create gardens and make tea." She continued to spend summers in her gardens in Dedemsvaart. Her staff often accompanied her, and everyone who came to work in her studio was obliged to spend some time weeding in the experimental gardens. To her great sorrow, she was no longer able to do any weeding herself. She had a lot of help and support from her friend Rosette Zandvoort, who was now editor in chief of *Onze Eigen Tuin*. Mien was still interested in politics and felt drawn to pacifism. She took part in the mass peace demonstration in Amsterdam in 1981, against siting cruise missiles in the Netherlands. She had more time for her hobbies: she painted, read a lot, and listened to music. And at the end of every day, she invariably drank two shots, no more and no less.

▲ Mien in 1980

▼ Mien and Princess Juliana of the Netherlands in 1988, in conversation on the bench in the Old Experimental Garden

Time to Hand Things Over

Hans Veldhoen and Arend Jan van der Horst, now fellow directors, were taking over more and more of the design work. Although Mien still always contributed ideas during the design process, they were the main designers for the assignments. Mien chiefly focused on making planting plans, which she was now able to do in only a few hours due to her vast knowledge and experience. "I start dancing with pleasure working at my squared paper," she once said. In 1981, Arend Jan van der Horst left to start his own design studio, and in 1985, Anet Scholma joined the studio as a landscape gardener and landscape architect. Experiments in the experimental gardens continued, not only conducted by Mien, but also by Hans and later Anet, as a means of acquiring experience with plants and materials. Mien's last book appeared in 1981. She wrote *Van vensterbank tot landschap* (*From Windowsill to Landscape*) in conjunction with her friend Rosette Zandvoort. The book is about the relationship between humankind and nature, about how the Netherlands is set up, and the importance of designing it as well as possible so that nature can be experienced. Mien felt that this was something we all had a responsibility toward. Now, over 40 years later, this is still a topical subject.

Open Gardens

Gardening, creating gardens, and especially visiting gardens became "hot" in the 1980s. Gardening magazines, gardening programs, model gardens, garden days, gardening clubs, and garden routes appeared. The many organized coach trips to open gardens were very popular, such as to Ton ter Linden's Tuinen, Rob Herwig's Modeltuinen (model gardens), Henk Gerritsen's Priona Tuinen, Ada Hoffman's Vijvertuinen (pond gardens), and of course, Mien Ruys Gardens.

◄ Mien Ruys and Rosette Zandvoort at the book presentation of *Van vensterbank tot landschap* (*From Windowsill to Landscape*) in 1981

Gardener's Garden (1981)

Around 1900, a small house for staff was built on the Moerheim site. The gardener, Dirk Jan Koning, moved in there and created his own private garden around the house. When working in the other gardens, he followed Mien Ruys's wishes, but he was able to arrange this garden in the way he wanted. No straight, clear-cut lines here or plants that had proved themselves, but unpaved, meandering paths and wild, natural planting. The site, partly peaty soil and partly sandy, contained differences in height due to large holes left after oak trees blew down. These different circumstances made it interesting to let nature take its course. While Mien believed that naturalization had to be kept in check, Dirk Jan wanted to see what happened if you didn't intervene. According to Dirk, there were no such things as weeds in "his" garden, but it did not prove easy to leave the plants entirely alone. There were always new plants enticing him to try them out, and other plants that needed protection in order to survive. The gardener's house is now the Foundation's office, and the garden has been included in the tour.

▲► The plants in the Gardener's Garden are mainly shade-loving, with a great deal of contrast in leaf shapes.

◄ The gardener's house, built around 1900, in 2023

Yellow Garden (1982)

Close to the experiment with flower-meadow mixtures stood a pergola with no obvious function. One of the remaining larch hedges was in a position relative to the pergola such that both elements could be connected to each other relatively simply. Another circle was made in the curve of the hedge—a single soap bubble—flowing completely naturally from the pergola. The circle was accentuated by a couple of strips of yellow bricks with a lawn between them. On the advice of Mien's friend Fred Zandvoort, the lawn was lowered slightly toward the middle. It was only a few centimeters, but the effect was and still is quite obvious. The dip creates a sense of being enclosed; you have more of a feeling that you are inside the space and in between the plants than if the circle had been flat. A border was created between the circle and the larch hedge, whose width tapers off due to the arbitrary curve of the hedge. Mien chose plants with flowers or foliage in shades of yellow, ranging from almost white to warm yellow. For the other side of the circle, she chose perennials and shrubs in yellow and orange. The larch hedge is about 1.40 meters high so that it is possible to look over it. As such, the Yellow Garden forms its own space, but there is still contact with the surrounding area. The parasol-shaped *Prunus* just beyond the circle gives the garden a roof and reinforces the line of sight between the pergola and the Yellow Garden. Mien called this garden her "magic circle."

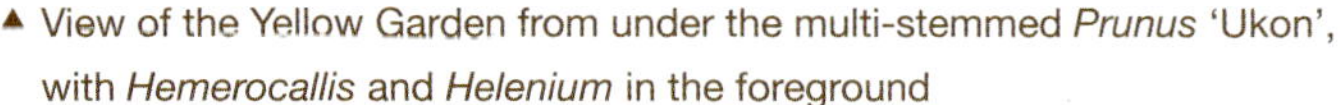

▲ View of the Yellow Garden from under the multi-stemmed *Prunus* 'Ukon', with *Hemerocallis* and *Helenium* in the foreground

▶ The Yellow Garden with the variegated foliage of *Hosta sieboldiana* 'Frances Williams' and *Phlomis russeliana* in the foreground. The *Prunus* is due for replacement. A new multi-stemmed *Prunus* 'Ukon' was planted in 2024 (opposite, above).

▶ The yellow of *Hemerocallis* 'Corky' and *Ligularia stenocephala* 'The Rocket' (opposite, below left)

▶ The larch hedge beside the Yellow Garden is a remnant of the "Bubbles" from the 1970s (opposite, below right)

Blue Border (early 1980s)

The Blue Border was planted around one of the other remaining larch hedges, another experiment in planting in a single color. Mien found blue a tricky color since not all blues look attractive together. In the end, she gave up on the idea of a border in a single color. She viewed it as a fad and, personally, she loved contrasts too much to allow herself to be restricted in this way. The Blue Border was therefore not granted a long life, in contrast to the Yellow Garden. There, the use of a broad palette of colors ranging from almost white to orange did ensure sufficient variation.

The Blue Border bounded by one of the comma-shaped larch hedges (above and below). Neither of them is there anymore. The photo below shows the Kitsch Mound in the foreground.

The planting plan for the Blue Border as depicted in the planting plan booklet published in 1984

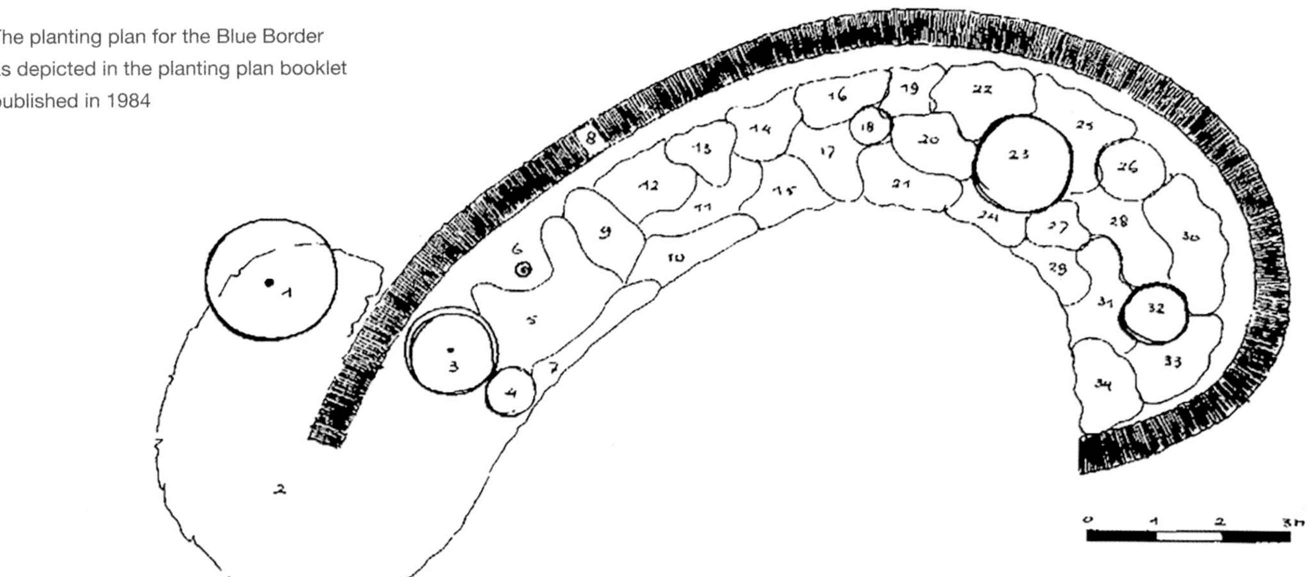

List of plants for the Blue Border

1 *Viburnum plicatum*

2 Bulbs and annuals in blue

3 *Ceanothus* 'Gloire de Versailles'

4 *Agapanthus orientalis*

5 *Hosta amethystina*

6 *Magnolia soulangeana*

7 *Viola cornuta* 'Hansa'

8 Hedge of *Larix kaempferi*

9 *Campanula lactiflora*

10 *Nepeta nervosa*

11 *Scutellaria incana*

12 *Aconitum* 'Bressingham Spire'

13 *Aster cordifolius* 'Ideal'

14 *Delphinium* purple

15 *Geranium* 'Mrs. Kendall Clark'

16 *Galega officinalis* + forget-me-nots

17 *Platycodon grandiflorus* 'Mariesii'

18 *Caryopteris* ×*clandonensis*

19 *Delphinium* blue

20 *Aconitum wilsonii* 'Barker'

21 *Salvia* ×*sylvestris* 'Blauhügel'

22 *Salvia uliginosa*

23 *Hydrangea villosa* + *Vinca minor*

24 *Centaurea montana*

25 *Delphinium* pale blue

26 *Aster* 'Climax'

27 *Delphinium* 'Arnold Bocklin'

28 *Veronica longifolia* 'Blauriesin'

29 *Veronica teucrium* 'Shirley Blue'

30 *Echinops ritro* 'Veitch Blue'

31 *Campanula persicifolia*

32 *Hibiscus syriacus* blue

33 *Lupinus perennis*

34 *Geranium* 'Johnson's Blue'

Flower Terrace (1982)

From as early as the 1960s, Mien regularly put her idea of a flower terrace into effect. It is a way of connecting a house with its garden. A patio is often laid against the outside wall of a house, which means that the view from inside the house is always of the paving and garden furniture. To get around this, she added "patches of flowers" in her grion tile paving, interspersed with various places to sit in the sun or in the shade. The staggered beds of plants create the impression that you are surrounded by plants, wherever you are in the garden. The view from the house is also of plants everywhere.

Despite this, there had never been a flower terrace planted in the experimental gardens. Good reason, therefore, to create one in 1982. It was the first time that a garden was to be planted not to experiment on, but to "immortalize" an idea. A free piece of land behind the Bredero wall was elevated and two square terraces were laid in a staggered formation, with a small difference in height. The paving was not grion tiles this time, but narrow concrete bricks laid in straight strips. Beds for plants were dug haphazardly in the paving in this otherwise streamlined design.

The flower terrace in Dedemsvaart was not just intended as a design solution for connecting a house and garden; it was also an experiment with plants. In this garden, Mien made an exception to her creed of matching plants to the available soil and not the other way around. Because she wanted to experiment with calcicole species, which thrive in lime-rich soil, she replaced the existing peaty soil with clay mixed with rock flour. Planting beds surrounded by paving required quite a different approach in terms of layout than a traditional border. She also believed it was important that the garden was attractive year-round. She chose a combination of a few early-flowering shrubs, miniature conifers, ornamental grasses, and perennials.

The idea of a flower terrace is still relevant as a solution for connecting a house with its garden.

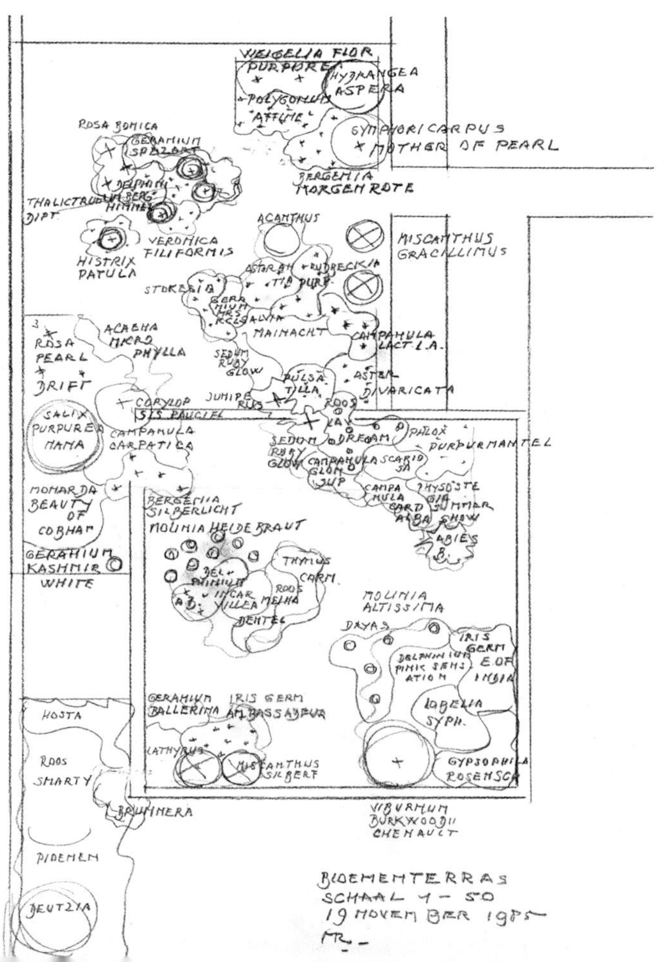

◀ Mien and Princess Juliana of the Netherlands on the Flower Terrace in 1988 (left)

◀ Modification of the planting plan for the Flower Terrace from 1985 (right)

▼ The Flower Terrace was designed as if it were a backyard, with the house on the side where the lawn is. The staggered beds mean plants can be seen across the whole width of the garden.

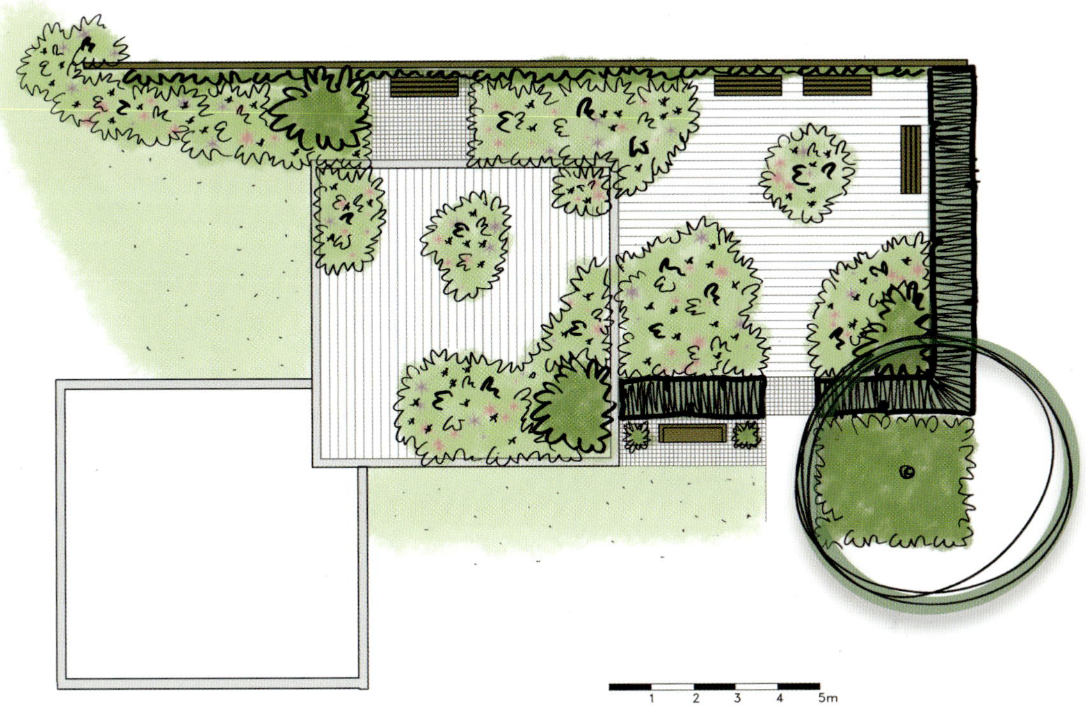

Circle in the Woods (1987)

The popularity of garden tours brought coachloads of visitors to the Gardens, and it was extremely busy at times. Too busy, in Mien's view. "It feels as though you're on Kalverstraat in Amsterdam." When it was so busy, she felt that people couldn't see what she meant by the Gardens. The avenue of larches was the only access route between the oldest and newer parts of the Gardens. In between lay the hundred-year-old oak woods that had been planted as a windbreak for the nursery. To steer the stream of visitors somewhat, a second access route between the two parts was laid through the woods. Mien had never been interested in the woods. There's not much you can do with them, she felt. They only became interesting if there was an open clearing. When surveying the trees, it became clear that (because a few trees had been felled) the tops of the trees did not quite meet each other, and a round clearing had emerged. On that spot, where the light shone through the tops of the trees, a raised circle was created, surrounded by a path. At first, Mien filled the circle with shade-loving plants such as ferns, fall-blooming anemones, and Solomon's seal, but they did not produce a satisfying result. She felt it was too much like a "little garden in the woods." It had to be simpler. She chose a single species, the indigenous *Oxalis acetosella*. Rhododendron and holly were planted along the edges of the path as a green wall around the circle. The *Oxalis* forms a pale green blanket, illuminated by rays of sunlight through the gap between the tops of the trees. A second magic circle was born. Mien called the spot her "cathedral." Its simplicity is what makes it one of the most beautiful, peaceful spots in the garden.

In addition to *Oxalis*, moss is allowed to grow in the circle. Seen from above, the circle displays a variety of different shades of green.

Sheared hedge cubes, an element that Mien and her followers often used, outside the PTT shipping center

PTT Shipping Center (1986–1987)

Mien Ruys produced an unusual design for the outdoor areas around a new building for the PTT (Postal, Telephone, and Telegraph Service) in ’s-Hertogenbosch, the Netherlands. She devised a grid of square privet hedge cubes with narrow paths between them across a large part of the site. The measurements of the cubes were such that the whole cube could be trimmed with hedge clippers. As a contrast to the austere, symmetrical shape of the hedge cubes, she planted less constrained, bushy shrubs to screen off the parking spaces.

The KNSM park in the 1950s

KNSM Island, the Last Project (1993–1994)

During the 1950s, Mien had been involved in the design for the KNSM (Royal Dutch Steamboat Shipping Company) business park in Amsterdam. When the designated use of the site was changed in 1993, she was asked to redesign the park. She drew up a design and a planting plan. It was her last project. In 1999, the year in which Mien Ruys died, the park was given the name *Mien Ruysplantsoen* (Mien Ruys Park), and the wheel had come full circle.

1990-1999

THE NETHERLANDS: PEACE AND PROGRESS

The fall of the Berlin Wall in 1989 ushered in a new era. Tensions between East and West subsided, and the threat of World War III appeared to have been averted. Europe became a single entity, which had a positive effect on trade and the economy. Computers, internet, and even the stock market became accessible to a large group of people. There seemed to be no end to prosperity. Society changed too: the church, marriage, and the division of roles between men and women were no longer beyond question. Immigration—which had begun in the 1960s—had brought a sizable group of people to the Netherlands who had different cultural and religious backgrounds. The population grew—partly due to immigration—and with it, the demand for housing. Expansive housing developments were built, often in rural areas around the major cities. These were dubbed "*Vinex*" estates after the name of a government policy document on regional development.

Government campaigns with catchy slogans, like "A smart girl is prepared for her future," encouraged women to join the labor force and become economically independent. Women were no longer expected to focus solely on keeping house and bringing up children. Increasing numbers of men began to do their share of domestic tasks.

The End Approaches

Mien's long career was drawing to a close. By the time she was in her early nineties, work was no longer possible. This brought her great sadness, as work had been her life. She herself called it a sort of obsession. "It's sad that it's coming to an end; I'm nowhere near finished," she said. After a while, she moved permanently to Wiekend, her cottage in Dedemsvaart. A group of friends, family, and staff took care of her. She was unable to walk any distance and was confined to a wheelchair, in which she was often pushed around the Gardens. She was terrified of losing her memory and so continued to practice the scientific names of plants for as long as she could. She died in her sleep at Wiekend on January 9, 1999, at the age of 94. It was the anniversary year of the Gardens, 75 years after her first experiment that began her career: her first "act of landscaping."

◄ Mien in 1994

▼ The Clipped Garden in the winter of 2017. The garden was laid out in 1999, the year in which Mien Ruys died and in which the Gardens celebrated its 75th anniversary.

Continuing in the Style of Mien Ruys

Work had stopped for Mien, but not for her design studio, Buro Mien Ruys. Hans Veldhoen and Anet Scholma took over at the helm, still in the same premises on Amstel in Amsterdam where Mien had begun over 50 years before. The staff worked on both major projects and designs for private individuals. Always in the style of Mien Ruys: austere, clear-cut lines, and lush vegetation. Sometimes garden owners asked for renovations of gardens Mien had previously designed, or there was a need for past projects to be modified, such as the garden of the provincial government building in Zwolle. The Gardens in Dedemsvaart still served as experimental gardens for the design studio, and the staff visited Dedemsvaart regularly. Mien remained interested in their work right up to her death. She always asked about the assignments the studio was currently working on.

Growing Awareness of Historical Value (1995)

Halfway through the 1990s, there was a growing awareness that the experimental gardens—as well as being a laboratory for the design studio—also had historical value. When the railway sleepers in the Sunken Garden were found to have rotted, the initial idea was to dig up the garden and start afresh. That was until people realized that there would then be no garden at all in the Gardens with railway sleepers, since the old Railway-Sleeper Bench had been removed a while ago. Because the use of railway sleepers was extremely characteristic of a particular period in Mien Ruys's career, the decision was made—for the first time—to renovate a garden instead of replacing it. The idea was discussed with Mien, and she gave her permission for the plan, because "if it's good for the studio, it's a good thing."

75 Years of Mien Ruys Gardens

Many more experiments in design and planting—including with roses—were carried out in the "bubbles" corner where roses had originally been planted in circles. None of them were very successful, and they were dug over again. The current design in this part of the Gardens only came about on the occasion of the 75th anniversary. When Mien Ruys died in January of that year, preparations for the anniversary were in full swing. To celebrate the anniversary, two new gardens, the Clipped Garden and the Corner Garden, were laid out. Mien was aware of the preparations but did not live long enough to see their outcome.

The Clipped Garden and the Corner Garden in 2023

The Dutch Wave

A new movement developed in the 1980s, based on the ideas of a group of garden designers and growers. It was only later, in 1992, that the movement was given a name by the Swedish botanist Rune Bengtsson: The Dutch Wave. The group initially comprised Henk Gerritsen, Rob Leopold, Ton ter Linden, and Piet Oudolf. They were in contact with each other and shared ideas, but each of them had their own opinions on gardens and plants. What linked them, however, was their commitment to unstructured, natural, informal planting, with nature as its source of information. Not only was the flower of the plant important, its structure, form, and winter interest also played a part in their plant combinations. Perennials and ornamental grasses, sometimes supplemented with annuals and bulbous plants, were used to ensure that the landscaping was rewarding all year round. "Gardening in tune with nature" was the rationale; sustainability and biodiversity figured prominently. The use of artificial fertilizer and chemical herbicides was absolutely forbidden. The group was inspired by the botanical gardens of Jac. P. Thijsse and C. Broerse. The way Mien Ruys made use of perennials was also a revelation for Piet Oudolf and Henk Gerritsen in particular. Perennials with a natural appearance, which were needed to achieve the look they were seeking, were hard to find at that time. Piet Oudolf therefore began his own nursery, and others too (including Coen Jansen, Hans Kramer of De Hessenhof, Fleur van Zonneveld and Eric Spruit of De Kleine Plantage) began to grow a new range of natural-looking plants and ornamental grasses. The movement became well-known internationally, was copied by many garden designers and growers, and inspired garden photographers and authors of gardening books.

◄▲ Examples of "Dutch Wave" planting in Piet Oudolf's garden in Hummelo (2018) and in the *Vlinderhof* (butterfly garden) in Máximapark in Utrecht (2016–2018)

► Beth Chatto, Dirk Jan Koning, and Piet Oudolf on a visit to Mien Ruys

Marsh Garden (1990)

In the 1970s, Mien Ruys was asked by a manufacturer to come up with designs for plastic ponds with irregular edges. She had difficulty with this assignment because she preferred rectangular ponds, to create a contrast between form and vegetation. Nonetheless, she did her best, using one of the irregular-shaped ponds in the farthest corner of the site newly acquired in 1974. She laid a rocky path around it, but "the unmotivated shape remained a strange element." After a few years, she decided to let the pond sink and to lower the ground around it. The result was a sort of marsh, which provided new opportunities for experiments with plants. The Rock Garden became the Marsh Garden, a name that is actually contradictory, as is "heath garden." "Marsh is part of the landscape; the emphasis in a garden is on seclusion." She considered the garden a failure, since the plants she wanted disappeared and unwanted plants proliferated, but most of all because it had no shape. The garden was therefore tackled rigorously in the winter of 1990. By then, recycled plastic had appeared on the market. A manufacturer of this new material asked the studio to use it in an experiment with decking. The little plastic pond was dug up and replaced by a rectangular pond with a natural base and sloping banks. A long deck connected one bank with another, and square decking tiles were placed in an alternating pattern in the water. The disadvantages of this decking are that it is not very strong, it expands in the heat, and it shrinks when cold. A substantial construction was required below water level to make it sturdier. Natural, partly indigenous marsh and water plants were planted. Mien was proud of the result. She liked the recycled material: it did not become slippery when it rained, and—even better—it was a sustainable alternative to tropical hardwood. But the main reason the experiment was a success was that a clearly defined shape had returned to the garden.

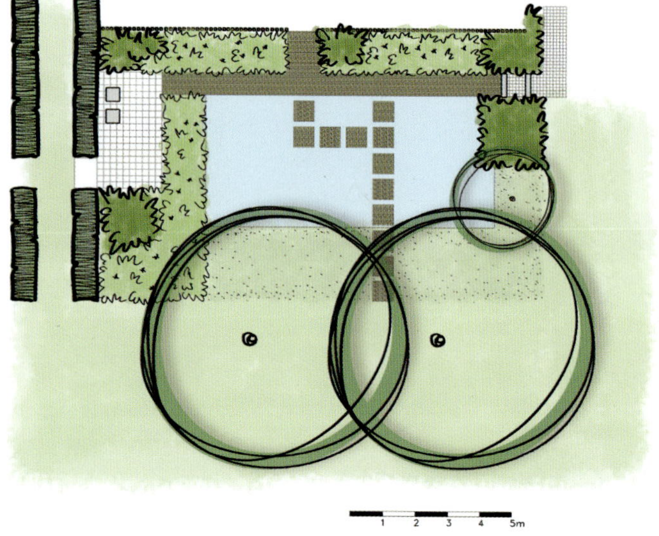

▲ The Marsh Garden in the winter of 2017 with *Halesia carolina* in the foreground

▶ Laying the decking tiles in the Marsh Garden in 1990 (above)

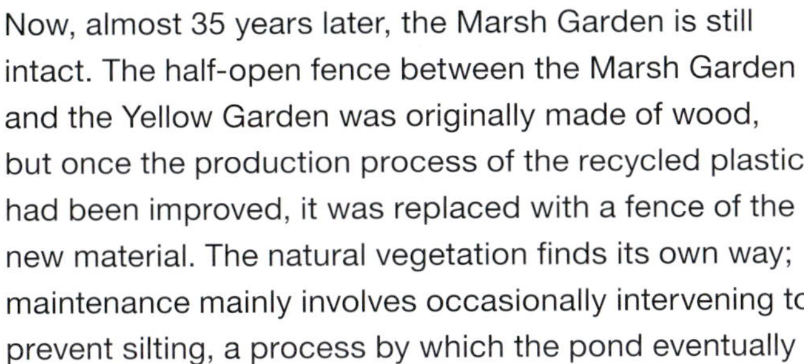

Now, almost 35 years later, the Marsh Garden is still intact. The half-open fence between the Marsh Garden and the Yellow Garden was originally made of wood, but once the production process of the recycled plastic had been improved, it was replaced with a fence of the new material. The natural vegetation finds its own way; maintenance mainly involves occasionally intervening to prevent silting, a process by which the pond eventually becomes woodland. It was one of the last experiments Mien Ruys was closely involved in. An interesting aspect is its similarity to the Wilderness Garden, her first experiment in 1924. The strong square shape of both gardens and the untamed vegetation that is allowed to grow naturally create a powerful and exciting contrast.

Grass Garden (1993)

Mien Ruys mainly used ornamental grasses as solitary features. When many more new species of ornamental grasses began to be grown and planted in the 1980s, she wanted to experiment with them. The Blue Border was dug up to make room for a new experiment. A sunken square bed was dug next to the Flower Terrace to test various ornamental grasses in terms of sturdiness and winter interest. At the same time, the experiment provided an opportunity to try out new materials. Large concrete elements were used to form the edge of the sunken bed. Asymmetrical beds were planted with ornamental grasses and a few perennials in a layer of Flachkorn, a type of gravel made from flat, slate-like stones. The surface created by the flat stones can easily be walked on, since they do not roll like ordinary gravel. A raised concrete tank filled with water is an eye-catcher in the otherwise rather austere garden. On sunny days, the water reflects the grasses and the blue sky. Various grasses have been replaced over the years because they proved to be unsuitable for growing in the garden. They had become messy, overgrown, or had fallen over. When, after several years, the bamboo beside the water tank grew too big in relation to the rest of the garden, the whole garden was dug over. The bamboo roots had spread right under the concrete edges. The bamboo was replaced by a smaller species that does not spread, and the old bamboo is now nowhere to be seen.

▲ When the Grass Garden was renovated in 2016, the roots of the bamboo were discovered to have spread throughout the garden. (above)

◀ The round concrete tank provides a water feature reflecting the sky.

▶ Modifying the planting plan for the Grass Garden in 1994

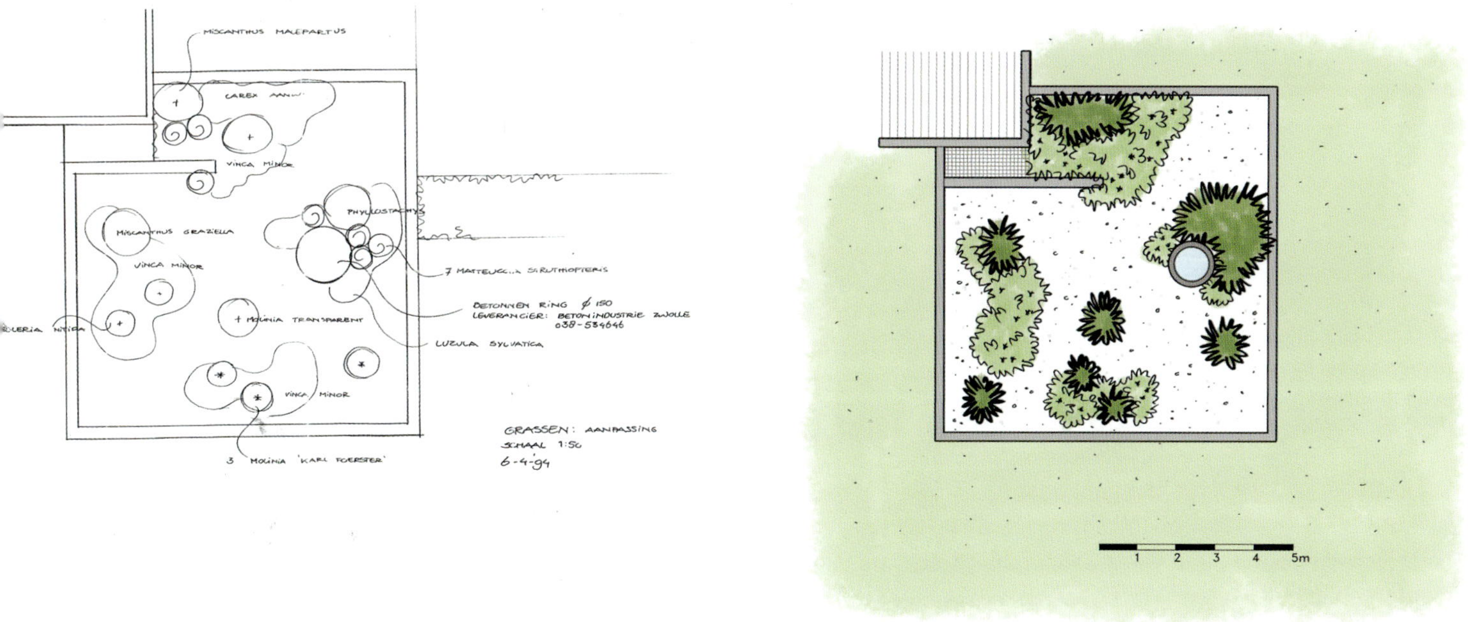
MISCANTHUS MALEPARTUS
CAREX AANW.
VINCA MINOR
PHYLLOSTACHYS
MISCANTHUS GRAZIELLA
VINCA MINOR
7 MATTEUCCIA STRUTHIOPTERIS
BETONNEN RING ∅ 150
LEVERANCIER: BETONINDUSTRIE ZWOLLE
038-534646
MOLINIA TRANSPARENT
LUZULA SYLVATICA
VINCA MINOR
3 MOLINIA 'KARL FOERSTER'
GRASSEN: AANPASSING
SCHAAL 1:50
6-4-'94
1
2
3
4
5m

Clipped Garden (1990)

The Clipped Garden was one of the gardens planted for the 75th anniversary. The garden, designed by Anet Scholma and Hans Veldhoen, is an experiment in having a garden without flowers. The basis for the garden is an elongated pond surrounded by tiled paving, with water elements by the artist Henk Rusman. High yew pillars screen it from the central lawn. At the other side of the garden, low square hedges of red *Berberis* connect the Clipped Garden to the Corner Garden. The plants were mainly chosen for their form and texture; there is little color and there are almost no flowers. It is a typical example of the austere, minimalist style of the 1990s, with few plants and a focus on hard elements. A recurrent element in the Clipped Garden is the "stripe": in the leaves of the ornamental grasses and the *Hosta*, in the tiles, and on the trunk of the *Acer davidii*.

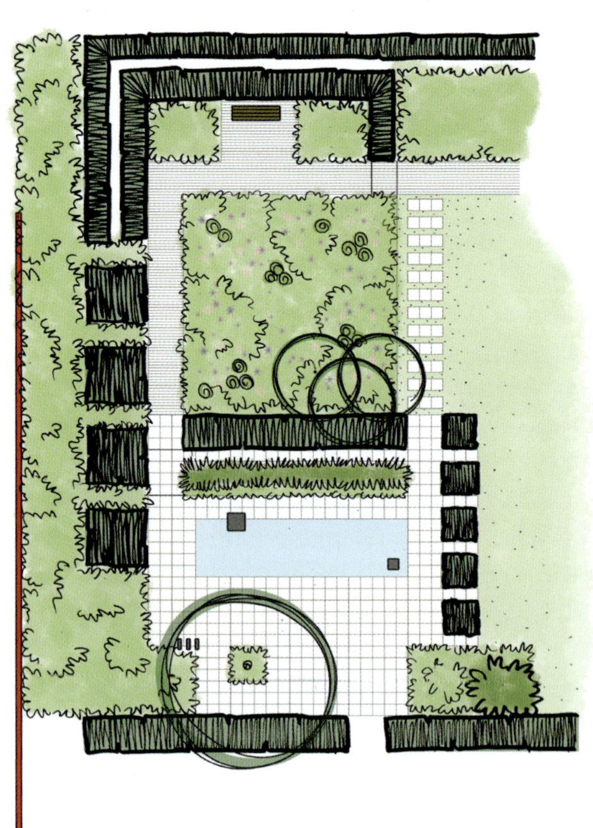

◀ The Clipped Garden seen from above, with the New Border in the foreground (above)

◀ One of the yew pillars between the central lawn and the Clipped Garden. The crown of the *Acer davidii* can be seen behind it (below).

▶ The opening of the Clipped Garden by councilor Joost Liese in the anniversary year of 1999

▼ The blocks of *Berberis* connect the Clipped Garden to the Corner Garden.

Corner Garden (1999)

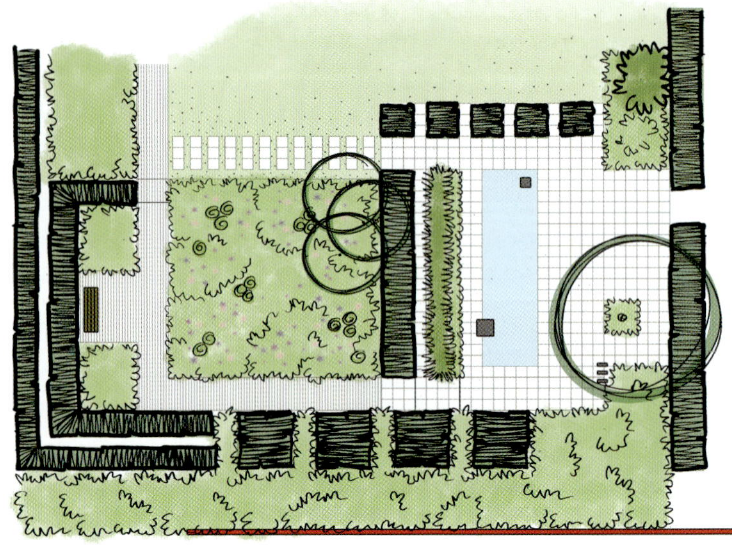

The second anniversary garden was planted between the Clipped Garden and the Mixed Border from 1974. This corner of the garden had previously been raised to give the experiment with roses a chance to succeed. The new design was simple in shape: straight lines with a double hedge of red beech and *Cotoneaster* and the hedge blocks of *Berberis*. A few roses were permitted to remain; otherwise only a limited number of species were planted. The basis for the planting is the large central bed of low-growing *Asters*. These *Asters* form a green blanket that changes to a pale purple sea of flowers late in the season. The *Clerodendrum trichotomum*, or harlequin glorybower, provides a magnificent dome for the Corner Garden. This tree is sometimes also known as the peanut butter tree, as its foliage smells like peanut butter.

The flowering *Symphyotrichum novi-belgii* 'Professor Anton Kippenberg', together with *Sedum* 'Matrona' and *Panicum virgatum* 'Rehbraun' ensure spectacular color in fall.

A NEW CENTURY: THE EXPERIMENTAL GARDENS AFTER 1999

All her life, Mien Ruys looked forward, not back. She hardly ever revisited the gardens she had designed. Experiments in her own experimental gardens were regularly cleared away to make room for a new experiment. She once told Theo that she made the experimental gardens for the visitors. “Rubbish,” Theo had replied, “you only do it for yourself.” Later, Mien admitted that Theo might have been right. And yet, in an interview she gave when she was about 90, she wondered what would happen to her beloved experimental gardens after her death. “I’d love to be able to look into the future; I’d love to know what will happen with all this later. How is it all going? We’ll never know. That’s a pity.”

Tuinen Mien Ruy, a Monument

Visits to gardens were less popular in the new century than they had been in the 1980s. The number of visitors to the Gardens declined considerably. The Foundation was in trouble financially and the Gardens were at risk of being closed. The garden staff, the studio, the board, and the volunteers undertook to save the *Tuinen* from catastrophe. One of the initiatives to save Mien Ruys Gardens was an application to The Cultural Heritage Agency of the Netherlands, *Rijksdienst voor Cultureel Erfgoed* (RCE), to have the Gardens listed as a heritage site. The three oldest gardens were awarded this status: the Wilderness Garden, the Old Experimental Garden, and the Water Garden. The Municipality of Hardenberg granted the other gardens designed by Mien Ruys the status of listed site on its register of municipal historic sites. Another six gardens from the post-war reconstruction period became heritage sites in 2014: the Ready-to-make Borders, the Sunken Garden, the Sun Borders, the Pond with Reeds, the City Garden, and the Shady Borders. Various reasons are given in the description of the heritage sites as to why the complex is one of public interest. The Gardens were seen as a representative example of modernist landscape gardening, designed and laid out by Mien Ruys in the period 1924–1999. The perfectly conserved principal structure, the thematic coherence of the gardens, their importance for the history of landscape gardening and landscape architecture, and the influence of Mien Ruys on the development of public and private landscape gardening in the Netherlands were also reasons to grant the oldest gardens the status of national heritage sites.

▼ Pond with Reeds, one of the gardens from the post-war reconstruction period that was granted the status of national heritage site in 2014

pages 202–203: The path along the Shady Borders, another of the gardens from the post-war reconstruction period

Dealing with a Green Heritage Site

The description of the gardens with heritage status provides guidance for managing and maintaining them. But as Mien Ruys said, "A garden is a process." After all, the plants, the basis for the garden, are continually changing. Trees that cast a shadow on places that were previously sunny, diseases and infestations that threaten certain species, and a changing climate are just some of the factors that ensure a garden constantly needs to be modified. Choices have to be made, and in doing so, the interests of the heritage site are considered. What is the essence of the garden, what are its characteristic elements? In the period prior to the gardens receiving heritage status, the plants, and sometimes the design too, changed on a regular basis; after all, they were experiments. So which period is the one to follow, and to what extent is that—decades later—realistic? Often the correct information is missing, because many design drawings and planting plans for the gardens have sadly been lost. Since 1984, the planting plans have been recorded annually, but for the preceding period, only a few drawings remain. The following sections give a selection of the countless examples of the dilemmas faced in maintaining a green heritage site.

The Yew Ball in the Old Experimental Garden

There is a large yew in the Old Experimental Garden that has been clipped in the form of a ball. It is one of the characteristic elements mentioned in the description of the heritage site, but in fact, this element came about more or less by accident. The story goes that Mien was once sitting on a bench with Dirk Jan, the gardener at the time, and, on a whim, suggested that the yew at the northern end might be clipped into the shape of a ball. Dirk Jan duly followed her suggestion. The next time Mien was back in Dedemsvaart, she was astonished and shouted: "But that wasn't my intention!" Nonetheless, the yew ball remained, but over the years, it became bigger and bigger and began to sag. In 2005, the decision was made to intervene, and the ball was pruned back to bare wood in two phases, something from which yews (unlike other conifers) can recover successfully. Scandalized reactions came from all sides that a unique element of a heritage garden had been treated in this way, but sometimes rigorous intervention is necessary in order to achieve a better result in the end. The ball now has its attractive round shape again.

Storm and Fungus in the Water Garden

That it is not easy to maintain a green heritage site was made clear in 2009, when a storm felled the old weeping birch in the Water Garden. A new one was planted, but it will be many years before it comes close to equaling the appearance of the ancient, 100-year-old birch. The gray-green hedge of *Chamaecyparis lawsoniana* 'Triomf van Boskoop' had also grown in the 50 years since it was planted to become a wall several meters high, which was impossible to maintain without risking one's life. Not only that, it was now no longer in proportion to the garden. During the renovation of the Water Garden in 2002, the hedge was replaced several times, but without success, until soil tests revealed that the ground was infested by a fungus. The gray-green conifer provided an attractive combination with the gray-leaved plants in the dry section, but planting the same species would lead to the same problems. Out of necessity, a dark green yew was chosen that has now grown to become a substantial hedge. Rebuilding the natural stone dry-stack walls was another challenge: no one could be found to do this specialist work. Again out of necessity, the stones were fixed with cement, but this does not have the same effect as the dry-stack walls.

The Dome in the Square Garden

From the start, the Square Garden had a little covered terrace where people could shelter from the rain. When the Square Garden was altered in 1984, the original wooden roof was replaced with a plastic dome, similar to the material that was then often used to cover open-sided shelters, such as carports. After 30 years, the transparent material of the dome was so weather-beaten that, despite tireless efforts to clean it, it could no longer be called transparent. The combination of the weather-beaten dome, the lichen-covered tiles, and the austere wall of concrete blocks made the whole Square Garden look rather dilapidated. Visitors often passed the garden by. The tiles were turned over and an architect was asked to design a new shelter. The existing terrace with the dome was taken down in the spring of 2014 and replaced by wooden decking with a bench and a roof. Once again, criticism came from various angles: a characteristic element had disappeared, and the atmosphere of the Square Garden had been altered. The dome had not been mentioned in the very brief description of the heritage site of the Square Garden, but with hindsight, the critical comments were valid. This incident underlines the importance of thinking very carefully before carrying out radical alterations to the gardens with heritage status. A plan of action was drawn up for major interventions needed in the coming years; it was discussed with the town council in their capacity as the responsible body. A number of these interventions have since been carried out, while others have been postponed for various reasons.

The Water Ball

One of the interventions mentioned in the plan of action was to renovate or even replace the water ball. This ball is a characteristic element beside the Bench by the Water Ball, having been made in the 1970s from wire and concrete by the artist Auk Fock van Coppenaal. Some 50 years later, the continuous flow of water has worn away the concrete in certain places, exposing the wire. It would be tricky to repair the cement layer in a way that would not show. A new ball was an option, but an artist or at

◀ The yew ball in 2016, almost ten years after the rigorous intervention

▶ The "ravages of time" are clearly visible on the moss-covered water ball least a skilled craftsperson would have to be found who could make it. Replacing the ball using modern material such as blue stone would not be appropriate. Opinions varied, but eventually the decision was made not to replace the ball (yet). The fact is, the ball is an artwork, and its decay also has a certain beauty.

Problems with *Buxus*

From about 2010, a plague of box tree moths appeared, first attacking *Buxus* in the south of the Netherlands, but soon the little black-and-white moth reached Dedemsvaart. In the early years, it was possible to limit the damage by catching the caterpillars and moths, but in the summer of 2020, there was no stopping them. The *Buxus* beds in the Herb Garden became completely infested within a few days. Because no pesticides are used in the Gardens, there were two options: uproot them or radically cut them back and then hope that the plants would recover by themselves. The second option was felt to be the best; if it did not work, they could always be uprooted. The plants were cut back and given a good dose of manure to help them produce new shoots again. The decision proved successful, as most of the plants recovered well. Some new plants were acquired to replace the ones that did not. Unfortunately, these new plants turned out to be affected by a notorious boxwood fungus,

and so, in spite of all our efforts, all the *Buxus* plants had to be uprooted. The plague of box tree moths has now receded. Birds and hedgehogs have added the caterpillars to their menus, and the moth has become a victim of its own success, since many *Buxus* plants have disappeared. It is too late for the *Buxus* in the Square Garden, however. The fungus is in the soil and will also affect any new plants. A replacement was sought and found in the form of the low-growing privet *Ligustrum vulgare* 'Lodense', a species Mien Ruys also often used. What's more, this privet is even mentioned in a planting plan and in the list of plants for the Herb Garden dating from 1965 as an option for the beds. The privet was most likely later replaced by *Buxus*.

Before the box tree moth reached the Netherlands, *Buxus* plants frequently succumbed to two different fungal diseases. The beds of *Buxus* in the Square Garden were also affected by one of these fungal diseases in 2015. The green, austerely sheared beds are an essential part of this garden, so a good alternative was required. The beds were replanted with *Ilex crenata* 'Dark Green', the species used in the gardens of Het Loo Palace instead of *Buxus* for the same reason. The *Ilex* is reasonably satisfactory, but sometimes gaps appear in the beds when a plant (or part of one) occasionally dies. They also require more frequent pruning. Varieties of *Buxus* have now been grown that are unaffected by the box tree fungus and also offer good resistance against the box tree moth. Once these plants have proved themselves and are widely available, it is likely that they will reappear in the Gardens.

Circle in the Woods

A monoculture is always vulnerable, and this certainly applies to the *Oxalis* in the Circle in the Woods. Depletion of the soil's fertility and diseases lie in wait. Retaining this plant has already required a lot of time and care: applying manure, adding more plants, reseeding, and keeping it free of other plants that threaten to gain the upper hand. Until a few years ago, the moss was regularly removed to give the *Oxalis* more space, but this was not particularly successful. Eventually it was decided to leave the moss alone, because it did not spoil the effect of a large, green,

soft, and round cushion in the woods. Since then, the *Oxalis* has improved; it often grows with moss in the wild. Sometimes it's better to let nature take its course rather than always trying to fight it. In all fairness, it should be said that the circle has been regularly watered during the recent dry summers, because *Oxalis* likes damp soil.

Future Interventions

A major intervention still on the wish list is the alteration of the strip of plants between the Shady Borders and the gardens at the northern end of this strip. This was where Mien Ruys planted a variety of her Ready-to-make Borders to experiment with in the early 1960s. The plants in the strip in between include a few very tall conifers. Their tops were sawn off several times in the past so that they would not grow too tall. This was quite a long time ago now, and the conifers have become enormous giants. These trees are quite out of proportion to the small-scale gardens around them. Furthermore, the huge trees deprive the plants below them of a lot of light and moisture, and these were plants originally intended for sunny gardens, such as the City Garden and the Sun Borders. The Shady Borders, originally planted as borders for partial shade, are now in deep shade due to the oak trees on one side and the conifers on the other. Over the years, the plants in the various borders have been altered in line with this change. By replacing the conifers with new vegetation of shrubs and smaller trees, the surrounding gardens can be returned to their original state, as far as possible and desirable. Removing the conifers is, however, a rigorous intervention that will have an enormous impact on the current appearance of this part of the Gardens. On the other hand—as is often the case with such interventions—the result will ultimately be an improvement compared to the old situation.

Experiments Continue

Besides maintaining the heritage gardens, the core issues for Mien Ruys Gardens are still experiments with design, planting, and materials. Even after 1999, the year of Mien Ruys's death, gardens were altered and new gardens laid out, and this is still happening today. In 2006, some of the gardens were no longer in the same condition as they had been when Mien designed them, and so they were not granted heritage status. These gardens—the Roof Garden, for instance—present opportunities for new experiments. Part of the larger site was also brought into the Gardens in 2006. Experiments with design, materials, and planting will continue in this New Experimental Garden.

◀ The blocks of *Buxus* in 2007, before the box tree caterpillar attacked them

▲ The Circle in the Woods in 2010

New Border (2000)

The development of a new, more natural type of planting, which had begun at the end of the twentieth century with The Dutch Wave, called for experiments to be carried out in Mien Ruys Gardens. The selection of plants and the way they are planted are different from that in traditional border planting. Natural-looking perennials are used, combined with ornamental grasses. The plants do not need to be constrained by having a fixed spot in the border but are mixed together and allowed to develop naturally. Repetition of species creates a restful look. Maintenance is less labor-intensive than in a traditional border, because it is no longer necessary to support, tie up, or trim the plants. The experiment with this New Border in the Gardens was directly prompted by one of the plants in a newly discovered assortment: *Persicaria amplexicaulis*. Mien was enthusiastic about this plant, but its large leaves and relatively small flowers proved to be rather inappropriate for a traditional border. Beatrice Krehl, who worked as a gardener in the Gardens from 1996 to 2005, made a planting plan for part of the Gardens bordering the new Clipped Garden, where previously other experiments had been carried out. She drew inspiration from the theories of the German professor Richard Hansen. Based on years of experience, he had developed a system in which perennials are classified according to the requirements of their natural habitat and their growth characteristics. The method requires considerable knowledge of plants to make the right decisions about combining plants, the distance between them, and their vigor.

The parameters for choosing plants for the New Border were damp soil in an open space and dry soil on the edge of the woods toward the large *Acer cappadocicum* 'Aureum'. Other characteristics were also pivotal for the selection: Is it a naturally solitary plant, one that provides structure, one that serves to connect others, or one that gives good groundcover? Is it a short- or long-lived plant? Taking all these characteristics into account, species were carefully chosen, planted, and allowed to develop in their own way and at their own speed. Various things have changed over the years: certain species have disappeared, while others have been added or have spontaneously blown in. After about 20 years, radical action was needed, since the *Persicaria amplexicaulis*, no less, had taken over a large part of the bed, and a *Hemerocallis* planted later had also appropriated far too big a role. The alterations to the planting were governed by the experience gained over the previous years. The concept of this border—selecting plants on the basis of their natural habitats and growth characteristics—remains the same.

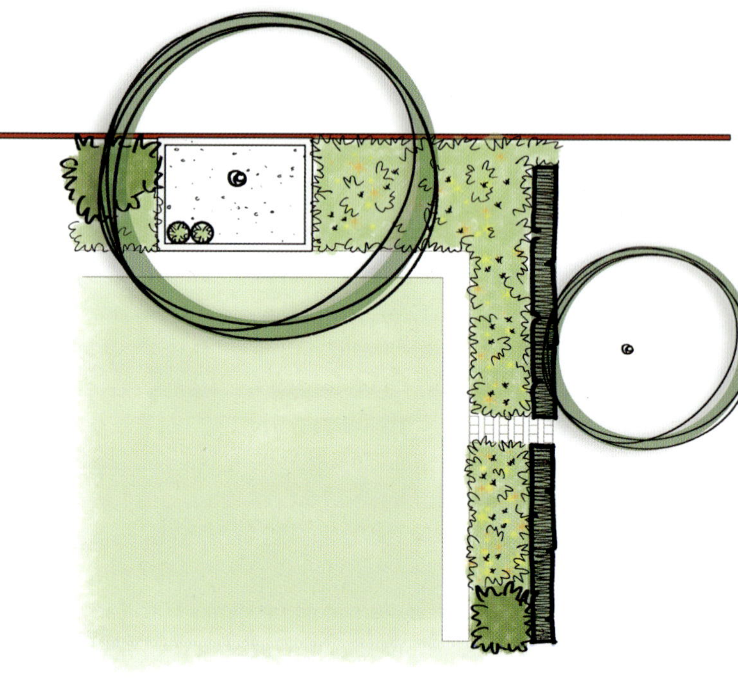

The New Border is separated from the Clipped Garden by a slatted fence made from scaffold boards. The boards have been treated with Falu Rödfärg: original Swedish red wood paint with a matte, velvety look.

pages 210–211: The New Border with the orange *Hemerocallis* 'Margaret Perry' in the foreground

Autumn Garden (2002)

Frost and mycosis had damaged the heathers in the Heath Garden over time. Increasing numbers of heathers were replaced by nectar plants for bees, and a beehive was installed, leading to a change of name from the Heath Garden to the Bee Garden. The beds of *Buxus* had survived all these changes and still formed a green architectural basis in the garden. Eventually, the shade cast by the surrounding trees became too much for the nectar plants, and moreover, the "hedge on legs" of golden alder became infested by the alder leaf beetle. Two *Gleditsia* trees that formed a gateway to the City Garden had become too big and were felled. All these changes meant it was time for a new experiment. In 2002, the garden was transformed into the Autumn Garden, a garden with an emphasis on a single season. A path was laid between a combination of perennials, shrubs, and ornamental grasses, whose flowers, foliage, and berries provide spectacular color in fall. Pruning the "hedge on legs" had always been a job for daredevils, and so it was replaced by a low-maintenance variant: a screen of Virginia creeper, which turns a beautiful red in fall. Later, in 2019, more changes were made. The "hedge on legs" returned, no longer in the form of golden alder, but of sweetgum, *Liquidambar styraciflua* 'Worplesdon', which produces magnificent fall color. The only path through the garden ran mainly alongside the plants and not through them. In the past, there had always been two paths leading to the Square Garden, which still seems logical when seen from that garden. A second path was laid, making the garden more accessible. The plants required intervention too, as some species had commandeered more space than they should. The whole garden was cleared (apart from a few shrubs), and a new plan was laid out.

Plants in the Autumn Garden from left to right: *Astilbe* 'Rosenschleier', *Geranium ×oxonianum* 'Laura Skelton', *Epimedium pubigerum* 'Orangekönigin', and *Euonymus alatus*

pages 214–215: The new "hedge on legs" of *Liquidambar styraciflua* 'Worplesdon'

New Experimental Garden (2006)

The Foundation acquired the site on the other side of the Wiek in 1991 but did not give it a specific function until 2006. Buro Mien Ruys constructed a grid inside a clearly defined, minimalist design of paths, hedges, and a block of trees. Different spaces were created within the grid, in which neatly mown lawns alternated with unrestrained flower meadows. The original idea was for the garden to be a sculpture garden, but very soon, the spaces were being used for all sorts of experiments with plants. Beds of flowering shrubs and borders for bees and butterflies appeared, borders were designed and laid out by students from Delft University of Technology, and experiments were carried out with borders of annuals and dahlias. These were usually temporary experiments: conclusions were drawn from the results, and the plants were dug up, given a new purpose, and something new was devised again. A few experiments, such as the "Grow and Flower" Border, the Mix Border (2018), and the *Helenium* Border, were granted a longer life.

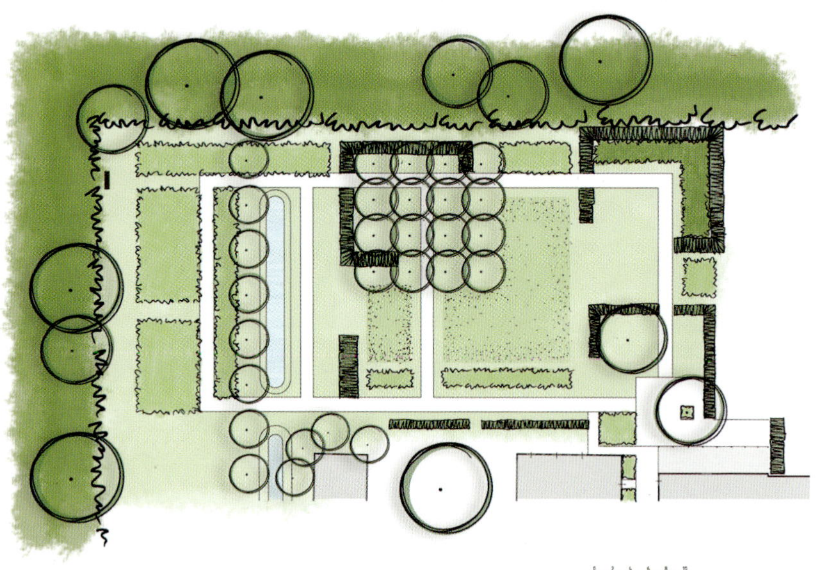

▲ View through the hedges of the *Helenium* Border on the right and the Mix Border (2018) on the left (above)

▲ A place to sit under the *Malus* 'Bramley's Seedling' apple trees (below)

► One of the lines of sight from beneath the apple trees in the New Experimental Garden. An artwork by Kees Bierman can be seen on the left; it has since been moved to a new position.

New Experimental Border (2007)

The place where Mien Ruys began testing flower-meadow mixtures in the 1970s had had various functions. It had been a kitchen garden for many years before being planted with 90 different annuals to commemorate Mien Ruys's 90th birthday in 1994. A few years later, in the anniversary year of 1999, the New Experimental Border was laid out: a place to display and track the progress of the increasingly extensive range of perennials. The existing perpendicular pergola was replaced by an L-shaped one with a framed transparent divider on one side. Matched by an L-shaped beech hedge on the other side, they border a square, enclosed garden. The basic paving is standard paving stones measuring 30 × 30 cm, within which the arrangements can easily be altered. The assortment of plants changes regularly. New cultivars of *Geranium* and *Helenium* were mainly tried out in the early years. In 2007, the space was arranged in its current form: one large central bed surrounded by seven small beds measuring 2.4 × 2.4 meters. The idea behind the small beds was that a traditional border is now too big for most people's private gardens in the Netherlands, since gardens have become smaller over the years. Seven well-known growers (Henk Jacobs, Piet Oudolf, Brian Kabbes, Heilien Tonckens, Wim Willemsen, Coen Jansen, and Hans Kramer) were each asked to come up with an exciting, varied planting plan for one of the small beds that would be practical for a small garden. To create a restful interlude between the seven different plantings, the central bed was filled with a single species of ornamental grass, *Deschampsia cespitosa* 'Goldtau'. The planting has been modified over the years, but the specification is still to try out new species and different combinations to create exciting combinations of plants in such a small bed. The *Deschampsia* fell victim to root damage by grubs and has now been replaced by *Pennisetum alopecuroides* var. *viridescens*.

◂ Winter sun on the bed of *Deschampsia cespitosa* 'Goldtau' in 2016

▸ The bed created by Coen Jansen, with *Phlox ×arendsii* 'Utopia' and *Agastache* 'Blackadder' in 2007 (above left)

▸ The bed created by Brian Kabbes, with *Agastache* 'Kolibri' in 2008 (above right)

▸ The seven growers planting plans in 2007 (below)

pages 220–221: The bed with *Deschampsia cespitosa* 'Goldtau' in 2014. *Sedum* 'José Aubergine', *Nepeta manchuriensis*, and *Miscanthus sinensis* 'Purple Fall' can be seen in the foreground.

1. **Hans Kramer**
1 *Chelonopsis moschata*
2 *Clematis heracleifolia* 'Cassandra'
3 *Melittis melissophyllum* 'Lilaroze'
4 *Codonopsis mollis*
5 *Euonymus cornutus quinquicornutus*
6 *Polystichem setiferum* 'Plumosum Bevis'
7 *Geranium wallichianum* 'Crystal Lake'

2. **Wim Willemsen**
1 *Helleborus ×nigercors* 'Candy Love'
2 *Heuchera* 'Melting Fire'
3 *Helleborus* 'Snow Love'
4 *Hemerocallis* 'Spits Margaretha'
5 *Echinacea purpurea* 'Maxima'
6 *Hosta* 'Touch of Glass'
7 *Sedum* 'José Aubergine'
8 *Agastache* 'Pink Beauty'
9 *Hemerocallis* 'Bela Lugosi'

3. **Henk Jacobs**
1 *Carex comans* 'Bronze Form'
2 *Sporobulus heterolepis*
3 *Kalimeris incisa* 'Blue Star'
4 *Geranium* ×'Blue Cloud'
5 *Veronicastrum virginicum* 'Curly'
6 *Helenium* 'Kanaria'

4. **Heilien Tonckens**
1 *Veronica chamaedrys*
2 *Euphorbia cyparissias*
3 *Origanum vulgare*
4 *Galium verum*
5 *Succisa pratensis*
6 *Hypericum perforatum*

5. **Brian Kabbes**
1 *Salvia nemorosa* 'Pink Friesland'
2 *Agastache* 'Kolibri'
3 *Geranium phaeum* 'Sunburst'
4 *Erigeron* 'Saturnus'

6. **Piet Oudolf**
ER = *Eryngium bourgatii*
TR = *Tricyrtis formosanum*
AM = *Amsonia tabernaemontana var. salicifolia*
1 *Limonium gmelinii* + *Origanum* 'Herrenhausen'
2 *Stachys officinalis* 'Hummelo'
3 *Echinacea* 'Vintage Wine' + *Knautia macedonica*
4 *Pycnanthemum muticum*
5 *Aruncus* 'Horatio'
6 *Panicum virgatum* 'Shenandoah'
7 *Deschampsia sespitosa* 'Goldtau'
8 *Scuttelaria incana* + *Calamintha nepeta*
9 *Trifolium rubens*
10 *Salvia* 'Dear Anja' + *Perovskia* 'Little Spire'
11 *Sedum* 'Matrona'

7. **Coen Jansen**
1 *Phlox* 'Utopia'
2 *Agastache* 'Blackadder'
3 *Sanguisorba* 'Pink Brushes'
4 *Thalictrum delavayi* 'Ankum'
5 *Geranium saguineum* 'Ankum's Pride'
6 *Epimedium* 'Black Sea'

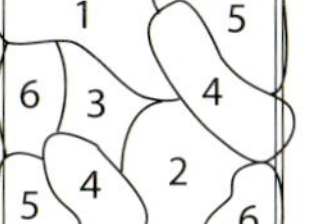
7

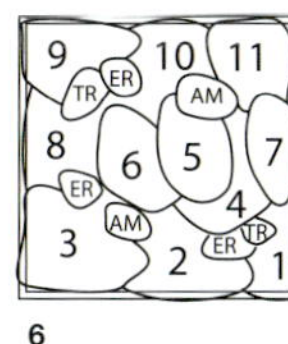
6

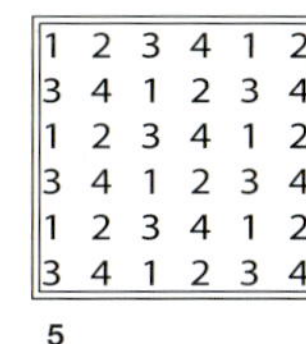
5

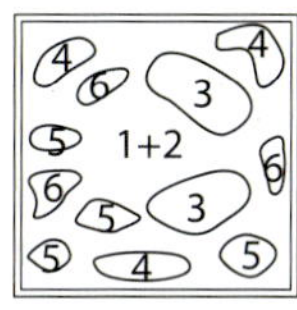
4

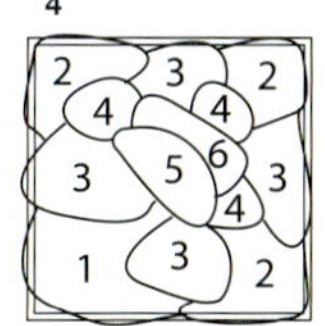
3

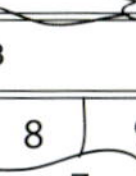

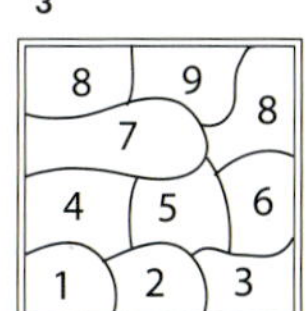
2

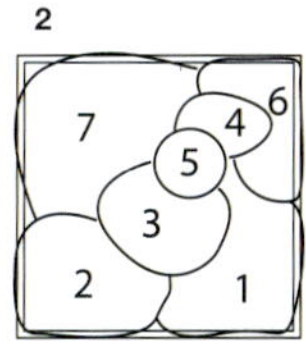
1

Helenium Border (2010)

The collection of *Helenium* assembled over the years by Beatrice Krehl was the basis for a border that was planted in 2010, featuring a single plant species in the starring role. The planting plan was made by Tineke Grin, head gardener at the Gardens from 2005 to 2015. It is a combination of the most attractive and strongest *Helenium* with ornamental grasses and other perennials. The rest of the collection was transferred to Kwekerij Jacobs, a nursery in Vriescheloo, Groningen, which is the keeper of the *Helenium* plant genus collection.

◂ From top to bottom: *Helenium* 'El Dorado', 'Little Orange', and 'Rubinzwerg'

▾ The long flower spikes of *Digitalis ferruginea* give the border its strong vertical form

▶ The New Experimental Garden from the *Helenium* Border, featuring *Phlomis russeliana* and *Nepeta grandiflora* 'Bramdean'

▶ Most day lilies flower in shades of yellow, orange, and red. This *Hemerocallis* 'Princess Blue Eyes', with its purple flowers, is an exception.

pages 224–225: *Helenium* 'Mien Ruys', created from one of the seedlings of the assembled *Helenium* collection. It was raised from seed by Henk Jacobs of the Kwekerij Jacobs nursery and named after Mien Ruys due to the seedling's resilient nature.

“Grow and Flower” Border (2011)

Mien Ruys once said: “If an alphabet of only 26 letters is enough to say everything you want, you ought to be able to make any garden with a limited number of plants.” *Vereniging Groei & Bloei* (Grow & Flower Association) was inspired by this statement to introduce its “26 plants plan” to encourage people to create green gardens. A group of experts selected 26 strong, easy-to-maintain plants. The selection comprises a couple of small trees, shrubs, perennials, ornamental grasses, and a rose. From this list, 16 species were chosen to be planted in a square bed measuring 5 × 5 meters between two hedges in the New Experimental Garden. Tineke Grin designed the planting plan, and one of the plants she chose was *Cercis canadensis* ‘Forest Pansy’, a small tree (or, actually, a shrub) with pink flowers on its stems, dark red foliage, and wonderful fall color. Two years later, the tree had become much bigger and was casting a lot of shadow on the plants beneath it. The shrubs selected had also grown considerably, so much so that the bed had become too overcrowded. Intervention was needed: almost all the shrubs were removed and some perennials were moved elsewhere, while others were replaced by different species from the list of 26 plants. It is a clear example of changing circumstances, which make a garden a process that requires modifications time and time again.

▸ The “Grow & Flower” Border in 2014, 2016, and 2023. The growth of the little tree *Cercis canadensis* ‘Forest Pansy’ greatly affects the development of the plants around it. (from top to bottom)

pages 228–229: The flowering of *Cercis canadensis* ‘Forest Pansy’ in April. The pink flowers present a striking contrast to the shoots of the reddish-brown foliage.

▸ The colors that the leaves of *Cercis canadensis* turn in fall (left)

▸ *Hemerocallis* ‘Ed Murray’ (right)

▸ The original planting plan for the “Grow & Flower” Border in 2012 and the modified planting plan in 2023 (below)

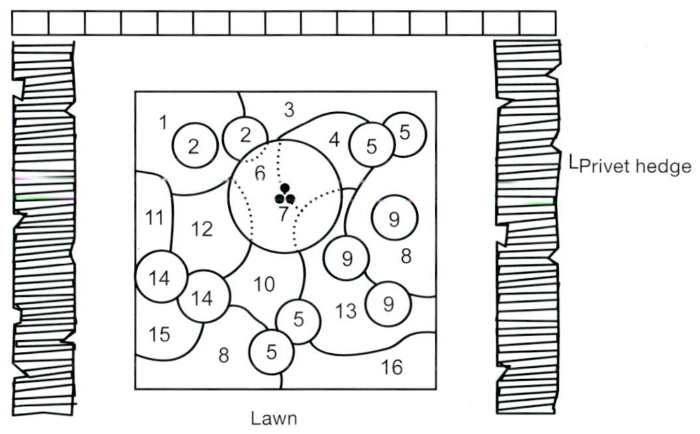

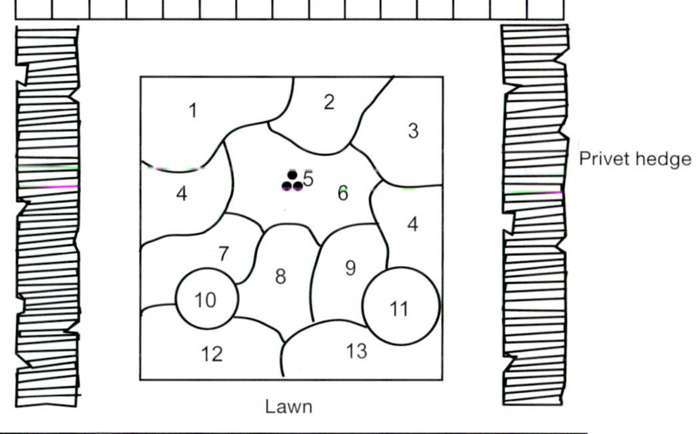

List of plants for the 2012 "Grow & Flower" Border

1 *Anemone ×hybrida* 'Honorine Jobert'
2 *Euonymus alatus* 'Compactus'
3 *Alchemilla mollis*
4 *Aster ageratoides* 'Stardust'
5 *Miscanthus sinensis* 'Kleine Silberspinne'
6 *Brunnera macrophylla* 'Jack Frost'
7 *Cercis canadensis* 'Forest Pansy'
8 *Geranium* 'Anne Thomson'
9 *Hydrangea quercifolia* 'Burgundy'
10 *Kalimeris incisa* 'Madiva'
11 *Hemerocallis* 'Ed Murray'
12 *Persicaria amplexicaulis* 'JS Caliente'
13 *Salvia nemorosa* 'Caradonna'
14 *Buddleja davidii* 'Nanho Blue'
15 *Sedum* 'Matrona'
16 *Heuchera* 'Mocha'

List of plants for the 2023 "Grow & Flower" Border

1 *Anemone ×hybrida* 'Honorine Jobert'
2 *Aster ageratoides* 'Stardust'
3 *Brunnera macrophylla* 'Jack Frost'
4 *Hemerocallis* 'Ed Murray'
5 *Cercis canadensis* 'Forest Pansy'
6 *Carex morrowii* 'Variegata'
7 *Persicaria amplexicaulis* 'JS Caliente'
8 *Phlox ×arendsii* 'Utopia'
9 *Kalimeris incisa* 'Madiva'
10 *Miscanthus sinensis* 'Kleine Silberspinne'
11 *Hydrangea quercifolia* 'Burgundy'
12 *Geranium* 'Anne Thomson'
13 *Alchemilla mollis*

Changeover Border (2012)

When visitors walked between Wiekend and the Barn into the New Experimental Garden, the view was quite austere. The flower meadow does not flower very abundantly, and the various planting experiments were not immediately visible, as they were hidden by the hedges. There was a need for a colorful eyecatcher for those entering this section. The aim of the planting in this strip is to have exuberant flowers that are different every year. Combining annuals with dahlias results in a profusion of flowers blooming from June well into fall, exerting a powerful attraction for butterflies, bumblebees, bees, and other insects. As of 2020, the plants have been supplied by Verver Export in exchange for monitoring and reporting on their development in terms of growth and flowering, maintenance, and attractiveness to people and insects.

◀ Peacock butterfly on *Dahlia* in 2020 (above)

◀ Common swallowtail butterfly on *Verbena bonariensis* in 2020 (below left)

◀ *Zinnia elegans*, *Ocimum basilicum*, and *Agastache mexicana* in 2017 (below right)

▶ Planting in 2016 with different species of *Dahlia*, *Artemisia ludoviciana* 'Silver Queen', and *Foeniculum vulgare* (above)

▶ Planting in 2017 by Joyce Oomen of Blooming Business (below)

page 232: The Changeover Border in 2015 (above) and the one from Verver Export in 2021 (below)

page 233: The Changeover Border from Verver Export in 2020

Ruysend Riet (2014)

Ruysend Riet, a wooden summerhouse between the reeds beside the Wiek and next to Wiekend, was built in the 1960s. The house was intended as accommodation for the Ruys family. In 1991, after the Foundation acquired the site on which the house was built, the summerhouse served as accommodation for various gardeners and later as an office. Since the office work has been moved to the old gardener's house, the space is now used as an exhibition room and is accessible to visitors. The garden at Ruysend Riet did not get its current form until 2014, when the Gardens celebrated its 90th anniversary. It was designed by Conny den Hollander, who has been a gardener in the Gardens since 2012 and is the author of this book. Anet Scholma of Buro Mien Ruys supervised the design process. Mien Ruys's design principles were initially adhered to, with minimalist, clearly defined shapes and lush vegetation. On the other hand, the garden has been designed to meet the needs of our age: modern and sustainable material, low-maintenance, and with sufficient room to sit, eat, and live in the garden. The large concrete tiles measuring one square meter give the garden its contemporary look. Some of them have been laid to create a large terrace, and others have been used as stepping stones. Mien Ruys's functionalism is still our starting point because, as Anet says, "Every tile must have a function."

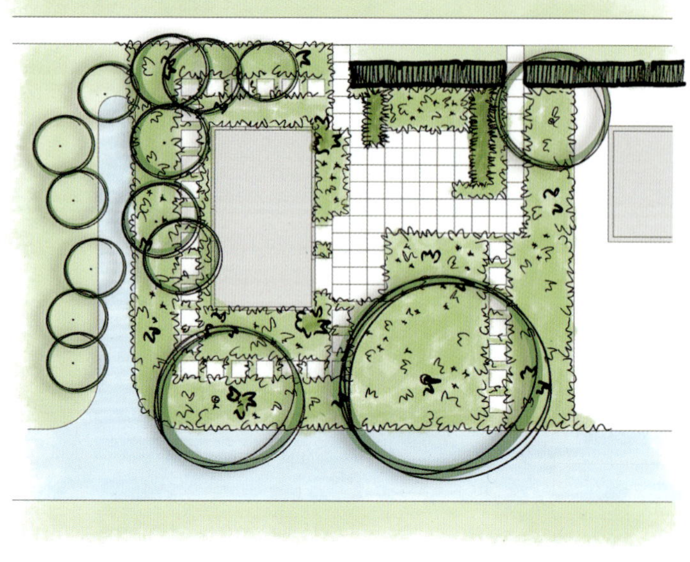

The garden used to be hidden behind high hornbeam hedges. Removing one hedge and creating a second entrance made the garden more connected to its surroundings and therefore more accessible. The huge *Acer saccharinum* 'Laciniatum' that has been there for decades is a visually dominant element in the garden. The beds around the terrace are mainly filled with cultivated species. Otherwise, the planting is primarily indigenous species that seek their own spot, disappear, self-seed, or blow in. As such, little maintenance is needed, but this does not mean that everything can simply be left to go its own way. Intervention is needed if the boundary between naturalized and neglected is crossed. In recent years, the plants have visibly suffered from the hot, dry summers; competition from the maple tree that sucks in water from the other plants; and the large tiles, which radiate a lot of heat. Changing circumstances such as these require the planting to be altered.

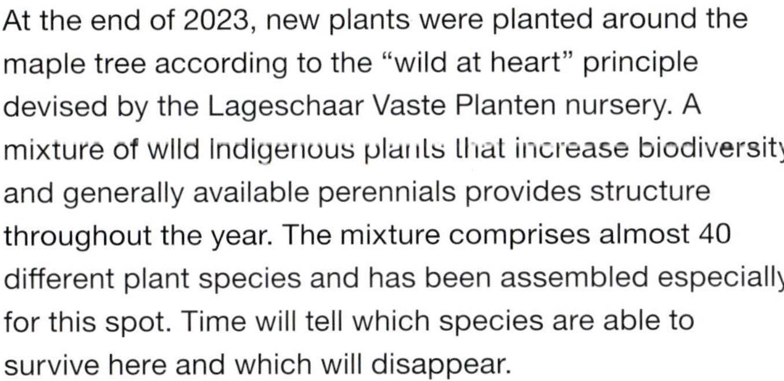

At the end of 2023, new plants were planted around the maple tree according to the “wild at heart” principle devised by the Lageschaar Vaste Planten nursery. A mixture of wild indigenous plants that increase biodiversity and generally available perennials provides structure throughout the year. The mixture comprises almost 40 different plant species and has been assembled especially for this spot. Time will tell which species are able to survive here and which will disappear.

◂ Ruysend Riet in the 1960s

▴ Planting *Molinia arundinacea* ‘Karl Foerster’ in the spring of 2014 (above left)

▸ The garden of Ruysend Riet with the façade of Wiekend in the background (above)

▸ *Lunaria annua* (center)

▸ The large terrace seen from under the *Acer saccharinum* ‘Aureum’ (below)

Mix Border (2018)

At the beginning of the new millennium a change occurred in green public spaces from the rather boring planting of shrubs to the use of colorful, flowering perennials. What was known as "concept planting" made an entrance, in which strong, healthy perennials formed the basis for an attractive, colorful landscape in public gardens, on verges, and on roundabouts. Because the plants are planted close together, there is less opportunity for weeds to grow, and so little maintenance is needed. The plants also increase biodiversity and make the living environment more attractive. *Zorgeloos Groen* (carefree greenery) is an example of such concept planting, an initiative of Buro Mien Ruys in conjunction with growers and landscapers. Perennials are combined with a new generation of strong roses and ornamental grasses.

▲ *Crocosmia*

▼ Hundreds of plants ready to be planted in the layer of lava rocks in the spring of 2018

Buro Mien Ruys felt the need to try out this concept, and so laid out a model planting of Zorgeloos Groen in the New Experimental Garden in 2010: the Rose Border. Despite the improved rose species, the combination of roses and perennials in the acidic, damp soil of Dedemsvaart once again proved to be tough going. After a few years, the Rose Border was replaced by the Mix Border, another example of concept planting for public green spaces by Lageschaar Vaste Planten. This concept consists of strong perennials and ornamental grasses with a natural look, which are not planted in groups but mixed and then repeated over and over. A layer of lava rocks prevents the soil from drying out during a drought and ensures good drainage during heavy rain showers. A variety of plant mixtures were planted in the three beds of the Mix Border in 2018. Just as in the other plantings, species disappear after a while and others spread extensively. Adjustments are occasionally made by removing plants or adding new ones, but the general look remains colorful and natural. The layer of lava rocks has several advantages, including reducing maintenance. There is often no need to weed and any weeds that do grow are easily removed. Furthermore, the rocks are comfortable to work on. There is no risk of the soil being compacted by the weight of the person weeding. And watering—despite the hot, dry summers—is hardly needed at all.

▲▶ One of the three beds contains plants that flowers in shades of orange, red, yellow, and pink: an electrifying combination of colors. The layers of flowers of *Phlomis russeliana* provide striking winter interest.

pages 238–239: The Mix Border in 2022 with *Lythrum salicaria*, *Geranium*, *Phlomis russeliana*, and *Veronicastrum virginicum*

Middle Garden (2023)

The Middle Garden is in between the New Experimental Garden and the Roof Garden. The garden's layout is simple. In the center is *Tetradium daniellii* with an underplanting of *Waldsteinia ternata*, surrounded by paths made of square cobblestones. The layouts of the Middle Garden and the Roof Garden were altered during the winter of 2020–2021. There were various reasons for this, and one of them was that the planting in the Middle Garden looked messy and needed replacing. The route to the Roof Garden was also modified so that visitors are now led diagonally through the Middle Garden rather than along one side of it. The existing strip of plants was widened and divided into two beds because of the new pathway. After having experimented with seed mixtures of annuals for a couple of years, staff remade the garden with new plants in the spring of 2023. The hot, dry summers with occasional heavy downpours and the mild, wet winters of recent years had led to a need to experiment with "climate-proof" plants that would withstand these extreme conditions. Plants for hot, dry summers are easy to find among Mediterranean plants, but they are generally plants that like some lime in the soil and do not like wet winters. These are not exactly ideal plants for the peaty, acidic soil in Dedemsvaart. For this reason, plants were sought that have few demands when it comes to the type of soil, can successfully withstand changing water levels, or plants that naturally lay down reserves. Plants such as *Amsonia*, *Sanguisorba*, *Geranium*, *Hemerocallis*, and *Baptisia* were chosen. Time will tell whether these plants are indeed "climate-proof."

European Garden Award (2023)

The Mien Ruys Gardens won first prize in the category "Management or development of a historic park or garden" of the 2023 European Garden Award, made available by the European Garden Heritage Network (EGHN). The jury's report stated that "the Gardens are a sequence of 30 gardens designed and laid out according to both old and innovative ideas with a well-balanced combination of plants. New combinations of plants and garden materials are tried out. The Mien Ruys Gardens give an overview of 20th century garden architecture and current trends." This Award represents tremendous recognition of the unique nature of the Gardens and appreciation for its staff, board, and volunteers who put their heart and soul into maintaining and innovating in the Gardens.

◂ Colorful annuals in the summer of 2021 (see also pages 242–243)

▸ View from the Middle Garden through the Roof Garden to the old *Salix alba*

▸ Planting plan for the Middle Garden, an experiment to discover which plants can withstand extreme weather conditions

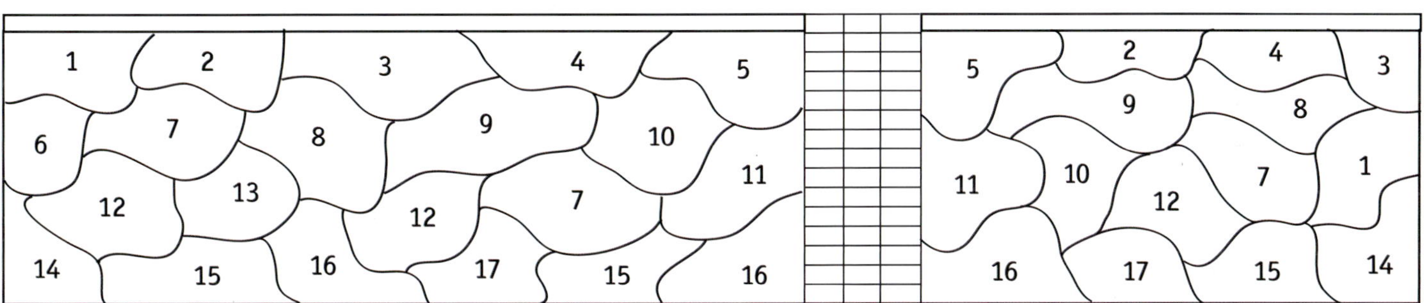

List of plants for the 2023 Middle Garden

1 *Aster ageratoides* 'Ezo Murasaki'

2 *Sanguisorba canadensis*

3 *Anemanthele lessoniana* 'Sirocco'

4 *Veronicastrum virginicum* 'Erica'

5 *Amsonia tabernaemontana*

6 *Nepeta govaniana*

7 *Baptisia* 'Blueberry Sundae'

8 *Sanguisorba officinalis* 'Lum'

9 *Euphorbia characias* subsp. *wulfenii*

10 *Kniphofia* 'Elvira'

11 *Schizachyrium scoparium* 'Standing Ovation'

12 *Hemerocallis* 'Nummer 4'

13 *Asclepias incarnata* 'Ice Ballet'

14 *Heuchera villosa* var. *macrorhiza*

15 *Nepeta* 'Neptune'

16 *Geranium renardii* 'Tcschelda'

17 *Centaurea montana* 'Jordy'

THREE NEW INSPIRATIONAL GARDENS

In 2024 it is 100 years since Mien Ruys laid out her first garden, the Wilderness Garden. She used her gardens in Dedemsvaart to experiment with planting and materials, and she also wanted to inspire as many people as possible to start gardening. One hundred years later, in addition to maintaining the heritage gardens, Mien Ruys Gardens continues to experiment and inspire. To emphasize this point, three new gardens are being planted for the anniversary year. Three designers from Buro Mien Ruys have each designed a garden measuring 5 × 7 meters to inspire owners of similar small gardens. They are modern versions of the City Garden Mien Ruys created in the 1960s (see page 102). The specification was to make these gardens green and sustainable, and, as far as possible, to use materials that have been recycled. Each garden has its own theme.

The Playground

The Playground was designed by Evy Blom for a family with young children. Smart solutions have been devised to incorporate play into the garden as efficiently as possible without making it a playground. A toy kitchen and a sandpit are built into the long bench against the fence. A climbing rope hangs from the pergola, and a timber sheet has been cut to form the front of a playhouse. Some of the tiles in the path through the garden are set out as a game of hopscotch. And this small garden even includes a tree, a small terrace, a lawn, and a border of perennials. The lawn runs across the entire width of the garden, making it look bigger. The border is against the back wall of the house, so that the flowering plants can be seen from inside. The species used are from the "typical Mien Ruys" assortment: strong, colorful, and long-flowering.

List of plants

Tree
- *Sorbus* 'Joseph Rock'

Hedge
- *Prunus lusitanica* 'Angustifolia'

Climbing Plant
- *Clematis armandii*

Perennials
- *Phlomis russeliana*
- *Hemerocallis* 'Happy Returns'
- *Brunnera macrophylla* 'Jack Frost'
- *Helenium* 'Moerheim Beauty'
- *Campanula poscharskyana*
- *Achillea* 'Coronation Gold'
- *Salvia nemorosa* 'Mai Nacht'
- *Verbena bonariensis*

Ornamental Grasses
- *Calamagrostis ×acutiflora* 'Karl Foerster'
- *Pennisetum alopecuroides* 'Hameln'

Bulbs
- *Narcissus* 'Juanita'

The Easy Garden

The Easy Garden was designed by Ward Maaswinkel as a garden for people who have little time to work in their garden but still want to enjoy it. The style chosen is minimalist and modern, with a spacious terrace. A large part of the garden is taken up by a "rain garden," or *wadi*, a hollowed area planted with vegetation and designed to collect rainwater. The tree in the rain garden, *Alnus glutinosa* 'Imperialis', can withstand damp soil and can even stand in water for a while. The tiles to be used are made from recycled concrete. The rain garden and the beds of plants will be covered with a layer of lava rocks, which will reduce the number of weeds and help regulate the water balance for the plants. This means that the plants will not have to be watered so often. The fence of composite tongue-and-groove planking is an experiment to see whether this material will last in the long term.

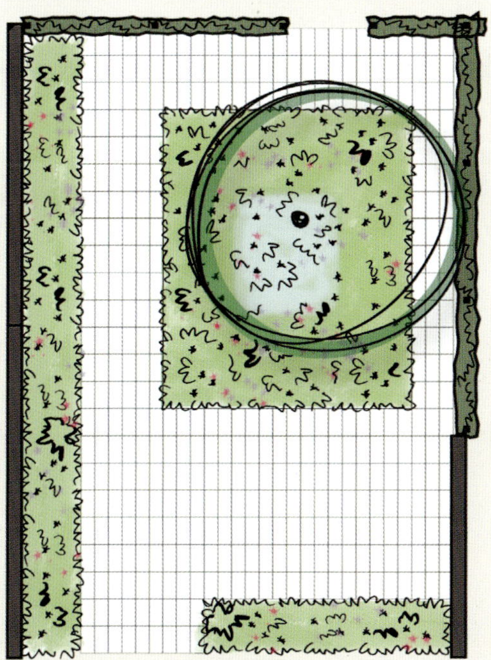

List of plants

Tree
- *Alnus glutinosa* 'Imperialis'

Hedge
- *Trachelospermum jasminoides*

Climbing Plant
- *Clematis* 'Mrs Cholmondeley'

Perennials
- *Echinacea purpurea* 'Alba'
- *Iris sibirica*
- *Lythrum salicaria* 'Robert'
- *Digitalis purpurea* 'Alba' (biennial)

Ornamental Grasses
- *Carex muskingumensis*
- *Molinia caerulea* subsp. *caerulea* 'Moorhexe'
- *Calamagrostis ×acutiflora* 'Karl Foerster'

Bulbs
- *Leucojum aestivum* 'Gravetye Giant'
- *Camassia leichtlinii* 'Caerulea'

The Nature Garden

The Nature Garden was designed by Ilona Dekker with a focus on food from your own garden, as well as on sustainability and biodiversity. Currant bushes, an apple tree, and a pear tree will be planted in the garden. The paving will comprise used tiles and olivine, a mineral that absorbs carbon from the air. Part of the boundary line will be fenced by piling up used plastic plant crates. The crates will be filled with pots of plants and materials in which insects can nest. In due course, we will discover whether this experimental fence will stand the test of time. A few of these plant crates will also be used to create a little kitchen garden. The plants in the border comprise indigenous plants that attract bees and butterflies. The hawthorn hedge provides ideal nesting opportunities for birds.

List of plants

Trees
- *Malus domestica* 'Sterappel'
- *Pyrus communis* 'Gieser Wildeman'

Shrubs
- *Ribes rubrum* 'Jonkheer van Tets'

Hedge
- *Crataegus monogyna*

Perennials
- *Lamium maculatum*
- *Leucanthemum vulgare*
- *Salvia pratensis*
- *Alchemilla xanthochlora*
- *Veronica longifolia*
- *Lythrum salicaria*
- *Aster linosyris*
- *Digitalis purpurea* (biennial)
- *Aquilegia vulgaris*

TYPICAL MIEN RUYS
Characteristic Elements

Mien Ruys developed several innovative materials and design applications during her career. She frequently incorporated them into her designs for private gardens and gardens for offices, factories, and institutions. These "typical Mien Ruys" elements can also be seen in her own experimental gardens, often as basic features with which to experiment.

The decking tiles in the Marsh Garden. The use of squares and other geometric shapes is characteristic of Mien Ruys's designs.

"The rectangular material was simple to make and consistent with the modernist architectural style of the period."

Grion Tiles

Shortly after the war, there was a shortage of paving material for gardens. Natural stone materials such as flagstones were rarely available anymore, and bricks were rationed. Standard concrete paving stones measuring 30 × 30 centimeters were abundantly available, but even Mien Ruys found them boring. The rough tiles that had been made and used for the paths in the nursery for as long as anyone could remember did attract her interest, however. The tiles were made of concrete mixed with gravel, and wear and tear had brought the gravel to the surface. The rectangular material with its natural-looking upper layer was simple to make and consistent with the modernist architectural style of the period. And so, the *grion* tile was born, a name Theo had come up with by combining the Dutch words *grind* (gravel) and *beton* (concrete). Production of these tiles started in the early 1950s, at first manually in a shed in Amsterdam. Wooden templates in two sizes, 40 × 40 centimeters and 40 × 60 centimeters, were lined with newspaper and filled to the brim with concrete. The top layer was treated with hydrochloric acid, which washed away the concrete to reveal the gravel. Later, the tiles were produced mechanically by a concrete manufacturer. The grion tiles were well suited for use in Mien's designs with their straight, austere lines and planes. Mien often used them as stepping stones in a lawn, allowing the grass to grow between the stones, or with several centimeters of grouting. The idea of using grion tiles was adopted on a grand scale in the decades that followed, with the 1970s being a high point. The washed gravel tile began to lead a life of its own, acquiring various top layers, sometimes in contrasting colors. These tiles no longer had the natural look Mien Ruys had in mind. "The industry quickly adopted my idea and now half the country is covered in them," she said in *Mijn Tuinen* in 1987. Grion tiles can still be seen in various gardens in Dedemsvaart.

▲ The precursor of the grion tile surrounding the pond in the Wilderness Garden created in 1924

◄ New grion tiles were made for the terrace at Wiekend when it was renovated in 2013.

The Diagonal Line

Mien Ruys often used a diagonal line as the basis for her garden designs in the 1950s. She discovered that the diagonal line works well as a way of subdividing rectangular spaces. Straight lines divide a long, narrow strip into straight rows, emphasizing their length. By using the diagonal, more interaction is created, and the space appears to be bigger. She never placed the diagonal at a 45-degree angle, but rather at about 60 degrees, to avoid having sharply defined, impractical corners. The City Garden and the garden at Wiekend were designed around the diagonal line.

"By using the diagonal, more interaction is created, and the space appears to be bigger."

▲ The diagonal line in the park next to the Tomado factory

▼ The diagonal line in the City Garden makes the garden look bigger.

The Ready-to-make Borders

The idea for the Ready-to-make Borders came from Theo, who was inspired by the modular construction methods used during the post-war reconstruction period. If prefab houses could be built, Theo reasoned that it ought to be possible to do the same for gardens. Despite a certain amount of skepticism on Mien's part, she devised a few ready-made packages for borders of different sizes. She chose strong perennials that flower for a long time, do not spread, and do not require too much maintenance. The type of soil (sandy or peaty/clay), the amount of sun (sunny or partial shade) and various color combinations (pink to carmine red, blue-gray, or mixed colors) determined the choice of plants. The standard borders were included in Moerheim's annual catalog, and a specific order form was designed. Apart from giving their name and address and a signature, customers also had to select the type of soil, amount of light, color combination, and measurements. The standard borders were supplied at a discount by Moerheim Nursery, accompanied by a planting and maintenance plan, and were affordable for "ordinary people." The concept of the Ready-to-make Borders was popular for a very long time, with even a well-known department store including them in its range of goods. These borders were not tailor-made, but ready-made, removing the need for a landscape gardener. Several Ready-to-make Borders can still be found in the Gardens in a modified form.

▼ The Ready-to-make Borders in Mien Ruys Gardens partly comprise the old assortment that Mien Ruys used in her ready-made packages for borders.

▶ Order form for the Ready-to-make Borders supplied by Moerheim Nursery in the 1960s

AAN DE KWEKERIJ MOERHEIM TE DEDEMSVAART

Naam ....

Straat ....

Plaats ....

Met blokletters schrijven a.u.b.

Mijne Heren,
Ik verzoek U een border voor mij te reserveren volgens de hieronder ingevulde cirkels. Wilt U, wanneer de beste planttijd is gekomen, de planten voorzien van plattegrond, plantenlijst met de namen der bloemen en nauwkeurige aanwijzing voor het planten en onderhoud, naar onderstaand adres zenden. Het verschuldigde bedrag wordt overgemaakt op postgiro nr 800005, per postwissel of via Twentse Bank Amsterdam, binnen 14 dagen na ontvangst der goederen.

Handtekening

A	Grondsoort	O zand O klei of veen
B	Belichting	O zon O halfschaduw
C	Kleurencombinatie	O rose-karmijn, blauw-grijs O gemengde kleuren
D	Afmetingen	O 3 x 1,5 m à f 19,50 O 4 x 2 m à f 31,20 O 5 x 2 m à f 39,— O 10 x 2 m à f 78,—

Invullen van A, B, C, D is noodzakelijk. Onvolledige bestellingen kunnen niet worden uitgevoerd

ZO ZIJN ONZE STANDAARD-BORDERS
KONINKLIJKE KWEKERIJ „MOERHEIM" DEDEMSVAART

MOERHEIMS STANDAARD-BORDERS

Nu ook in Uw tuin een border

Wat geeft in een tuin meer vreugde dan een bloemengroep, of een gehele border, die men slechts éénmaal een plaats gaf om de planten daarna, jaar in jaar uit steeds voller, dus mooier te zien terugkomen? Dit is het wat Moerheims standaardborders onderscheidt van een rand met eenjarigen: de overblijvende planten komen steeds weer op dezelfde plaats. Bovendien bezitten vaste planten een veel grotere verscheidenheid van bouw, van groei, van hoogte zowel als van kleur dan b.v. rozen of dahlia's. Heesters en bomen verschaffen meestal met het gazon de basis van de tuin, rozen vormen kleurvlakken maar de vaste planten brengen er het boeiende element in, de afwisseling, het leven.
Het is niet zo moeilijk een vaste plantenrand samen te stellen die op één moment mooi is, maar het vraagt grote vakkennis en ervaring een border te ontwerpen, die de gehele zomer, van mei tot september, kleur geeft, terwijl bovendien rekening moet worden gehouden met zon of halfschaduw, met zware of lichte, met droge of natte grond. Slechts weinigen kunnen zelf de vaste planten op de juiste wijze kiezen en rangschikken.
Daarom komt Moerheim met dit plan, waardoor elke bezitter van een tuin, zelfs van een zeer kleine, de jaarlijks terugkerende vreugde van een bloemenborder kan genieten. De tuinarchitecte Mien Ruys ontwierp hiertoe verschillende borders, zowel voor klei als voor zandgrond, voor zon en halfschaduw, borders in rose-karmijn-blauw-grijs en in gemengde kleuren.
Er zijn miniatuur-borders van 3 x 1½ meter als kleurige mozaiekjes voor slechts f 19,50. Hierin zijn voornamelijk lage planten gekozen met een enkele iets hogere er tussen oprijzend, zodat deze groepen het minste onderhoud vragen.
Dan volgen borders van 4 x 2 meter voor f 31,20 en van 5 x 2 meter voor f 39,—. Hierin zijn al wat forsere groepen opgenomen met een langere bloeitijd, waarbij de hogere bossiger soorten uit de aard der zaak ook iets meer steun vragen. Tenslotte zijn er dan de borders van 10 x 2 meter voor f 78,—. Hoe groter de bloemenrand, des te meer variatie er kan zijn in kleur en bloeitijd.
Wie geheel andere maten heeft of een afwijkende vorm, kan zich wenden tot het „Tuinarchitectenbureau Mien Ruys", Amstel 157, Amsterdam. Indien U een situatietekening zendt met opgave van maten, grondsoort, windrichting en wensen, dan kan men een apart beplantingsplan samenstellen, geheel aangepast aan ligging en grondsoort, waarbij ook eventueel aanwezige planten in het schema kunnen worden opgenomen. De kosten voor zo'n plan bedragen dan 15% van de prijs van de te verwerken planten, vermeerderd met een klein bedrag voor lichtdruk- en administratiekosten.
Maar wie in zijn tuin plaats heeft voor een border in de hierboven genoemde maten doet wijs gebruik te maken van deze goedkope aanbieding. Niet alleen de prijs van de planten per stuk is lager dan de gewone catalogus-prijs, bovendien is het bijbehorende beplantingsplan gratis terwijl tenslotte nog een boekje wordt ingesloten over de behandeling van de planten zowel als over de verzorging daarna.
Wanneer U ons achterstaand biljet ingevuld toezendt, ontvangt U in het voorjaar — in de loop van april — een mand of pakket met de planten, het beplantingsplan (waarnaar U zelf gemakkelijk kunt planten), de plantenlijst en de handleiding voor de verzorging. De verzendkosten worden bij ontvangst door de besteller betaald, terwijl Moerheim het verpakkingsmateriaal voor zijn rekening neemt. Om technische en administratieve redenen kunnen deze „standaardborders" niet tegelijk met eventueel andere bestelde planten worden verpakt. Ze worden dus geheel apart verzonden.
Hoewel deze standaardborders dus een unieke goedkope aanbieding betekenen, wil dit niet zeggen dat er mindere kwaliteit planten voor wordt geleverd. De keuze is gedaan uit het beste, sterkste en mooiste wat Moerheim op zijn uitgestrekte bloemenvelden bezit en de plantenschema's zijn ontworpen na jarenlange proeven, zodat men nu een border kan bezitten voor minder geld en toch van „Moerheim-kwaliteit".

The Repeat Borders

A noteworthy form of the Ready-to-make Borders was the Repeat Borders. These were large borders in which a limited number of perennial species were repeated according to a fixed pattern of geometric shapes. The plants Mien used were carefully chosen based on color, form, flowering schedule, and competitive ability. The Repeat Borders were particularly suitable for larger communal outside spaces and gardens around offices, factories, and institutions. The view of the colorful beds of flowering plants from the higher floors of a building was an added advantage. The Repeat Borders were also offered as standard borders for private gardens, available from Moerheim. For the price of 97.50 Dutch guilders, people would receive plants for a border measuring 2.5 × 8 meters, featuring colorful flowers from June to September for a sunny spot and requiring little maintenance. "The bigger it is, the more fascinating." If people had a larger space available, they could order several of these packages. The borders contained only five species, repeated in a pattern: *Helenium* 'Moerheim Beauty', *Achillea filipendulina* 'Coronation Gold', *Salvia nemorosa* 'Lubecca', *Geum coccineum* 'Borisii', and *Geranium ×johnsonii* 'Johnson's Blue'. Obviously, Mien chose strong, healthy plants for these borders. All the species used in them are still available today.

"The Repeat Borders were particularly suitable for larger communal outside spaces and gardens around offices, factories, and institutions."

Mien often chose a combination of *Salvia nemerosa*, *Achillea filipendulina,* and *Helenium* 'Moerheim Beauty', a striking contrast in flower color and shape.

The Sunken Garden is the only remaining example of the experiments with railway sleepers in Mien Ruys Gardens.

The Railway Sleeper

In 1958, Mien was asked by the architect Gerard Holt to design a garden for his house. He had designed the house himself in the modernist style, against a slope in the dunes of Overveen. When she visited the site, Mien immediately noticed that the dune, when seen from the house, was very obtrusive. She wanted something to counteract it but wasn't sure how to do this. Brick walls would need strong foundations to prevent them from sinking into the weak sand of the dunes and, in any case, they would be inappropriate for the surroundings. She decided that old timber would be a suitable material. She traveled a lot by train and had seen a pile of old railway sleepers (called "railroad ties" in the United States) along the track. This gave her the idea of using old railway sleepers to deal with differences in height. She was so enthusiastic about the possibilities of the material that she immediately arranged for a truckload of railway sleepers to be brought to Dedemsvaart to experiment with. Mien Ruys went on to use railway sleepers frequently in gardens with height differences. The substantial beams were especially ideal for soft, pulpy soil due to their large bearing surface. To her horror, the idea was adopted indiscriminately, and railway sleepers began to be used in every housing estate and every front yard, whether relevant or not. The Sunken Garden is an example of Mien's experiments with railway sleepers.

"To her horror, the idea was adopted indiscriminately, and railway sleepers began to be used in every housing estate and every front yard, whether relevant or not."

“Throwing Dice”

From her “very first landscaping endeavor” in the Wilderness Garden, Mien Ruys made use of the square shape. In the 1960s, she began employing the square haphazardly, or “throwing dice,” as she called it. She created designs in which she cut out square beds in the paving, staggering them. The beds were filled with roses, perennials, or blocks of hedges. As such, planting was always visible, irrespective of the angle from which the garden was viewed. The Square Garden is a good example of a garden in which Mien “threw dice.”

◀ ▼ “Throwing dice” with square shapes in the Square Garden (left and below)

▶ An example of a “throwing dice” project with rose beds in Enschede (above)

“Blowing Bubbles”

A comparable way of employing a rigid geometric shape in an apparently random pattern was the use of “bubbles.” By acting as if she were blowing bubbles, Mien placed circles of various sizes in her design. She used this method in the part of the nursery that was acquired by the experimental gardens in 1974. Although the “bubbles” experiment has long gone, the circle is still the principal shape in the Yellow Garden and in the Circle in the Woods. The influence of structuralism is clearly visible in her work of this period. As well as “throwing dice” for squares and “blowing bubbles” for circles, she also occasionally used hexagons.

▸ “Bubbles” in one of the communal gardens of the Patrimonium housing association

▾ “Bubbles” in the Gardens, with circles of roses separated by comma-shaped larch hedges

The Flower Terrace

The Flower Terrace was a type of design Mien Ruys often used from the 1950s on. Flowerbeds with irregular edges were cut out of the paving of rectangular or square terraces. Here, too, just as with "throwing dice," the planting can be seen from any angle. A flower terrace was also laid in the Gardens in Dedemsvaart in 1982.

And Of Course ... the Plants

Many of Mien Ruys's contemporaries, fellow landscape gardeners and landscape architects, regarded the use of colorful perennials as decoration, which was incompatible with the new post-war modernist style. For Mien, however, they were an essential part of a garden. Planting wasn't a means, but an end. All her life, she was a steadfast champion of the use of exuberant, colorful combinations of perennials. In her book *Leven met groen in landschap, stad en tuin* (*Living with Greenery in the Landscape, City, and Garden*), published in 1960, she said this about the modernist garden: "Het Nieuwe Bouwen [functionalism] threw overboard everything that was expendable in order to rediscover its baseline; but in landscape gardening it was the essence—living plants, precisely the basis for a garden—that was discarded. After a while, garden owners refused to put up with this and understood that a garden from which plants were excluded, wasn't actually a garden at all."

A list of the 100 plants Mien used most frequently in her designs is provided on page 264.

"The typical Mien Ruys elements, her books, and her articles in *Onze Eigen Tuin* helped to make a beautiful garden—in which people could experience nature and the seasons—accessible to everyone."

▲ A private garden with flower terrace

► The Flower Terrace with *Rosa* 'Lavender Dream' on the left

pages 260–261: Squares, rectangles, and circles were typical of Mien Ruys's style.

MIEN RUYS'S FAVORITE PLANTS

Mien Ruys had an assortment of trees, shrubs, and perennials that she often used because she felt that they had sufficiently proved their worth. Anet Scholma, director of Buro Mien Ruys, worked with Mien Ruys for many years. Drawing on her experience and knowledge, she has compiled a list of Mien Ruys's 100 favorite perennials, trees, and shrubs for the 100th anniversary of Mien Ruys Gardens. Many of the plants on this list can still be seen in the Gardens. Many species and cultivars are still widely available and very rewarding in a garden.

Helenium 'Waldraut'

PERENNIALS

Achillea
yarrow

All *Achilleas* crave the sun and can generally withstand dry soil. They are strong and flower profusely for a long time, with a flowering season between June and September. Apart from being excellent garden plants, they are also good as cut flowers. One of Mien Ruys's classic combinations is *Achillea*, *Salvia*, and *Helenium.* The cultivars Mien Ruys often used are the shorter *Achillea filipendulina* 'Coronation Gold' and the taller *Achillea filipendulina* 'Parker's Variety'. The foliage of 'Coronation Gold' is fine and grayish green, and its umbels are lemon yellow. The flower of 'Parker's Variety' is more golden and its foliage pale green.

Aconitum
monkshood

Aconitum is one of the oldest known garden plants. It requires partial shade and grows in any soil, provided it is not too dry. All *Aconitum* are toxic. *Aconitum carmichaelii* 'Arendsii' has stiffly upright spires and bright green foliage. A striking feature is its late flowering in October. The flowers are a rich blue. *Aconitum henryi* 'Spark's Variety' has a wide, airy spire with dark midnight-blue flowers. It is slightly taller than the first one and flowers earlier: between July and August. One of Mien Ruys's classic combinations is *Aconitum* with *Monarda*, *Echinops*, and *Phlox.*

Alchemilla mollis
lady's mantle

Alchemilla is a worthwhile plant not simply because of its greenish-yellow flowers, but also because of its attractive foliage on which drops of water lie like pearls. It forms a strong, dense clump and is therefore ideal along the edge of a border. Self-seeding.

Anemone ×hybrida 'Honorine Jobert'
windflower

Mien Ruys combined this white Japanese anemone with other autumn-flowering plants such as *Aster*, *Aconitum*, and *Sedum*. It likes some shade and soil that is not too dry.

Aster

Asters regularly appear in Mien Ruys's planting plans. Commonly used species are the *Symphyotrichum novi-belgii* 'Professor Anton Kippenberg', a late-flowering, low-growing species with lavender blue flowers, and *Aster ×frikartii* 'Wunder von Stäfa', a slightly taller aster that flowers earlier and has lilac blue flowers. Of the tall species, *Symphyotrichum novi-belgii*, Mien Ruys mainly used the 'Crimson Brocade', which is carmine red with a yellow center, and the 'Marie Ballard', with its grayish blue flowers.

Astilbe
false spirea

A perennial Mien Ruys used a lot in the 1960s and 1970s. The most frequently used cultivars are *Astilbe* 'Fanal', a compact, clump-forming plant with dark foliage and dark red, compact flower plumes, and *Astilbe* 'Spinell', which is taller and has bright red, loosely branched plumes.

Brunnera macrophylla
Siberian bugloss

Mien Ruys used this plant mainly because of its large, heart-shaped leaves. The plant puts out shoots very early in spring, retains its foliage until frost hits, and produces small flowers similar to forget-me-nots in April to May.

Campanula
bellflower

Both the taller and low-growing species were often used in planting plans. The ones most often selected were *Campanula lactiflora* 'Loddon Anna', with its loose clusters of pale pink flowers, and the lower-growing, compact *Campanula lactiflora* 'Prichard's Variety'. The latter has rich violet-blue flowers and does well in sun or partial shade. The profusely flowering, low-growing *Campanula portenschlagiana*, with its violet-blue flowers in June and July, was also frequently used as groundcover. *Campanula poscharskyana* also provides good groundcover but is less delicate in terms of growth, height, and foliage. It tends to put out tendrils and is ideal for covering the edges of ponds or low walls.

Cimicifuga (Actaea)
bugbane

Luminescent white or cream spikes that grow well in shade and flower late in the season. The most used species were *Cimicifuga ramosa* (or its new name *Actaea simplex* 'Prichard's Giant'), which can grow to a height of two meters with long, narrow spikes. *Cimicifuga simplex* 'White Pearl' (or *Actaea simplex* 'White Pearl') is altogether more delicate and lower growing.

Delphinium
larkspur

Her father's nursery had hundreds of cultivars of *Delphinium*; too many, in Mien Ruys's view. She compared and assessed them and chose the ones she thought were the best. A distinction can be made between two groups. The *belladonna* forms are branched and relatively low-growing, up to a meter and a half tall. The *elatum* forms are taller, up to two meters, and have compact flower spikes with larger flowers. The most frequently used belladonnas are 'Lamartine', which has dark violet-blue flowers; 'Moerheimii', which has white flowers; and 'Völkerfrieden', which has gentian blue flowers. The most frequently used *elatums* are 'Berghimmel', which has pale, sky-blue flowers; 'Finsteraarhorn', which has dark blue flowers with even darker hearts; and 'Perlmutterbaum', the tallest, with lilac blue flowers.

Dicentra
bleeding heart

Mien Ruys used two variants of this plant: *Dicentra formosa*, with its delicate divided leaves, and *Dicentra spectabilis*, with fleshier leaves that form a higher clump. Both flower in May with rose-pink flowers.

Echinops bannaticus 'Taplow Blue'
blue globe thistle

Has round, steel blue flowers in July to August. Can withstand drought and can be planted in groups to form a background for a border.

Eupatorium purpureum subsp. *maculatum* 'Atropurpureum'
gravel root or Joe-Pye Weed

Good in the background of a large border because this plant can grow to a height of over two meters. Despite its height, Joe-Pye Weed remains bolt upright.

Euphorbia polychroma
cushion spurge

A clump-forming, compact plant that flowers in April and May with acid-yellow flowers. Attractive in combination with *Geum* and *Brunnera* in the foreground of a border. The new name for *Euphorbia polychroma* is *Euphorbia epithymoides*.

Fuchsia magellanica 'Longipedunculata'

In fact, this is a small shrub rather than a perennial, but because its stems freeze in hard winters and the plant subsequently puts out shoots again from its base, it is often used as a perennial. It flowers profusely and for a long time, from July to October, carmine red with violet. Even does well in a north-facing spot in the shade.

Geranium
cranesbill

Suitable for the foreground or center of the border, this was almost always included in Mien Ruys's planting plans. The species planted most often are listed here. *Geranium endressii* has pale green foliage and rose-pink flowers, which bloom from June to September; tends to spread and will withstand a lot of shade. *Geranium ×johnsonii* 'Johnson's Blue' has large, open, lavender-blue flowers. It flowers prolifically but only for a short time in June. *Geranium ×magnificum* is one of the strongest geranium species; will also withstand shade. Has coarse leaves and large, purple-veined flowers. Tends to fall over and should be cut back after flowering to allow a new clump of leaves to grow.

Geum coccineum 'Borisii'
avens

This almost turf-forming perennial is often seen along the edge of planting plans for borders. Upright stems with orange flowers that "dance" above its leaves. The plant is also more or less evergreen.

Lavandula 'Munstead'

Lysimachia punctata and *Campanula poscharskyana* 'Stella'

Phlox paniculata 'Spitfire'

Viburnum opulus 'Compactum'

Rudbeckia fulgida 'Goldsturm'

Salvia nemorosa 'Ostfriesland'

Metasequoia glyptostroboides

Viola cornuta 'John Wallmark'

Achillea filipendulina 'Coronation Gold'

Prunus ×yedoensis

Symphyotrichum novi-belgii 'Professor Anton Kippenberg'

Helenium 'Moerheim Beauty'

Delphinium 'Völkerfrieden'

Echinops ritro 'Taplow Blue'

Euphorbia polychroma

Hemerocallis 'Black Prince'

Hemerocallis 'Bonanza'

Geum coccineum 'Borisii'

***Gypsophila* 'Rosenschleier'**
baby's breath

Open panicles of small white flowers create the appearance of a cloud. Requires a sunny spot. Pretty combined with roses but is also suitable in a border combined with *Campanula*, *Nepeta*, *Potentilla,* and *Salvia*.

Helenium
sneezeweed

These composites were included in almost every planting plan. The one most often used is *Helenium* 'Moerheim Beauty', a bred strain originating from Moerheim Nursery in 1930 that is still one of the best *Heleniums* in the assortment. 'Moerheim Beauty' is one of the first to flower in June with deep orange flowers. 'Rubinkuppel' is darker in all respects: darker stems and darker coppery-red flowers. It blooms later, in September. 'Waltraut' has warm orangey-yellow flowers in July–August. *Helenium* 'Wyndley' is shorter and produces yellow flowers in July–August.

Hemerocallis
daylily

This genus has countless cultivars, and Mien Ruys used the following: *Hemerocallis* 'Black Prince', with its very dark brown to orange flowers; 'Bonanza', with its wide-open yellow flowers with dark terracotta hearts; and 'Tejas', with its delicate, reed-like leaves and thin stems supporting orange flowers.

Hosta
plantain lily

These plants are mainly used for their beautiful foliage, but they are susceptible to slug damage. The species Mien Ruys used are *Hosta* 'Albo-marginata' (*Hosta sieboldii*), which is relatively low-growing and has a white edge to its leaves, making it a bright, cheerful addition to plants in the shade, and *Hosta sieboldiana* var. elegans, whose broad, heart-shaped leaves form a considerable clump. Its thick, blue-gray leaves are apparently less attractive to slugs.

***Iberis sempervirens* 'Snowflake'**
candytuft

Compact, evergreen groundcover with little umbels of pure white flowers. This plant was often used at corners of low walls or along steps to camouflage sharp corners.

***Iris sibirica* 'Perry's Blue'**
Siberian iris

An iris with striking sky-blue flowers. Although this iris is by its nature a marsh plant, it will withstand dry soil remarkably well. It was frequently used along the edges of ponds.

Kirengeshoma palmata
yellow wax-bells

For a place in the shade in damp soil. Produces nodding, bell-shaped, creamy yellow flowers in August–September. The attractive shape of its foliage also makes this plant worthwhile.

Lavandula
lavender

This evergreen woody plant is actually a shrub, but Mien Ruys often used it in borders in the same way as perennials. She frequently used *Lavandula angustifolia* 'Hidcote': clumps of lanceolate, gray foliage with deep violet-purple flower spikes in July–August. Requires a spot in the sun. She also made regular use of *Lavandula angustifolia* 'Munstead', which has a shaggier appearance, gray-green foliage, and lighter, pale-blue flower spikes.

Ligularia
leopard plant

Almost all are tall plants with yellow flowers, often also with eye-catching foliage. Mien Ruys frequently used *Ligularia dentata*, a substantial plant with large round leaves measuring up to 50 centimeters in diameter. Its orange daisy-like flowers grow on tall stems of over a meter high. The cultivar 'Othello' is more compact and darker; its foliage is maroon on its underside and its stems are also dark red/purple. Or *Ligularia przewalskii*, which has clumps of deeply palmately cut leaves and flower spikes with orange or yellow flowers on tall, dark stems. Can withstand shade; in fact, this plant is quick to droop in the sun.

Lupinus
lupin

Mien Ruys only used two cultivars of this species in her borders: *Lupinus* 'Chandelier', which produces bright yellow flower spikes in June/July, and the dark-red-flowered *Lupinus* 'My Castle'.

Lysimachia
creeping Jenny, dotted loosestrife

Mien Ruys used two different species of *Lysimachia* in her designs. The round leaves and bright yellow flowers of *Lysimachia nummularia* (creeping Jenny) provide strong groundcover. Occurs naturally in damp, grassy places. The plant is evergreen and ideal for covering the edges of ponds. *Lysimachia punctata* (dotted loosestrife) is a strong border plant that spreads somewhat. Its flower spikes can grow up to a meter tall, producing yellow flowers from June to August. Withstands sun and shade; can be in damp or dry soil.

Macleaya cordata var. *yedoensis*
plume poppy

Mien Ruys considered this plant to be the most attractive *Macleaya*, with its very decorative blue-green leaves and creamy-white plumed flowers. Growing to a height of two to three meters, this plant works well toward the back of a broad border or as a way of masking an ugly fence.

Monarda
bergamot

Almost all *Monardas* are susceptible to mildew. Mien Ruys considered 'Mahogany' to be one of the healthiest. Its pinkish-red flowers combine well with many border plants, even with the tricky colors of *Phlox* 'Spitfire' and *Centranthus ruber*.

Nepeta 'Six Hills Giant'
catmint

Mien Ruys considered this gray-leaved plant with pale lilac flowers to be a fantastic basis for combining with roses or as the foreground of a border. The plant can withstand drought and burning sun.

Phlox paniculata
perennial phlox

There was almost always a place for phlox in planting plans for borders. Its flowering season is from July to August, and its height varies from 80 to 140 centimeters. The ones Mien Ruys used most frequently were 'Lavendelwolke', a tall species with pale lilac flowers; 'Purpurmantel', the darkest purple in the assortment; 'Rembrandt', a pure white cultivar; 'Spitfire', a lower-growing species with rather dazzling orange-pink flowers; and 'Starfire', comparable to 'Spitfire' but darker in all aspects (foliage, stems, and flowers).

Rudbeckia fulgida var. *sullivantii* 'Goldsturm'
coneflower

Relatively low-growing, forming tight clumps of dark green leaves with warm yellow flowers and darker flower heads. The stems and their flower heads remain upright through winter.

Salvia nemorosa
sage

An indispensable border plant for Mien Ruys. The species she used the most are *Salvia nemorosa* 'Ostfriesland', strong and healthy with a profusion of deep blue flower spikes, and *Salvia nemorosa* 'Mai Nacht', which flowers a little earlier, with its slightly coarse, deep purple flower spikes.

Hylotelephium spectabile (Brilliant Group) 'Brilliant'
ice plant

This plant's thick, fleshy stems and leaves mean that it not only withstands drought very well, but also dappled shade. Its large, bright pink umbels attract butterflies and bees in fall. The flower stems remain upright, even in winter.

Solidago [Golden Gate] ('Dansolgold')
goldenrod

A strong perennial with yellow flower plumes that was frequently used in large groups in a summer border.

Tradescantia
spiderwort

A strong border plant that can withstand drought and damp. The plants need to be supported by twigs or sticks, because they tend to fall over even as they flower. There are cultivars in white and all shades of blue. Mien Ruys had a preference for 'Leonora'. Its flowers are deep violet-blue and, because it is relatively low-growing and more compact, it is also the most robust.

Viola cornuta
horned pansy

These pansies are ideal for the foreground of a border. 'John Wallmark' produces prolific pale lilac flowers and is completely winter hardy. It can suddenly die off after a few years, but it is worthwhile replanting this little pansy, if only because it flowers endlessly until December.

TREES

Crataegus ×lavalleei 'Carrierei'
hawthorn or hybrid cockspur thorn

Mien Ruys frequently used this cultivar in her planting plans, particularly in the 1960s. The tree develops a broad, parasol-shaped crown and is an excellent source of nectar and pollen. Its clusters of white flowers attract honeybees and bumblebees. In fall, the tree produces an abundance of large orange-red berries, which remain on the tree well into winter.

Gleditsia triacanthos f. *inermis*
thornless honey locust

Unlike most of the other *Gleditsia triacanthos*, this tree has no large thorns. Mien Ruys used this species because of its unstructured, open crown and its delicate bipinnate foliage that turns a magnificent buttery yellow in fall.

Malus hybrids
flowering crab apple

Mien Ruys often included crab apple trees in her planting plans, not just because of their profuse flowering, but also because of the little coloured apples they produce in fall. She chose species that she considered to be the most resistant to scab and that also had an attractive crown. Examples include *Malus ×zumi* 'Golden Hornet', with its large flowers and deep yellow crab apples; *Malus ×zumi* 'Professor Sprenger', with its small yellow and orange fruit; and *Malus ×floribunda*, which produces a profusion of blossoms and has a broad crown.

Metasequoia glyptostroboides
dawn redwood

This tree was raised from seed and multiplied by Bonne Ruys, Mien Ruys's father. It had been thought that this fossilized tree was extinct, but the seeds proved to be viable. However, no one had any experience of how this tree would develop and Mien Ruys did not realize that this tree would grow to such an enormous size.

Prunus
flowering cherry tree

Mien Ruys liked to often include flowering cherry trees in her planting plans. The species and cultivars she used the most are mentioned here. *Prunus ×yedoensis* (own root) is a species that grows into a substantial tree with a broad, parasol-shaped crown. Abundant blossom appears very early in spring, before any leaves emerge. *Prunus ×subhirtella* 'Autumnalis' grows to a modest size, and its most important ornamental value is the blossom it produces in winter. This bloom of small, pale pink flowers starts to appear in November or December and can continue into April. The modest size of *Prunus padus* 'Colorata' makes it ideal for smaller gardens. Mien Ruys's main reason for using it was its red-purple foliage, which appears from early spring until it falls, providing a colorful note in plantings.

SHRUBS

Corylopsis pauciflora
winter hazel

Its early blossom and especially the way it spreads were the reasons Mien Ruys liked to include this shrub singly amongst perennials.

***Cotinus coggygria* 'Rubrifolius'**
smoke bush

Mien Ruys often used this shrub, obviously because of its red-purple foliage (often combined with gray-leaved shrubs) but also because of its finely branched, rarefied inflorescence and spectacular color in fall.

Cotoneaster simonsii
Himalayan cotoneaster

One of the many *Cotoneaster* species Mien Ruys frequently included in her planting plans. She often used it to create hedges, until fire blight (or bacterial blight) struck the *Cotoneaster* assortment at the end of the 1970s, and she stopped using these shrubs.

Elaeagnus submacrophylla
oleaster or silverberry

Not a spectacular shrub, but exceedingly strong and one that can withstand drought and shade. It retains its leaves in winter and produces unflamboyant but deliciously scented flowers in January.

Euonymus alatus
winged spindle

The compact, spreading way this shrub grows makes it ideal as a solitary shrub in smaller gardens. Its most important ornamental value is its spectacular bright red color in fall.

***Hypericum ×hidcoteense* 'Hidcote'**
St John's wort

This evergreen or semi-evergreen shrub is reliably strong, spreads extensively, and provides good groundcover. It is excellent along the edges of shrubberies. *Hypericum ×hidcoteense* 'Hidcote' flowers for a long time, producing yellow blooms from July to September.

***Ilex ×meserveae* 'Blue Prince' and 'Blue Princess'**
blue holly

This compact miniature shrub has dark bluish-green foliage. Mien Ruys often used it to create low hedges. A mixture of the male 'Blue Prince' and the female 'Blue Princess' was usually planted so that berries would appear.

Ligustrum vulgare 'Atrovirens' and 'Lodense'
privet

Mien Ruys liked to use privet to make hedges. It is a strong and healthy shrub that grows well in any soil. 'Atrovirens' is the most evergreen species, while 'Lodense' is compact and low-growing; ideal for low or cubed hedges.

***Philadelphus* 'Belle Étoile'**
mock orange

This mock orange admittedly only flowers for a short period in June and July, but the scent of its flowers is something to look forward to all year.

***Potentilla fruticosa* 'Abbotswood'**
shrubby cinquefoil

"There is no such thing as an ugly plant, just the wrong place for it," Mien Ruys often said. She combined this rather unspectacular but exceedingly strong shrub with other gray-leaved shrubs, such as purple willow, oleaster, butterfly bush, and lavender.

***Rosa* 'Bonica'**

Still one of the healthiest and longest-flowering roses in the assortment. Ideal for combining with perennials such as *Salvia* and *Nepeta*.

***Rosa* 'Nevada'**

This botanical shrub rose was used because of its shape: elegant, arching branches producing abundant white, saucer-shaped flowers. The rose variant 'Marguerite Hilling' was likewise often used.

***Rosa virginiana* 'Harvest Song'**

A low-growing, compact shrub rose, ideal in the foreground of a shrubbery. As well as pink flowers, this rose produces an abundance of orange-red rosehips, and its foliage turns an attractive yellow in fall.

Sinarundinaria murieliae
bamboo

This bamboo, now called *Fargesia murielae*, was included in almost all planting plans from the 1970s on. After this bamboo started flowering and then dying in large numbers at the beginning of this century, it was often replaced by *Fargesia* 'Jiuzhaigou'.

***Spiraea ×arguta* (Spiraea ×cinerea)**
bridal wreath

This shrub—with its elegant, arching branches and bright green, small leaves—was pruned into a spherical shape and used to create small hedges, as in the Ready-to-make Borders.

Spiraea veitchii
Veitch's spirea

This upright shrub was always carefully pruned so that its arched branches formed a green gateway or canopy over the path, similar to that near the sundial in the Old Experimental Garden.

***Symphoricarpos ×doorenbosii* 'Mother of Pearl'**
snowberry

Another example of a shrub that was not chosen for its blossom but rather for its berries—in this case, large pearly-pink berries. Incidentally, its insignificant flowers attract considerable numbers of bees, as they are an excellent source of nectar and pollen.

Syringa sweginzowii
Chengtu lilac

A lilac that grows more freely than *Syringa vulgaris*; its flower plumes are more delicate and flared. Producing pale pink flowers, this lilac was often combined with brown-leaved shrubs.

***Syringa vulgaris* 'Andenken an Ludwig Späth'**
common lilac

Mien Ruys frequently used this lilac because of its deep purple flowers and, of course, because of its scent.

Viburnum opulus
Guelder rose

A vigorous shrub primarily for landscape designs. Produces white flower umbels in May–June, and large clusters of bright red berries appear in fall.

***Viburnum plicatum* f. *tomentosum* 'Mariesii'**
Japanese snowball

Another shrub that produces white flower umbels and clusters of red berries in fall. The way it grows and how it is used are quite different, however. Mien Ruys sometimes used this more cultivated snowball, with its horizontal, wide-spreading branches, as a solitary shrub at a corner of a border.

Symphyotrichum novi-belgii 'Crimson Brocade'

Hemerocallis 'Tejas'

Phlox 'Starfire'

Viburnum opulus

THANKS

Writing this book was a process I didn't accomplish alone: many other people were involved too. I would therefore like to take this opportunity to thank everyone who helped—in whatever way at all—to make this book a reality. A few people deserve to be mentioned by name.

First and foremost, Hélène Lesger, who was enthusiastic right from our first contact and was confident that it would become a beautiful book. Thank you for believing in us enough to embark on this project. I am thrilled this book will now also be available in English, so thank you Makenna Goodman at Timber Press for also believing in this project.

I would also like to thank my fellow readers, Anet Scholma and Ineke den Hollander. Anet collaborated with Mien Ruys for many years, continued her work, and knows the Gardens as no other. She used her experience to cast a critical eye over the texts, checking for their accuracy. And Ineke, who as a "layperson" was just as critical but in a different way, was even more meticulous than I am. Thank you, too, to Kay Dixon for her translation, that is true to the text and to the spirit of Mien Ruys.

The photographers, Erwin Zijlstra, Wouter van der Tol, and Carlo van Tartwijk, were prepared to take wonderful photos at the most impossible times. Thank you for your commitment and flexibility.

Thanks also go to Wouke Boog and Wouter Eertink, whose skills have transformed the texts and images into a coherent, colorful book.

And obviously, all the people around me, especially my colleagues, Monique Bruins Slot, Minie Nijboer, Nicoline van der Veer, and my partner Andreas, who had to manage without me for a year and a half when I was either physically or mentally absent. Thank you all for your support.

And lastly, the most important person of all: Mien Ruys. For her courage, perseverance, and creativity, which she put to use to make beautiful gardens throughout her long life. For this magnificent place she has left as her legacy, even though that was never her intention. Now, 100 years later, it is still a place to enjoy and be inspired by.

SOURCES

Books

Backer, Anne Mieke, *Er stond een vrouw in de tuin. Over de rol van vrouwen in het Nederlandse landschap* (Rotterdam, Uitgeverij de HEF, 2016)

Bijhouwer, J.T.P. and Mien Ruys, *Leven met groen, in landschap, stad en tuin* (Amsterdam, Moussault's publishing house, 1960)

Deunk, Gerritjan, *Nederlandse tuin- en landschapsarchitectuur van de 20ste eeuw* (Rotterdam, NAi Uitgevers, 2002)

Dulk, Leo den, Mien Ruys. *Tuinarchitect. Zoeken naar de heldere lijn. De complete biografie* (Rotterdam, Uitgeverij de HEF, 2017)

G.J. Pannekoek, *Bloemen en tuinen. Fleur en kleur rondom het huis* (Deventer, Uitgeverij N. Kluwer, 1966)

Onna, Edwin van and Norbert van Onna, *In Bergeijk. Gerrit Rietveld Mien Ruys* (Veldhoven, Uitgeverij Archehof, 2008)

Oudolf, Piet and Noel Kingsbury, *Oudolf | Hummelo* (Amsterdam, HL Books, 2020)

Ruys, Bonne, *Memoires van Bonne Ruys, 1865–1950* (Dedemsvaart, 1988)

Ruys, Mien, *Borders, hoe men ze maakt en onderhoudt* Amsterdam (Uitgeverij Kosmos, 1939)

Ruys, Mien, *Mijn tuinen* (Amsterdam, Uitgeverij Het Huis van Linnaeus, 1987)

Scholma, Anet and Conny den Hollander, *Proeven in de Tuinen Mien Ruys* (Dedemsvaart, Stichting Tuinen Mien Ruys, 2015

Steenhuis, Marinke and Fransje Hooimeijer, *Maakbaar landschap. Nederlandse landschapsarchitectuur 1945–1970* (Rotterdam, NAi Uitgevers, 2009)

Zijlstra, Bonica, *Mien Ruys, een leven als tuinarchitecte* (Amsterdam, Nederlandse Tuinenstichting, 1990)

Articles, publications

"Mien Ruys: 'Ik vecht voor open Gemeenschapstuinen'", in *de Volkskrant* (June 22, 1960)

Geertsema, Reinko, Mien Ruys. *Beschrijving en documentatie van haar beroepspraktijk* (thesis, 1982)

Groenstructuurplan Nagele (PDF), by *Uitvoeringslab Nagele* (2012)

Kreikamp, Esther, "*Gedeelde idealen: De tuinstadgedachte en de Amsterdamse School*", in *World Garden Cities* (August 5, 2022)

Niemeyer, Hans and Vivian, *Onze jaren bij* Moerheim en Mien Ruys, 1951–1971

Ruys, Mien, "*De architect en de tuin*", in *De 8* and *Opbouw* (volume 13, February 1942 no. 7)

Verslag Van Eesterengesprek 57 (PDF, March 12, 2017)

Various articles from *Onze Eigen Tuin* (1955–2010)

Interviews

Een leven lang radio (NOS, October 16, 1987)

Laat ze maar praten. Episode with Mien Ruys, landscape gardener. Presented by Koos Postema (NOS TV, February 9, 1983)

Various video and audio fragments the titles and dates of which are unknown

Websites

https://www.hvavereest.nl/lezen-kijken/geschiedenis/

http://www.bonmama.nl/dedemsvaart.html

http://www.bonmama.nl/verveners.html

https://www.quest.nl/maatschappij/geschiedenis/a36207231/roaring-twenties-nederland-charleston-dansen/

https://npokennis.nl/longread/7632/hoe-beleefde-nederland-de-eerste-wereldoorlog#id-2

https://www.historamarond1900.nl/maatschappij

https://www.canonvannederland.nl/nl/crisisjaren

https://www.examenoverzicht.nl/geschiedenis/beurskrach-1929

https://www.canonvannederland.nl/nl/overijssel/salland/zwolle/crisisjaren

https://npokennis.nl/longread/7625/waarom-is-nederland-in-de-jaren-dertig-in-crisis

https://nagele.nl/bezoek_nagele/het-begin-architecten/

https://emmeloord.info/nagele/

https://vaneesterenmuseum.nl/tuinsteden

https://www.hetschip.nl/de-tuinstad-gedachte-uitgebreide-info

https://www.ploegfestival.nl/historie/rietveld-ruys-weverij-de-ploeg-bergeijk

https://deploeg.com/over-ons/geschiedenis/

https://cultuurhuisbergeijk.nl/ontdek/gerrit-rietveld

https://cultuurhuisbergeijk.nl/ontdek/mien-ruys

https://historiek.net/vrouwen-tot-1956-handelingsonbekwaam/15127/

https://www.historischeinterieursamsterdam.nl/blog/villa-holt-een-split-level-woning-aan-het-duin/

https://atria.nl/nieuws-publicaties/feminisme/feminisme-20e-eeuw/

https://www.cultureelerfgoed.nl/onderwerpen/post-65-erfgoed

https://historiek.net/club-van-rome-grenzen-aan-de-groei-1972/80577/

https://isgeschiedenis.nl/nieuws/bezuinigen-en-hervormingen-in-de-jaren-80

https://www.degroeneluwte.nl/index.php/en/groene-blogtest/46-the-dutch-wave-piet-oudolf-ton-terlinden-e-a.html

https://anderetijden.nl/aflevering/58/Schitterende-hoogmoed-in-de-jaren-90

https://groei.nl/tuin/tuinonderhoud/plantenziekten-en-plagen/olivijn-klimaatvriendelijke-toversteen

https://www.kwekerijjacobs.nl/

PHOTO AND ILLUSTRATION CREDITS

The ground plans of The Experimental Gardens are by Nadine Schiller

All the photos and documents come from the archives of Tuinen Mien Ruys, with the exception of the following:

Atelier Couleur 23

Harry Bennink 161 below

Dick Bieuwenga 31 above, 46-47, 98 left, 99 left, 116, 123 left, 130, 157, 167 above, 191 above, 195 below, 209 center right, 210-211, 213 above, 216 above, 223 above, 235 below right, 238-239, 250, 252, 255 below, 282-283, and **back cover top**

Evy Blom 244 garden design

Henk Boudewijns 195 above

Ilona Dekker 245 garden design right

Foto Colson 63

Henk Gerritsen 120-121

Historische Vereniging Avereest 19

Marijke Heuff, ***Rijksdienst voor het Cultureel Erfgoed*** **(Cultural Heritage Agency)** 131 below, 136 below, 137 below, 138, 139 below, 140-141, 142, 144 above, 145, 148, 170

Marijke Heuff 158 below, 185 below

Conny den Hollander 26 below right, 36, 39 below, 43, 44, 45, 49, 59, 56 left, 61, 86-87, 92 below left, 93, 127, 133, 134-135, 154 center, below left and below right, 155 below, 176 above left, 181 below, 184, 185 above left and above right, 186 above right, 190, 191 above, 204, 205, 206, 207, 209 above left, center left, below left, above right and below right, 212 below left and below right, 213 below left and below right, 216 below right, 217, 218, 220-221, 222, 223 below, 224-225, 226 above right and center right, 227 above left and above right, 228-229, 230, 231, 232, 233, 235 above left, above right and center right, 236, 237, 240, 242-243, drawings 244, 245 and 274

Arend Jan van der Horst 144 below, 149

KLM Aerocarto 111

Joh. Krop 179

Ward Maaswinkel 245 garden design left

Maria Austria (Collection MAI) 64, 65, and **back cover middle**

Memoires van Bonne Ruys 21

Moerheim Dedemsvaart 100-101, 251

Bert Nienhuis 181 above

Onze Eigen Tuin 78, 79, 136 above, 139 right

G.J. Pannekoek 114

J.L. du Parant 249 above

P.D. v.d. Poel 74 below right

Dieneke van Raalte 162

Rijkswaterstaat **(Netherlands Directorate-General for Public Works and Water Management), Multimedia department** 74 below left

Dieuwertje Roebbers-van Eekelen 161 above

Lisa van Schagen, Dakdokters 154 above

Anet Scholma 152 above

Special Collections, Wageningen University & Research – Library 23, 25, 55 below right, 59, 144 below, 149

Studio Moni 51 above

Carlo van Tartwijk 2-3, 6, 68-69, 83, 104-105, 124-125, 168-169, 177, 183, 188-189, 194 above, 214-215, 249, 260-261, and **front cover**

Wouter van der Tol 1, 4-5, 8-9, 10-11, 12, 14, 16, 40-41, 72-73, 82 below right, 92 below right, 103, 108, 109, 116, 119, 123 right, 127, 164 above left, 165, 166, 167 below left and below right, 174-175, 176 below left, 194 left, 196-197, 202-204, 247, 248, 253, 254, 257, 259, 276, and **back cover bottom**

Gijs Woldhek 122

Rosette Zandvoort, Archives 94 left, 113

Fred Zandvoort 113

Erwin Zijlstra 26 below left, 28-29, 37, 66 above, 70 above left and above right, 80-81, 82 below left, 89 above, 90-91, 95, 96-97, 98 right, 99 right, 126, 128-129, 132 below, 143, 155 above, 156, 164 below left, 173, 187 below, 192-193, 201, 226 below right, 241

INDEX

Photo and illustration credits appear on page 277.

Timber Press
Workman Publishing
Hachette Book Group, Inc.
1290 Avenue of the Americas
New York, New York 10104
timberpress.com

Timber Press is an imprint of Workman Publishing, a division of Hachette Book Group, Inc.
The Timber Press name and logo are registered trademarks of Hachette Book Group, Inc.

Printed in Shenzhen, China (APO), on responsibly sourced paper

English translation: Kay Dixon
Book design: Studio Wouke Boog
Art direction images: Wouter van der Tol
Project supervision: Hélène Lesger
Layout: Wouter Eertink

ISBN 978-1-64326-533-9

A catalog record for this book is available from the Library of Congress.

ECHINOPS
RAPLOW BLUE
30
OBERON
SALVIA
SUPERBA
36
ACHILLEA FIL
39
MACLEYA
45
DELPHINIUM
Monarda
Adam
44
Aster
Royal Red
KENTRANTHUS RUBER
NEPETA SIX HILLS GIANT
VIOLA CORN. VELVET BEAUTY
alpina
CHYS LANATA
CAMPANULA
ASTILBE
IRIS
ARTEMISIA
IRIS GERM.
78